LADIES
&
GENTLEMEN
BOYS
&
GIRLS...

Welcome to . . .

Presented by
Your Ringmaster

Douglas McPherson

PETER OWEN PUBLISHERS
73 Kenway Road
London SW5 0RE

Peter Owen books are distributed in the USA by Dufour Editions Inc.,
Chester Springs, PA 19425-0007

First published in Great Britain 2010 by
Peter Owen Publishers

Unless stated otherwise, all photographs are from
the author's collection.

ISBN 978-07206-1352-0

A catalogue record for this book is available
from the British Library

Printed and bound in Great Britain by
Windsor Print Production Ltd, Tonbridge

In memory of Eva

HALF PRICES!!
Saturday, October 25, 1817.
HORSEMANSHIP,
IN ALL ITS VARIOUS DEPARTMENTS:
An Act of Horsemanship, by Master BATHURST.
Evolutions in Vaulting,
By Messrs. ORD, POWELL, SUTTON, GUNN, BATHURST, and JENKISON, Clown.
AN ACT OF HORSEMANSHIP, - by Mr. POWELL.
The Metamorphose of the Sack;
Or, the Clown Deceived, by a Woman on Horseback, by Mr ORD;
FRICASSEE DANCE.
ATHLETIC POWERS,
Of HEAVY BALANCING, by Mr GUNN.
The STICK DANCE, with The Egyptian Pyramids.
Grand Trampoline, by Mr Powell.
Slack Rope Vaulting, by Mr Gunn.
Horsemanship,
BY MR. ORD.
SACK RACE.
The whole to conclude with
The TAILOR's JOURNEY to BRENTFORD.
Doors open at Six o'Clock, and Performance to begin at Seven.

THE PROGRAMME

ILLUSTRATIONS
BETWEEN PAGES 128 AND 129

Danny Adams re-creates Houdini's escape from a milk-churn; *David Street/Blonde Street Images/Great Yarmouth Hippodrome*
The author meets Sonja the elephant; *author's collection*
The Chinese State Circus: lion dancing, swordplay, contortionism and bikes; *SeventhWaveImagery/Chinese State Circus*
The cast of the BBC's *Big Top*; *Big Bear Films*
Miguel Peris takes his sister Alicia for a spin; *David Street/Blonde Street Images/Circus Hilarious*
Gerry Cottle and his stars of the future; *Gerry Cottle/Wookey Hole*
Gerry Cottle's future stars training at Wookey Hole; *Gerry Cottle/Wookey Hole*
Joseph Micheletty, France's 'Diabolist Extraordinaire'; *David Street/Blonde Street Images/Great Yarmouth Hippodrome*
The Bio Brothers from the Ukraine; *David Street/Blonde Street Images/Great Yarmouth Hippodrome*
Danny Adams 'auditions' for the Chinese State Circus; *David Street/Blonde Street Images/Circus Hilarious*

Patrons will note that, owing to the HAZARDOUS nature of circus, all acts are subject to CHANGE without notice. Please do not try any of the following stunts yourself. Smoking is NOT allowed in the big top. Please turn OFF your mobile phone. We hope you ENJOY the show.

INTRODUCTION

WELCOME TO THE CIRCUS

What is circus? Perhaps the word brings to your mind a big top, an enormous striped tent with grass underfoot and the cry of 'Roll up, roll up' in the air. Maybe you think of a white clown face with a red ping-pong ball for a nose. Or a man on stilts. Or elephants in tiaras and tutus.

Perhaps the word conjures darker images: the sinister clowns of horror films; Victorian lion tamers with oily moustaches and cracking whips; cruelty hidden behind the curtain.

Maybe you hear such names as Barnum, Smart and Cottle. Or perhaps you picture the lavish Las Vegas spectacle of Cirque du Soleil.

When I began my journey into circus I had only distant childhood memories of an entertainment I believed long defunct. To my amazement, I discovered the most thrilling performances and exciting shows that I have encountered in any field of entertainment. I found people performing feats of agility and skill that seemingly made the impossible possible. I saw circuses aimed at nightclub audiences and circuses aimed at the arts crowd. I saw shows at the cutting edge of theatrical production values and others that kept alive the tradition of sawdust, elephants and tigers.

I also found that I was not the only person to have overlooked this world within the circus ring. While theatre, music and literary criticism abound, there was almost no serious writing about circus. The papers might report an animal-rights protest outside the big top or offer a perfunctory review of

Cirque du Soleil. But where was the authoritative comparison of one contortionist's routine with another? Where was the informed debate on the merits of narrative circus, or the changing character of clowning? Where were the celebrity circus stars, the poster boys and girls of their profession?

I wanted to redress the balance by looking critically at the many varied styles of circus being performed today: the rock'n'roll razzmatazz of the Great Yarmouth Hippodrome; the gymnastic lion dance of the Chinese State Circus; the breathtaking ice show of Cirque de Glace.

There is a rich history to be told, stretching back to the father of modern circus, Philip Astley, in eighteenth-century London, and beyond, to the arenas of ancient Rome and the variety theatre of China, more than 2,000 years ago. But it was not the history itself that fascinated me so much as the way in which the traditions of those past centuries live on, consciously and unconsciously, in the performers and performances of today.

Julius Fucik's century-old circus music, 'Entrance of the Gladiators', isn't history, because you can hear it today, with the smell of camel wee in your nose and horses galloping by as they did in the days of Astley. You can see the most progressive of clowns performing routines that nobody in the audience will realize were considered oldies but goodies eighty years ago.

In the pages that follow, you will therefore find all the famous historical figures that shaped circus, from the American showman Barnum, creator of the 'Greatest Show on Earth', to the Frenchman Jules Léotard, the original 'Daring Young Man on the Flying Trapeze'.

But rather than seeing them presented as a chronological circus history, you will find them mixed in with the contemporary performers whose lives and work they continue to inform. So the story of Joseph Grimaldi, the father of clowning, sits next to that of nineteen-year-old rising star Bippo. The Victorian freak show is described alongside today's Circus of Horrors. They mirror and illuminate each other in a world where the past and present (and doubtless the future, too) mingle as easily as the concepts of possible and impossible, reality and illusion.

Most of all, this book is about the characters that populate today's circus scene. People such as Britain's only female tiger trainer; the German tax-office worker who trained alone for years to become a sword-swallower; the great showmen such as Gerry Cottle, who ran away with the circus when he was fifteen years old.

They are a breed apart from any other entertainer. Their stories have seldom been told before, and I want you to hear them as they told them to me, in their own words, for it is in their personal testimonies, juxtaposed with descriptions of their acts, that the history and the spirit of circus are most fully revealed.

Chapter 1

EVA

In her last ever appearance . . .

I remember the elephants – just. It was a long time ago, and I was very small. But I can remember their legs, as thick and long as tree trunks, with a similar rough, cracked texture, and their big, disc-like feet as they marched along the high street. I remember looking up at their enormous curved sides – which looked black, in silhouette – and seeing each of their trunks holding the tail of the animal in front.

It's odd that I remember them in the street, not the big top. I couldn't tell you what they did in the big tent on my local park, but I remember being there. I remember the strange light beneath the canvas, the trampled mud and grass beneath my feet (because you notice the ground more when you're little; you're much closer to it), the dark red poles and the curved rows of wooden bench seats.

My memories of the show are fragmentary. I remember them clanging together sections of fence to build a cage around the ring and, particularly, a curved, barred tunnel that led through from the edge of the tent. I remember how flimsy those bars looked and how large the gaps between them seemed to be. I remember well the low growl – or perhaps it was a purr or maybe just the rasp of his breath on the chilled air – as a lion with lean haunches and a big shaggy mane ran through the tunnel to the ring. I was on the end seat, and he was very close. What the lions did in the ring, though, I am again at a loss to recall.

Memories of a row of lions sitting obediently on metal stands are from later, although not much later, television specials. Billy Smart's, perhaps, in black and white at Christmas.

The trapeze flyers were and are a blur. I can recall the tiny figures in their glittery leotards, with their swings and platforms glinting in the lights, high above my twisted-back head, in the vertiginous heights at the very top of the tent. But I was too young to appreciate their skill and daring, and their performance was too distant for me to engage with.

Naturally, I remember the clowns more clearly. One was dressed as what I would now recognize as a harlequin, with a shimmering pom-pommed outfit, white face and tall pointed hat. He seemed to be in charge, an aloof figure – a straight man maybe. Another clown wore a floppy brown suit and tramp-like trilby with a mop of orange hair sticking out from under it. He had a red nose like a ping-pong ball and a bucket of water balanced on a broomstick. We knew it was water because he and a pal had spent a lot of time soaking each other with bucketloads of the stuff. I remember the audience cringing back as he tottered towards them, then tripped in his outsize clown boots. But the bucket turned out to be fixed to the broom . . . and spilled only feathers or scraps of paper or some such.

They also had a terrific clown car that spluttered around the ring, losing doors and mudguards and backfiring with a firecracker BANG that made my mother jump right off the bench.

After the show we went backstage into another, smaller tent, rich with the tang of dung and hay, where we joined a queue to meet the animals – horses and maybe a camel or two – in their pens. It was a warm and cosy experience, not unlike visiting the police horses in their stables behind the police station on the high street.

We were animal lovers, whether hamsters and rabbits in the pet shop or ducks on the big pond in the cemetery.

Happy memories, then, but distant ones.

That first visit to the circus, at such an early age that I can't even guess at how old I was, was to be my last for decades.

As an older child I was taken to the cinema (the pictures, as we called it), museums, a *Dr Who* exhibition and even, occasionally, a zoo or wildlife park but never again to a circus. Not that other forms of live entertainment featured much in my cultural life either; it was the television age, and we weren't a theatre-going family.

Occasionally a circus was glimpsed on television, but as I grew older the word became sullied by a general acceptance, in my house at least, that if circuses weren't actually physically cruel to animals (and I can remember a few tabloid exposés that claimed they definitely were) then the idea of performing animals was in itself cruel or demeaning.

Gradually, circus faded, unmissed, from my radar – and I guess not only from mine. When I was a teenager and young adult, people talked about gigs, films, clubs, maybe stand-up comedy or even fringe theatre. But circus? It might have ceased to exist.

So when *The Stage*, the theatrical newspaper for which I have been reviewing plays, pantomimes and seaside variety shows, asks me to review the Hippodrome Circus in Great Yarmouth I really don't know what to expect. I certainly don't expect the steamy humidity of a jungle, the pungency of chlorine . . . and synchronized swimmers.

The Hippodrome, celebrating its hundredth anniversary as a circus venue, is a circular building, with steeply raked tiers of seats encircling its central ring – a Colosseum-like design that has earned it the nickname 'East Anglia's mini Albert Hall'.

As the show resumes after the interval, the red carpet that covers the ring has been removed to reveal glossy light-blue wooden boards. As the Weather Girls' disco hit 'It's Raining Men' fills the auditorium, six girl dancers are doing a 'Singing in the Rain'-style routine in short shiny macs and high heels. They put up their umbrellas as four fountains erupt into life from around the edge of the ring, shooting multiple jets of water maybe twenty feet into the air. It's a great accompaniment to the routine. But as the 'rain' cascades down upon the dancers, isn't the water sloshing around on the boards beneath their feet getting a little deep?

The dancers skip off and the music changes to the thunderous drama of the opening theme from the film *2001: A Space Odyssey* – which is also the music Elvis used to open his Las Vegas shows. Lights strobe and swirl around the darkened venue, distracting us, while the fountains continue to pour gallons of water into the ring, the surface of which has become a boiling cauldron beneath the ceaseless torrent.

When the lights and music finally still, the floor of the stage has disappeared completely. There's just blue water, from the middle of which six swimmers, in caps and goggles, suddenly leap like dolphins, ready to commence their synchronized routine.

A hundred years after its instigation by showman George Gilbert, the Hippodrome's party-piece transformation scene from circus ring to swimming pool has lost none of its magic. It even gets a smile and faintly disbelieving shake of the head from my host Peter Jay, the venue's current owner, despite the many times he has seen it before.

'It's hard to imagine what it would have looked like by gaslight in 1903,' says Jay. With a laugh, he adds, 'It might not have smelled very nice because they didn't have any filtration and they had elephants and horses performing directly above the water!'

Ah yes, the elephants. Peter used to have them. He talks fondly of how they would take their exercise out on the beach and go for a swim in the sea between shows. Like many circus owners, however, Jay dispensed with animals a decade or more ago. As one of the art form's leading modernizers his decision was pragmatic.

'People, and especially the press, can never think about circus without wondering whether it's got animals. Should it have? Shouldn't it have? Are they well looked after? They've always been fantastically looked after as far as I've seen. But now, without animals, it's an easier product to sell because there's no discussion about that.'

What Jay delivers instead of horses and lions is spectacle. He dresses circus up with an exciting blend of ear-splitting chart music, nightclub lighting and MTV-style dance routines – not to mention his fountains and swimmers. But behind all the razzle-dazzle are human circus skills that rely on one thing alone: the almost unbelievable skill, strength and bravery of the men and women who perform them.

Closing the first half of the show are perhaps the most daring performers of them all, the nut-brown, wire-muscled Valez Brothers on their enormous rotating Wheel of Death. How to describe the towering apparatus upon which they risk their lives twice daily? For the risk is real. Experienced performers have slipped and died doing this act. Imagine a windmill with two tapering sails, each about eight feet long and constructed from two layers of criss-crossed shiny metal, like the hollow gantry of a crane. Now picture a man-sized hamster wheel attached to the end of each sail . . . and the whole contraption revolving around its centre, the uppermost wheel rising nearly thirty feet into the air as the lower swishes just above the ground. While the lights flash and sweep around the arena, and chilli-pepper-hot Latin music blasts out madly, the Valez Brothers run around the inside of these two revolving hamster wheels and then around the *outside.*

Actually they don't run. They dance and leap. They jog backwards. They do handstands. They take huge bounds into the air as the wheel spins away beneath their feet, rejoining it with a clang, their weight and motion making it revolve ever faster.

My breath is held and my heart is in my mouth just watching, as I marvel at the apparent recklessness with which they flirt with death. One missed footing, one misjudgement, would mean a fall, a broken bone or worse. But these boys don't just ignore the danger, they embrace it; they *love* it.

Several times they use their balanced weight to stop the wheel so that it is completely horizontal or at 'ten to four'. Their black hair slicked down with oil and their brown chests glistening with sweat, they bare their teeth in the widest of grins as they swivel their hips in time to the music, revelling in their own daring. Whistling and shouting, Mardi Gras style, they slap their hands together, encouraging us to clap along. And then they're off again, leaping and running, perpetually seeming so close to missing their footing, but always making it, half a heartbeat from disaster, as the wheel rolls on.

It's as I watch the Valez Brothers that I first become fascinated with the circus breed and the mysterious glue that binds them to their life of peril. They are, there is no doubt, a breed apart. Somewhere between show business and sport, but standing apart from both, they seem to exist for no other purpose than to make the impossible possible.

I don't get to ask the Valez Brothers why they do what they do, although in truth I don't need to, because I can see the reason in their grinning eyes and teeth; no drug could give a man such a high.

But I do talk to Eva.

Eva Garcia performs on the aerial silk. It is a graceful act, equal parts artistic and gymnastic, a gravity-defying ballet performed in the air high above our heads. Climbing two broad but fine bands of silk that hang from the roof of the Hippodrome, she throws figures and strikes poses, letting go with her hands and trusting her weight to the silk as she rearranges it in loops and coils around her waist, a knee or ankle.

Eva is a stunningly attractive woman, whose green eyes and exotic features are evidence of her mixture of Spanish, English and Irish blood – and, perhaps more than anything, *circus* blood. Her suppleness in her red-and-white costume belies her thirty-eight years. In the spotlight, to the stirring music of the Hippodrome's closing theme, 'Time to Say Goodbye', she makes her routine look effortless.

In the cold light of a Great Yarmouth morning, Eva reveals the life of hard knocks and loneliness behind the glitter.

'There are a lot of good things about the circus,' she says in her strong Spanish accent. 'But then there are a lot of bad things. It's very tough, mentally and physically. You really have to love it to live in the circus.'

Already that week Eva had suffered bruises because the humidity was making her hands slip on the silk. Earlier in her career, injuries had forced her to change from a wire-walking act in which she performed back summersaults no other woman attempted. Yet, despite the scars, dislocations and operations, and the danger she is too superstitious to talk about, the modest, warm-hearted performer has no intention of giving up a life she has led from the age of seven and which has been in her family for over a hundred years. She has, in fact, just ended a nine-year relationship in favour of a nomadic existence travelling all over the globe, often driving alone at night with all her worldly possessions in the caravan behind her.

'He wasn't in the business and he could never handle me going away for months at a time. But I couldn't give up my life. I'm still too young.'

Estimating she has another ten years of performing ahead of her, Eva says the main change in circus during her lifetime has been in the area of presentation.

'The music, the lights, the costumes are all part of the act. If I still had the wire-walking act nowadays, I would present more and wouldn't do as many hard tricks.' With a laugh, she concludes, 'You still have to have good tricks, but these days you don't have to kill yourself.'

It's a good quote, and it comes out in *The Stage* the following Thursday. Whether Eva gets to read it, however, I don't know. The day after the interview appears, Eva falls thirty feet during her act. She dies instantly.

In shock and grief, the Hippodrome is closed for the weekend. But in circus, as in show business, the show must go on. For the rest of the season the Valez Brothers continue to dance and jump and gyrate on their rotating Wheel of Death. Vladislav, 'The Man Who Can Fly', grips thick straps in each fist, twists them two or three times around his steely wrists and soars like Superman through the glittering fountains.

Meanwhile, all along the prom, Eva gazes with a Mona Lisa smile from the gaily coloured posters that depict her in one of her poses on the silk. Her unreadable eyes silently remind us that there is no computer-generated trickery in what her colleagues do, nor are the risks they take for our entertainment anything less than real.

The word bravery is bandied about lightly in the arts. Often it refers to nothing more daring than an unusual choice of song. For the circus breed it is a nightly way of life and, sometimes, death.

Chapter 2

BACK TO THE HIPPODROME

Where better to find out what makes circus people tick than in the ghost-filled backstage corridors of Britain's oldest circus building?

'Circus Circus.' The red neon sign writes itself, flashes twice, blinks out, then writes itself again. Below it, tinny music spills out across Great Yarmouth's promenade.

The sign isn't advertising a circus. The single-storey, glass-fronted building is home to another of the brightly lit slot-machine arcades that line the prom in a gaudy approximation of the Vegas Strip: the Flamingo, the Silver Slipper and the Golden Nugget.

Stand far enough back, however, across the road, past the car park and the Victorian toilets on the edge of the esplanade, and above the 'Circus Circus' sign you can glimpse the central two of four domed terracotta towers, their once vibrant orange hue now dulled by time and grime. Between them you can just make out, in once golden, now faded yellow letters on weathered green tiles, the words that identify the towers as the uppermost part of a real piece of circus history, the Yarmouth Hippodrome.

Before circuses roamed the country in tents, many towns, and certainly the major cities and holiday destinations, had their own permanent circus building where shows were staged for weeks or months at a time. The most prestigious was Hengler's Grand Cirque, which stood on the site now occupied by the London Palladium. The last still used for its original purpose is the Hippodrome.

Before the amusement arcade was built in front of it, the Hippodrome faced the seafront across an open square. The grandest of the seven circus buildings that once graced the resort, it tempted holiday-makers with huge wooden cut-outs of dancing bears and white-faced, red-nosed clowns. Today the narrowness of the road behind the amusements makes it hard to stand back and appreciate the faded grandeur of the pillared art nouveau frontage, designed by Ralph Scott Cockrill, the son of the local borough surveyor, in 1903. But still the crowds come, queuing the length of the little road to see performers from around the world testing their skills and bodies to the limit in the most physically demanding arena of show business. Inside, the entire history of circus seems to hang in the shadows of corridors lined with framed posters advertising shows from before the war, dark concrete stairwells and cramped toilets unchanged in a century.

'If these walls could talk . . .' marvels the tanned, white-suited, shaven-headed roller-skater Miguel Peris in his chirpy Essex accent. 'Houdini worked here. Charlie Chaplin, they think.'

Great Yarmouth enjoyed a strong tradition of circus during the nineteenth century, when the arrival of the railways in the 1840s and the passing of the Bank Holidays Act in 1871 saw the small fishing community grow into one of Britain's three largest seaside resorts. In addition to the town's dedicated circus buildings, the resort played host to several of the large travelling circuses that flourished in the late 1800s. The biggest was Buffalo Bill's Wild West Show, which boasted a cast of 1,300 men and 500 horses, travelled in four special trains and played in an arena, erected for just one day, that could hold 14,000 people.

The Hippodrome was built by George Gilbert, a Norwich lad who, at the age of eleven, ran away with Hanneford's London Circus when it visited his East Anglian home town. Gilbert trained as an acrobat, trapeze artist and equestrian and later married Jenny O'Brien, the daughter of a prominent circus family. As a double act on bareback horses the couple performed all over the world, appeared before Queen Victoria at the newly built Olympia and toured the USA with the Barnum and Bailey Circus – the legendary 'Greatest Show on Earth'. When a knee injury ended Gilbert's performing career he turned to management, presenting Gilbert's Modern Circus of Varieties in Norwich and other towns.

Gilbert built Yarmouth's first Hippodrome, from wood and corrugated iron, on St George's Road in 1898. It proved so successful that five years later he replaced it on the same site with the current concrete building – buying up and demolishing the buildings in front so that it faced the seafront.

From the very first season the Hippodrome played host to a range of entertainments including bioscope shows – the forerunner of cinema, which the venue would later present on a screen suspended across the ring – as well as variety shows. Among the stars to appear were Lillie Langtry, Max Miller and Tom Major – the father of Prime Minister John. But with its circular structure and central ring, which could be lowered into a 60,000 gallon tank of water for aquatic displays, it was circus for which the Hippodrome was specifically designed and to which it remains uniquely suited.

Gilbert's ghost is said to walk the upper balcony, perhaps satisfied to see that his dream lives on, perhaps passing critical comment on a particular show.

Backstage, lighting designer Ben Jay, the oldest son of the Hippodrome's current owner, Peter, drapes himself from the upper curve of a German wheel – a kind of man-size freestanding hamster's wheel with hand grips and foot straps that Russian gymnast Denis Remnez will soon be rolling and bouncing all over the ring.

'Some of the lighting boys say they've been touched,' Ben assures me. 'Sometimes a bulb will blow, which we take as a warning that something is about to go wrong.'

It's midday, the semicircular backstage area is well lit and there are plenty of people around. It's too early for ghost stories. But it's easy to believe that after midnight, with the lights off, when you're the last one to leave, the Hippodrome is a far spookier place. So does Ben ever find it unnerving?

'Naw . . .' the big 32-year-old says, not entirely convincingly. Warming to his theme, Ben tells the story of a trapeze troupe whose members turned ghost-hunters and laced the balcony with trip-wires and tin cans in an attempt to trace the apparition's movements. When the cans began jangling wildly, they fled the building as if it were on fire. Only one sceptical soul remained and pulled aside a curtain . . . to find the troupe's joker gleefully yanking on a wire and laughing his head off.

This season's trapeze troupe are the Flying Neves from Brazil. It's a place that their giant catcher Montana – 'The Mountain' – is sorely missing. He's built like Mr Incredible, with enormous arms and shoulders, a barrel chest and triangular torso welded to snake-like hips and the long, almost dainty legs of a dancer. It's the classic all-top shape of a trapeze artist, exaggerated further in his role as catcher. But even the muscles of a cartoon superhero cannot protect him from the chill of an English seaside.

'How do they survive in this country?' Montana slaps his tree trunk-like arms and barks at the backstage area in general.

Joseph Micheletty, France's 'Diabolist Extraordinaire', can only roll his eyes in sympathy. In the ring the twenty-year-old Micheletty cuts a cool, streetwise figure. He is as lean and limber as a piece of string; with a square jaw and a floppy lady-killing fringe hanging over his eyebrows from beneath a jauntily sported black trilby with a white band, it's easy to imagine him on some sultry graffiti-decorated street corner in Harlem, where the pecking order is established not by fist fights but by break-dancing 'dance-offs' or skill with a basketball.

Micheletty's 'basketball' is the 'Devil on two sticks'. A diabolo is a double-ended spinning top, shaped like an hourglass, that rides up and down a length of string stretched between the two sticks, in the manner of a yo-yo that isn't actually attached to anything. Micheletty can do tricks with three of them spinning on the same piece of string. He can also hurl all three into the roof of the Hippodrome and catch them, one by one, on the string without breaking a sweat.

At the moment, though, Micheletty doesn't look so much cool as frozen. Hunched shivering on one of the battered crushed velvet sofas that litter the backstage area, he's wrapped in a blanket, like a racehorse. An hour before the afternoon show, the Hippodrome is everything a circus in warm-up should be. Montana picks up some scarlet clubs for an impromptu juggle. Denis Remnez, a Russian aerialist built like a squat blond bear, makes friendly kung-fu feints at the Bio Brothers, a pair of ghostly pale Ukrainians whose slender frames belie the almost superhuman strength and control displayed in their sci-fi-themed balancing routine.

In the otherwise empty auditorium, a gaggle of local school kids file in from a plate-spinning class that Micheletty has been hosting in the adjacent rehearsal studio.

Forty feet above their heads Montana's cousin Junior Neves is teaching his new girlfriend, a tiny porcelain-featured Russian ice skater called Svetlana, how to jump from the trapeze into the net below. She has bungee ropes attached to either side of a harness around her waist but still looks tense – it's a very long way down.

The couple met a few weeks ago on a tour of Italy. By the end of the Neves family's eight-week summer season at the Hippodrome Svetlana hopes to be flying well enough to join the act.

In the same period Junior's brother Aston hopes to have achieved the first quadruple somersault in Britain. It's the Holy Grail of trapeze and will propel the Flying Neves into the highest echelons of the circus world.

Such lofty aspirations, however, do not stop the flyers also selling merchandise from the stand in the foyer, while the giant Montana marches around the edge of the ring in the interval, looking as out of place as a Tyrannosaurus in a pinny as he sells dainty little battery-powered illuminated windmills to the kids. There are no divas in the circus.

'None of them is in it for the money,' says Peter Jay, who has run the Hippodrome with his wife Christine for the past thirty years. 'There are no egos. No drink or drugs. They're a totally different type of person to the rest of the showbiz world. For someone like Aston, it's just about getting that quad.'

A Subway sandwich bar on the corner has become the Hippodrome's *de facto* canteen. Dressed all in black, Peter perches at a window table, watching his clown car tootle up and down the windswept prom touting for business. It's an eye-catching vehicle: the entire top half is a ten-foot-tall clown's torso and head, gaily painted with yellow hair, whiteface, red nose and pink polka-dot tunic; its occupant is completely invisible.

'I've got a new driver, and I want to make sure he's driving slowly enough,' Peter explains. 'I want him to drive as slowly as he can without getting pulled over.'

At sixty-four Jay is a slight, bird-like figure with intense eyes and the hollow cheeks of a born worrier. Dressed entirely in black, and usually huddled in a capacious coat whatever the season, Jay's teased-up, raven-black hair betrays his past as a 1960s' rock star. His mostly instrumental band Peter Jay and the Jay Walkers, in which he played the drums, had a hit with 'Can Can 62' in that year and toured with the Beach Boys and the Rolling Stones.

Before that, Peter and Christine both grew up in families with entertainment interests along the Yarmouth seafront. His earliest memories are as a five-year-old, watching his mother produce variety shows at the Windmill Theatre, a couple of minutes' walk along the prom from the Hippodrome. Today the Windmill still stands, with its trademark windmill sails on the front, but Jay has transformed it into an indoor crazy-golf emporium. His other business interests include a cinema and a nightclub. While Yarmouth's holidaymakers pray for sunny weather, Peter and Christine are the only couple in the resort who pray for rain – to drive the punters inside.

'Christine was the girl next door,' Peter tells me. 'We literally lived within two doors of each other. Our families were bingo rivals. We were good friends, but we were battling with each other for business, because bingo was very cut-throat in those days. Christine's dad used to get up on stage and tell jokes and play the trumpet in their bingo hall, and we used to give away three-piece suites and rolls of carpet. When Christine and I started going out together everyone thought we were just trying to find out each other's family business secrets!'

It was the fear that another promoter might turn the Hippodrome into a rival bingo hall that prompted Peter and his father Jack to buy the building when it came up for sale in 1978.

'I actually hated circus at the time,' Peter admits. 'I'd been to the Hippodrome a few times as a kid, and I really didn't like it. They had terrible lighting, the worst musicians, and the music seemed to be stuck in a time-warp from the Swing era. For a young rock'n'roller like me it was totally uncool. My dad didn't like the circus, either. Originally we thought of turning it into a bowling alley or a disco. But there's a magic in that building that starts working on you. So, in a moment of madness, we thought, why not have a go at the circus thing but put a new spin on it and do it our own way?'

For his first two seasons Jay booked a travelling circus. After that he decided to book individual acts and produce the show himself. His interest in production began in his days with the band: 'We were never just a band standing on stage. It was always a produced show. We took lighting with us. We did comedy. We started the act backlit, in silhouette. The drums lit up. It was always very visual.'

By transferring his rock'n'roll sensibilities to the circus ring, Jay became one of circus's great modernizers – although at the time not everyone was ready for his innovations.

'We started doing simple things, like having the lighting move with the music – which is so basic. But at the time nobody was doing it. I had a lot of opposition from traditional circus fans, just for things like using music tracks with vocals. It doesn't sound possible now, but at the time it was ground-breaking. It was like "There's this mad rock'n'roller in Yarmouth doing all these things with flashing lights and loud music!"'

Before long, however, Jay had the satisfaction of seeing other circuses follow his style of presentation. 'I had acts coming to me who would say, "We want to come and work for you because our music's not very good and we know you'll put new music to it and do the lights." That's been my main pleasure really. Just seeing how putting new music and lighting to an act transforms it.'

From starting out as a complete outsider, Jay's reputation within the circus industry grew as he expanded to direct nine seasons at the Tower Circus, Blackpool, six seasons at the Blackpool Superdome and other events around the country, including the London Circus Festival in Docklands.

Peter describes his circus as the MTV version. 'Rather than go down the arty Cirque du Soleil route, it's a variety show for a seaside audience; something the man in the street who doesn't know anything about circus can come to and enjoy. But at the same time I'm trying to get back to the roots: daring acts that take immense concentration and years of practice, the excitement of watching someone attempt something they may not actually be able to do.'

Amid the pulsating lights and music Miguel Peris is a rotating blur on roller skates atop a circular platform the size of a small dining table. From a chain around his iron-hard neck, his sister Alicia is hanging by a harness around her own neck, spinning on her own axis as she whirls around him like a human helicopter blade.

In the wings, they collapse into plastic patio-style chairs. The darkly beautiful Alicia wraps a dressing-gown around her skimpy costume. Sweat is bursting out of Miguel's tanned shaven skull like a fountain. Typical of their peers, the siblings are fourth-generation circus stock. Their Spanish father and English mother met working for Billy Smart. They grew up in caravans all over the world and have been skating together for seventeen years, since their teens. The sprains and knocks are part of the job.

'There are no sick notes in the circus,' Miguel says with a grin, once he has recovered enough to lug his skating table backstage. 'You go on and do the same act with a smile on your face, even if you are in pain.'

The worlds of health and safety and circus appear to be mutually exclusive. The backstage of the Hippodrome is plastered with taped-up small posters on which someone has printed warnings to mind your head or watch your footing on the uneven floor. But they seem laughable when compared to the risks the performers take on the other side of the curtain.

Peter admits he worries constantly – a trait he inherited from his father. 'I was taught by a master!' he jokes. Jay senior seldom watched the shows, preferring to sit in his little office behind the box office until it was all over; he was always afraid something would go wrong. Peter, by contrast, watches every performance, usually from the very edge of his seat.

The strain shows in his face, and he admits the stress takes it out of him. But he says, 'It's a love–hate thing.' At the end of the season, when the audience has gone home, the performers have dispersed to the four corners of the globe and the Hippodrome stands cold and empty, he can't wait for the next season to come around.

'Because we don't have a big company, a lot of people are doing a lot of different things in the show, and it's not cost-effective to have understudies. So if someone hurts themselves and they're out of the show for any length of time, it can make life very difficult. But that's part of the addiction, I suppose – that thrill where every day you don't know what's going to happen. When you're watching the flying trapeze, in an instant something can happen that results in someone not being able to work. It then comes straight back to me to rearrange the show and make it work. So I get that same thrill ane audience has when it sees it for the first time. I get that every day, for different reasons.'

His skin snow-white in the spotlight, Danny Adams is handcuffed and lowered into a milk-churn brimming with water. As his head goes under and displaced water cascades over the sides, two volunteers from the audience tip fresh buckets of water into the churn on top of him to bring the level flush with the rim. Then they put the lid on and fasten it with four padlocks.

Danny is billed as Britain's top clown. His anarchic mix of broad slapstick and irreverent verbal humour could not be more British, nor more suited to a seaside audience. Although he wears a red nose and a multicoloured suit reminiscent of the Colin Baker-era Dr Who, Danny's highly verbal routines with his ringmaster father Clive Webb have less to do with the popular image of heavily made-up, mostly silent clowns than that of the classic straight man–funny man comedy double act. Clive's role is to be perpetually exasperated by Danny's pranks and interruptions.

'What did I tell you in the dressing-room?' Clive demands midway through their act.

'Don't do that in the sink,' replies Danny.

'Not that! After that!'

'Poke it down with a stick . . .' offers Danny.

The audience rolls up with laughter.

Danny's milk-churn stunt, however, is deadly serious; not an illusion, he insists, but a genuine escape that requires him to hold his breath under water in total darkness for a minute and a quarter.

As a black tent is drawn over the locked milk-churn, Clive invites the audience to see how long we can hold our breath. Peter Jay's youngest son, Jack, solemnly continues to count the seconds from a stopwatch long after we have been forced to take a gulp of air. By Jack's side a man stands with an axe, ready to break the locks on the churn if Danny fails to emerge.

As Clive keeps up an anxious commentary, some of the worry in his voice and demeanour is obviously showmanship, designed to keep us on the edge of our seats. But an equal part of it is clearly very real.

A split second after Clive has issued the slightly panicky command 'OK, let's get him out of there!' Danny emerges, staggering and spluttering through the curtains. It's hard to believe they don't always cut it that fine deliberately. But, Peter reveals, there were times during rehearsal when they really did have to rescue Danny from a claustrophobic watery grave.

Backstage, exhilarated, with water still dripping from his false red nose, Danny says, 'The first time I went in was horrible. You hear the padlocks go on. Your heart is racing . . . and I couldn't get out at all. It was the scariest, scariest thing ever. Two people have died doing it. One magician didn't realize they had dropped the churn on the way in and damaged it so that he couldn't get out. By the time they got him out and into hospital . . .' Danny tails off and looks away.

Discussing the dangers of circus in the Hippodrome, it's hard not to remember Eva who died in the ring just feet away. Yet this is a superstitious community, and the more heavily Eva's ghost seems to hang in the air the more taboo it seems to mention the ultimate risk that her colleagues take.

On the fifth anniversary of her death, Peter is understandably reluctant to discuss that dreadful day, except to say, 'It was a terrible time for all of us. We all lived through that. We're all friends. It was horrible, and it just reminds you how dangerous this business is.'

With a ghostly pallor in his face, the showman blows out his breath and raises his eyebrows as he reflects quietly, 'People are doing this twice a day for me.' Yet Jay says he has never come across an act he considered too dangerous to book. 'Not really. Because circus people are very precise. They know the risks they're taking, and they're very fastidious about their safety. The only things I don't like are things kids might copy: fakir-type acts with people sticking knives in themselves.'

Every showman should have a caravan. Peter Jay's is indoors. While the public swarm about buying popcorn before the show, he leads the way through the foyer and down a narrow corridor to a door set into the wall that you could walk past a hundred times without seeing. And there, parked in a cavernous storage space rammed with old props, is a huge metal trailer-home. Clanging up the steps to turn on the lights inside, Peter explains that his son sometimes sleeps here when he's been working too late to go home.

Making himself comfortable on the black leather upholstery, Peter explains that as a newcomer it took him many years to be accepted by the circus community.

'Most circus families go back hundreds of years. It's a small, quite close-knit community. So to come into it as an outsider, and with what were then fairly outrageous ideas about music and lighting, it was very hard to get accepted. For years it was like "Who is this person who doesn't know anything about circus and what's he doing messing about with our thing?"'

Yet, while Jay has helped to bring the style of circus into the twenty-first century, he has also become absorbed into the circus tradition; not least, the tradition of the circus family where every member is involved. His working relationship with his wife thrives on a strict division of labour, with Peter making the artistic decisions while Christine handles the administration.

'Christine is a fantastic back-up for me, because she's much more practical than I am. So I can come up with all these mad ideas like "Get me this act from Ecuador and this act from Kazakhstan", and she'll organize all the work permits and even travel to get them here. Once they're here, she's like a mother hen. If they need a doctor or a dentist, or they've run out of this or that and need to know where to get it, she'll organize it for them. So I get all the interesting bits and she gets all the boring bits!' Peter laughs.

The Jays' middle son, Joe, trained on the flying trapeze with legendary Mexican teacher Rene Ramos and toured Europe with Mexican troupe the Flying Rodogels, whom he met when they worked at the Hippodrome. Today Joe uses his aerial skills at the top of oil rigs and on the world's tallest construction sites, where the money is better.

Youngest son Jack, however, is a true son of the circus and determined to carry on his father's work. In the afternoon sunshine of the small yard at the back of the Hippodrome the twenty-year-old recalls, 'One of my first jobs was selling spinning plates – demo-ing them in the ring. That was the first skill I learned. I was probably seven or eight. Then I went on to selling programmes.'

The appeal of the circus for Jack is the camaraderie. 'More so than in regular show business, there are no barriers between the crew and the top act. Everyone is one unit. At the end of the season you may never see any of these people again, but for that six or eight weeks, you're family.'

Inheriting his father's musical ability, Jack was playing drums throughout the show by the time he reached his early teens. While his father has always been happiest behind the scenes, Jack has proved less shy about appearing in the spotlight. When Clive Webb was off work following a heart-bypass operation, Jack stepped into his shoes, quickly learning the straight-man routine for a theatre tour with Danny. Soon he'll be the Hippodrome's full-time ringmaster, as well as the show's co-producer.

Peter, in his caravan, is every inch the proud dad. 'Jack has been having ideas about the show his whole life. I remember when he was eight or nine, saying at the end of the show, "There were three or four things that could be improved. That bit was too long, or that bit wasn't funny." Now he's producing 50 per cent of the show. It's great for me, because my dad was never a fan of the circus. He just said, "If you want to do it, have a go at it." He was never involved. But I always kept his name on the posters while he was alive: *Jack and Peter Jay present*. . . So seeing that back on the posters again is fantastic for me.'

In time Peter sees himself handing the reins of the Hippodrome to his son entirely. 'Hopefully, I'll be able to do less of the day-to-day worrying,' he smiles. But, proving the truth of that old line from Cecil B. DeMille's film *The Greatest Show on Earth*, that you can shake the sawdust off your shoes but you can never shake it out of your heart, the man who once hated the circus admits, 'I'd find it very hard to let go of it completely.'

Peter still has plenty of plans for the Hippodrome, including a new entrance and cafeteria in the area where his caravan now stands. But, just as he has preserved the spirit of circus while updating its presentation, he is wary of altering too much the old building's unique character.

'I'm not a believer in ghosts,' Peter reflects, 'but it's a weird thing. It's almost like old theatres and places like this retain the spirit of great experiences. Many people experience good times, and it kind of stays there. It almost weaves itself into the fabric of the building. I've seen it happen too many times where they've destroyed the atmosphere of an old theatre by over-renovating. That's why I'm a great hoarder of old props and old bits and pieces. Ben keeps throwing things out, and I keep bringing them back in, because they'll go into the new parts to soften it.'

Backstage, while the show buzzes towards its climax behind the curtain, the talk has also turned to the future.

Montana, the 26-year-old catcher, says he plans to leave the circus and start a family in around ten years' time. 'Maybe I'll open a discotheque in Brazil.'

Miguel Peris is more typical of the circus breed when he says that the only person he would marry would be another circus performer with whom he could continue his nomadic life. 'The first time I worked in the ring I was six years old,' he says. 'It was a Western rope-spinning act. I've never wanted to do anything else.' With a laugh he adds, 'Even if I wanted to, I don't think I could do anything else.'

A few yards away a practice swing hangs from the ceiling. Junior Neves, having barely finished wowing the crowd on the flying trapeze, is again putting Svetlana through her paces. As she hangs from the bar, her face is rigid with concentration. Junior wears a broad grin.

'The Russians take training so seriously,' Junior teases.

Jumping down, Svetlana proudly displays tiny palms rippled with broken blisters.

'This is not from trapeze,' Junior points out. 'This is just from warming up.'

Half-a-dozen girls run by in swimsuits and a whiff of chlorine, their feet squelching on the tatty carpet. In bygone eras the Hippodrome's water feature was used to recreate hunting scenes, with real stags, dogs and horses galloping through the water. In the interval the audience were invited to dive into the pool for sovereigns thrown to the bottom. Today the only people in danger of a soaking are Danny and Clive as the son rows out in a boat to rescue his dad, who is stranded atop a stepladder in the middle of the pool.

Having barely had time to dry off and dress, Danny ends the show with a bang – as a human cannonball. This time the stunt is a comedy trick. As Clive begins the countdown, Danny slithers unseen from the base of the cannon and through the curtain into the foyer. Racing against the clock, he rips off his pristine boiler-suit to reveal a tattered one underneath. He blackens his face and hares off around the building to make his reappearance hanging from the balcony on the other side.

Running the merchandise stand, Christine Jay and her eldest son Ben cover their ears as a report shakes the hundred-year-old building. When the cannon is dragged out through the foyer and into the street, followed by a cloud of acrid gun-smoke and the cheers of the crowd, they break into huge grins.

Another show has been successfully completed, and everyone can relax. Until 7.30, when they do it all again.

Chapter 3

THE ELEPHANT IN THE ROOM

Circuses and animals have gone together since trick horse-rider Philip Astley built the first circus ring in London 250 years ago. But will animal circuses survive?

I'm in the pub when I first see the elephant. It's not pink, though, and I'm drinking nothing stronger than coffee. It's lunchtime, and the pachyderm is on the big screen behind the bar. It's standing outside a circus tent, with an old red car in the background. A burly silver-haired man in a red jacket and black top hat is standing beside the big, wrinkly brown beast, occasionally dipping into his pocket and feeding it what appear to be peanuts while answering questions from surrounding news crews.

The sound is off – the pub only puts it on for football – but the rolling subtitle beneath the Sky News logo tells me that animal-rights protestors are up in arms over the return of elephants to a British circus ring for the first time in a decade.

The next day the story is in all the papers. The coverage, predictably, focuses on the protests, as typified by the *Daily Mail*'s headline, 'Police on standby in war over the elephants.'

Dr Rob Atkinson, head of the RSPCA's wildlife department, is quoted as calling the return of the elephants 'a body blow for animal welfare in this country. Asking these majestic animals to behave in unnatural ways in the name of entertainment is a disgrace.' Tory MP Mark Pritchard, secretary of the all-party parliamentary group on wildlife and conservation, adds, 'These animals are being exploited for profit and nothing else.'

Elsewhere in the same report, the Captive Animals' Protection Society fuels the controversy by claiming that Delhi, one of the three elephants imported by the Great British Circus, has problems with her legs – she recently collapsed in Germany and needing to be rescued by firemen.

The report of the elephant's collapse appears to be unsubstantiated. In another paper it is claimed that firemen were needed to help Delhi from a lake in which she had gone for a swim with her trainer – a scene hardly suggestive of a cruel training regime.

The objections posted on newspaper websites read like the work of a small but vocal hard core of campaigners.

I find myself torn. In the past few months I have been increasingly impressed by the standard of circus productions, and the skill and dedication of its performers. I have become a circus fan. Yet the shows I have seen have been exclusively human spectacles. In the main they have been performed in theatres and arts centres – a modern and perhaps sanitized version of an art form that now seems happier to distance itself from its big-top origins by using the trendier, more media-friendly name 'cirque'.

The elephants call to me with the promise of a glimpse of an older, more raw tradition. They stir up almost forgotten but still potent childhood memories of what a circus should be. But the temptation is a guilty one, and my concern for the animals' welfare weighs heavily on me.

When I conduct a survey of my immediate circle I find that the feeling against animal circuses runs deep. Everyone I speak to harbours the instinctive conviction that animal circuses are cruel, even though nobody I speak to has been to one since childhood.

When I suggest to my partner that we should at least go along to judge for ourselves, she takes a lot of persuading. After all, animal circuses are cruel, aren't they? And so it is with a lot of baggage over the animal issue that we set out to see the Great British Circus at its first stop of the season, in Nottinghamshire.

It's not only ten years since circus elephants last worked in Britain. It's also a decade, almost to the month, since Mary Chipperfield was convicted on twelve counts of cruelty against an eighteen-month-old chimpanzee called Trudy, after undercover animal-rights campaigners filmed her kicking and beating the primate. At the same trial, Chipperfield's husband, a former director of Longleat Zoo, was found guilty of causing unnecessary suffering to a sick elephant.

Prosecutions of circus trainers for cruelty are rare, and in fact Chipperfield wasn't working in circus at the time; she was running a company training animals for film work. But the Chipperfield case was particularly damaging to the image of circus because her family name is one of the most famous in the business. The Chipperfields' association with animal training dates back more than three hundred years to 1684, when James Chipperfield presented animals at the Frost Fair on the frozen Thames.

Between the two world wars the Chipperfields moved into circus, and by the 1950s, which was a golden age for the popularity of circus in the UK, the family had established Britain's largest circus, with a herd of sixteen elephants, 200 horses and hundreds of other animals, plus a tent that could hold 6,000 spectators. In the 1970s ITV broadcast annual Christmas and Easter shows from Chipperfield's Circus in rivalry with Billy Smart's on BBC1.

Whether Mary Chipperfield's practices were typical of her profession is, of course, debatable – as is the question of what constitutes cruelty. Is it confined to painful training methods, or is simply constantly transporting the animals around the country in lorries bad enough?

In her memoir *Josser* (which is the circus word for an outsider who enters their world) Nell Stroud – now Gifford – presents a more positive picture of the way circus animals are kept and treated. During a gruelling year at the dirty end of circus, when she worked as an apprentice groom, travelling the country in a rusty showerless caravan, mucking out horses and elephants, she reports that the condition and welfare of the animals was always the circus's priority: 'It was the humans who were treated like shit.'

Julian Deplidge, company manager of the all-human circus on ice show Cirque de Glace, visited circuses in Russia, where most of his performers are from. In a bluff northern accent he tells me, 'I would be against cruelty to animals in any shape or form, and I've seen some things over there that I didn't agree with. When you have a bear juggling with fire . . . Wild animals have an instinct to run away from fire. But I noticed that at the start of the routine a whip was brought out. It was never used, but it was shown to the bear and put on the side of the stage. At that point you know that the bear was more frightened of the whip than it was of the fire. That's the kind of thing I thought wasn't right. On the other hand, I've been involved in shows where they had performing dogs and the dogs were better cared for than some of the people. There was no cruelty in their training. So I think every individual case has to be looked at on its own merits.'

Historically, circuses and animals have been inseparable. The word 'circus' dates from Ancient Rome: the Circus Maximus, Circus Flaminus, Circus Neronis and Circus of Maxentius, arenas that held chariot races, equestrian displays, gladiatorial contests and staged battles, with trained animals, jugglers and acrobats completing the mix. After the fall of Rome, itinerant groups of animal trainers and acrobats toured the fairgrounds of Europe, re-creating the spectacle of the Roman circus.

The father of modern circus was Philip Astley, a former cavalry officer and trick rider who opened his Amphitheatre of Equestrian Arts in Lambeth on 9 January 1768. One of his favourite tricks was to ride at full pelt while standing with one foot on his horse's back and another on its head while waving a sword in the air.

The son of a cabinet-maker from Newcastle-under-Lyme, Astley was born on 8 January 1742. He joined the Fifteenth Light Dragoon Regiment and was made a sergeant major after riding against the French in Germany when he was still in his teens. After leaving the army, Astley began performing on horseback on fields at Halfpenny Hatch at the south side of Westminster Bridge. His first arena was an open-air roped-off circle where his wife passed the hat while he rode, but he soon made enough money to build a wooden shed over part of the ring and charged for admission to the covered part.

By 1770 Astley had completely encircled his open-air ring with roofed seating and built a two-storey grandstand above the entrance, with stables beneath the seats. The sign said 'Astley's Riding School'. He gave lessons in the morning and broke horses on the side. But he performed shows in the afternoon and the exterior of his amphitheatre set the tone for the décor of circus box offices to this day, with gaudy illustrations of tightrope walkers, a pyramid of acrobats standing on each other's shoulders and a horseman riding two galloping horses, one foot on each. Along the eaves of the grandstand were a parade of wooden horsemen, and atop the peak of its central pitched roof was a figure of Astley, standing on horseback and brandishing his sword.

Before the performance, Astley would be found in his cavalry uniform astride a gleaming white charger at the end of Westminster Bridge, the original brightly costumed ringmaster, using his sword to point customers in the direction of the greatest show in London.

After his original wooden building burned down Astley built a grand new brick-built amphitheatre on a site where St George's Hospital would later stand. With three balconies, which could seat 3,000 people, it opened as the Royal Amphitheatre of the Arts in 1803 under the patronage of the Prince of Wales and Duke of York and would later simply be called Astley's.

By then a famous showman, Astley also opened the Amphitheatre Anglais in Paris and established circuses in eighteen other European cities. He died shortly after his seventy-second birthday at his French home in 1814 and was buried in the Père Lachaise cemetery in Paris.

Astley didn't call his show a circus – that name was adopted in 1782 by Astley's rival, Charles Hughes, who set up the Royal Circus a short distance away. But it was Astley who established the now standard diameter of the circus ring (which he called the 'circle') as 42 feet, or 13 metres; that being the optimum space needed for horses to reach a full gallop and create the centrifugal force required to ride while standing.

Astley also created the modern circus bill by adding novelty acts such as 'The Little Military Learned Horse', a strongman called Signor Colpi, jugglers, clowns, acrobats and riding displays that included a pyramid of men standing on each other's shoulders atop four horses galloping side by side. Trained wild animals began appearing in circuses soon after, and the first elephant in a British circus made its début at Covent Garden in 1810.

The word 'jumbo', meaning 'large', entered the English language because of the popularity of Jumbo, an 11-foot-tall Sudanese elephant who was bought from London Zoo by the American circus owner Phineas Taylor (P.T.) Barnum, in 1881 and became the star attraction of the Barnum and Bailey Circus – the famously self-declared 'Greatest Show on Earth'. It's believed the zoo staff derived the elephant's name from the Swahili words *Jambo*, meaning 'Hello', or *Jambe*, meaning 'Chief'.

During the first half of the twentieth century animal acts far outnumbered human performers in the circus ring. A Kayes Brothers circus poster from the 1950s promises Johnny Kayes and his lions, Paddy the unrideable mule, Cilla's Football Dogs, Comedy riding baboon Denaco, Jimmy Kaye's Streamline Greys, Pasha the High-School Horse, the Quadrilles Lady Equestrians, Kayes Liberty Horses and the Sensational Ranleighs – 'The fastest trick riding act ever presented to the British public'. The only human acts on the bill were clowns Andy and Atom, foot jugglers Levanda and Van and 'BBC ace accordionist' Chick Robini.

Before the advent of television, animal circuses had a unique educational role. If you lived in an English village at a time when foreign travel was a rarity and even a trip to a major city was not undertaken lightly, where but in a travelling circus could you see such exotic creatures as leopards, polar bears and camels? Even domestic animals were a major attraction, since circus horses tended to be rare breeds presented in a show condition unlikely to be glimpsed among the working horses encountered in everyday life.

Today, however, we can all watch the most exotic animals in their natural environments without leaving the comfort of our living-rooms. Do we need the moustachioed machismo of lion tamers with cracking whips and brandished chairs when we can have a comforting whispered commentary by David Attenborough?

By the 1970s a waning of interest in traditional circus shows was accompanied by a growing unease among the public over the animal-rights issue. During the same period a new movement of human-skills-based circus, called cirque nouveau, began to emerge simultaneously in France,

Australia, California and the UK. Performed by young companies and often attracting a student or arts-based audience, the movement had its roots in street entertainment. Eventually it would produce the biggest circus in the world, Cirque du Soleil – now a global corporation with several large-scale productions simultaneously on tour in the world's major cities.

In Britain the majority of traditional circuses gave up their animals during the 1990s for pragmatic reasons. Local councils, sensitive to the voice of protestors, banned animal shows from prime municipal grounds. The few mavericks such as Martin Lacey and his Great British Circus who refused to bow to pressure and kept their animals found themselves exiled to privately owned out-of-town grounds where protestors continued to picket the gates in an effort to keep trade away.

For Lacey, his elephant parade is something of a victory march. Standing amid the circled lorries, caravans and throbbing generators of his traditional travelling circus ground, the showman says, 'We waited until after the Department for Environment, Food and Rural Affairs report by the Circus Animals Working Group. The government did two years' research into animals in circuses, and the six scientists involved concluded that circuses are perfectly capable of meeting the welfare needs of animals in their care. To me, we now have the green light. Circuses have for far too long been the whipping boys of the animal-rights charities, and now that we've been officially cleared I thought it was right to bring back the elephants.'

Lacey is a big man, with a clipped voice and bearing in keeping with his military-colonial background. His father was in the Royal Artillery. Lacey grew up in barracks in Germany and India, and it was there, he says, that 'I fell in love with animals at an early age. I was taught to ride by the Royal Artillery. My father's regiment used to exercise the maharajah's horses, and I used to see the elephants the maharajah owned in their luxury stables. I was going to go to agricultural college and be a farmer. Instead I went to work in Chester Zoo. I worked in zoos for a long time but rapidly realized I was a glorified gaoler. Zoos put animals in cages for life, whereas I wanted to work with animals.'

Having trained tigers and lions for more than forty years, Lacey says, 'Our animals are a bit like police dogs or police horses. They have a very mentally and physically stimulating day and a super time working with people.'

The animals enjoy performing, then?

'Of course they do. Otherwise they wouldn't do it. It's organized play, and if they don't want to play then you have a problem. That's why any suggestion of cruelty is entirely spurious. If one mistreats any animal they tend not to forget. They will quite possibly want to get their own back, and in the case of tigers you're talking about the most perfectly designed killing machine there is. They know who their friends are and who they enjoy working with. To train them you have to be rather nice to them.'

Lacey is a passionate man who has been known to lose his temper with the animal-rights brigade or journalists who deliberately push his buttons. He's 'quite an angry man', according to his one-time boss, the veteran showman Gerry Cottle. But Lacey's prickliness is understandable. When Cottle took the business decision that, given the hostility towards animal circuses, it was easier to go with the flow and do without animals, Lacey chose the harder route.

It's easy to see Lacey as a Canute-like figure, defying the tide of changing times out of sheer cussedness – for in the current climate regarding animal circuses he's surely not in it for the money. On the surface, he's bullish about the protestors, arguing, 'There's no such thing as bad publicity. If these people didn't protest about them, you probably wouldn't be interested in my elephants.' But, when he thinks no one's looking the tension shows in Lacey. Outside the ring it's Lacey, not his tigers, who paces. In the interval he circles the inside of his tent. Between shows I find him walking around the perimeter of his circled lorries and caravans as if they were battlements. Like any showman Lacey is king within this medieval encampment. But Lacey's is a kingdom besieged, and the conflict is one he would sooner do without.

Indeed, he claims that running a circus is only a means to the end of working with the animals he loves. With a smile that could only be genuine, he confides, 'I'm like the guy who has a white Rolls-Royce and has to take it out on a Saturday to do weddings in order to fund his hobby.'

There are no protesters or police at the gate when I arrive at the Newark Showground, in Nottinghamshire, for the first show of the day at five o'clock on a Friday afternoon. Nor are there many paying customers. The showground is a windy expanse of land close to the A1 but little else. It's a long drive across a desert of concrete car park to the short row of cars parked in front of the looming big top and its surrounding articulated lorries. Having in recent weeks attended near sold-out circus shows in large theatres, it's a disappointing turnout.

The entrance to the tent is equally low key. After a short walk from the box-office wagon, across some well-trampled grass and dry mud, we're let in through a plain flap in the corner of the tent.

Inside, it's hard to escape the sense that you are entering another world. The first impressions are of size and darkness. Supported by thick king poles of criss-crossed steel, the roof of the tent looms high above, like a black sky. There are gold stars printed in the roof lining, but they are almost impossible to make out. The only light, from four banks of football stadium-style spotlights attached to the king poles, is focused on the ring – a gleaming oasis of near-white sawdust. Standing patiently inside the ring fence are a sturdy brown and white horse and a camel with a deep pile coat of thick brown fur, ready to provide rides around the ring for children.

Around the perimeter of the ring are three or four rows of loose plastic chairs, standing on the rough grass and mud floor. Encircling them are a wide walkway, then wide banks of gently raked fixed seats. Pulled up, just inside the entrance is a tea and burger wagon of the sort normally found in roadside lay-bys. In the far corner is a brightly painted popcorn stand. Walking through the heat coming off the food stands provides fleeting relief from the generally frigid air that is a constant reminder that, far from inhabiting a cosy theatre, we're in a tent in the middle of nowhere.

A short, old-fashioned-style clown, with a red nose, false white moustache and wide braces over a red-and-white striped T-shirt, is doing the rounds, selling spinning plates and the ubiquitous flashing windmills.

The ushers are Eastern European boys with big grins and little English. Ridiculously, considering the sparseness of the audience, there's a mix-up with my front-row seats, and it looks as though someone else is going to get evicted. I point out a couple of empty seats further down the row. How about we just take those two? But, no, these boys are determined to get it right. In the end it takes three of them. An evidently more senior woman, a mother-hen type who eventually turns up, counts the plastic seats from the end of the row – there are no numbers on them – and, with rolled eyes and an indulgent smile in the direction of her underlings, concludes that *these two* empty seats a little way along the row are mine.

I look around and realize that the rows of tiered seats behind me are going to remain empty. 'Mr and Mrs Wood and the whole Wood family', as circus folk describe a tent with more empty furniture than patrons. But as the lights go down it ceases to matter. In a theatre you would feel the emptiness of a poorly attended house sapping the atmosphere. The big top, by contrast, seems to close snugly around us, emphasizing only our proximity to the ring and the impending action. The sense of anticipation is palpable. I can feel the excitement not just in myself but in those around me, especially the little children who are standing in front of their seats in expectation. I can see it in the families opposite me, on the far side of the ring.

The spotlights converge on the closed dark red velvet curtains – the ring doors. Behind a desk off to the side, Lacey puts the music on – and that's when something extraordinary happens.

The music is 'Entrance of the Gladiators', the hundred-year-old circus theme tune that, next to 'Happy Birthday to You', must be a contender for the most recognizable piece of music on the planet. Few might know it by title or be able to name its composer, the unfortunately surnamed Julius Fucik, but say 'circus music' to anybody and they'll *dum-dum-dummy-dummy-dum-dum-da-da* it to you with a smile on their face. It's a piece of music so predictable that a modern, cirque-style show wouldn't play it in a million years. I should find it unspeakably naff – or, at the very least, ironic and amusing. But within the big top, with the trampled mud, the sawdust and the whiff of horses and camels, it hits me harder than any piece of music I have ever heard. Two hundred and fifty years of tradition, the circus magic, call it what you will – it hits me like a train.

Even typing this a month later, just remembering that moment brings a lump the size of a tennis ball to my throat, and I feel the tears welling up behind my eyes. *This is the real deal,* that simple little piece of music says to me. *This is circus, undiluted and unashamed. It's down, it's marginalized and there's not much of it left . . . but it's alive, it's powerful and it will live on.* When I mention it to my partner, who was so reluctant to accompany me, she confesses she was affected by the music in exactly the same way. In fact, she was overcome to such an extent that, at the time, she was too embarrassed to mention it.

Circus's trademark mixture of low budget and high spirits is evident in the opening number, as the Union Jack-waving dancers – just three of them – kick sawdust into the air in their high heels . . . and as Sophie Coles, the ringmistress, an orange-tanned blonde with a mysterious closed-lip smile and impossibly large eyes, rides into the arena on a horse to welcome the 'Ladies and gentlemen, boys and girls . . .'

It's a far cry from Las Vegas where tens of millions of dollars and hundreds of performers were poured into the five Cirque du Soleil shows currently playing different venues in the glitter city – some of the buildings completely remodelled or specially built for the purpose. But there's a heart to this tent show in Newark that transcends its bargain-basement tinsel and conspires to be far more engaging and enthralling than many a far artier or glitzier production.

The dancers aren't just ring candy. Early in the show they also perform a magic routine, two of them making the third appear from a glass case in the time it takes to whip a cloth over it and whip it off again. The illusion is impressive, but there's a formative quality to the act, a lack of poise and polish in the presentation that suggests they're still working on it. But they're young and have the potential to be good. In conventional theatre, actors learn their trade in stage schools and rehearsal rooms, behind closed doors. Circus performers learn in the ring, in front of an audience from the beginning.

There are a couple of moments that make the animal-lover in me cringe. The horse-trainer's party piece in which a stallion goes down on one knee to take a 'bow' is an awkward and unnatural movement on the animal's part, and he looks as uncomfortable performing it as I am watching. Am I supposed to clap the horse for achieving this trick? Or should I applaud the trainer for making him perform this humiliating little gesture? Moreover, the 'bow' seems unnecessary.

The five Dutch Friesian stallions presented by Helyne Edmonds are stunning creatures simply to behold. Their gleaming black coats attest to their pure breeding and the show-winner condition in which they are kept. I would defend the circus's right to exhibit these fine animals on the ground that it is a privilege for us to be able to admire them in motion at such close quarters. The children in the audience are especially entranced. But surely it's enough to watch the horses doing more naturally horsy things, such as cantering around the ring and turning on the spot at Helyne's command?

The cutesy curtsy is a bit like watching a dog owner squeeze a pampered poodle into human clothes. It's not so much cruel as distasteful – and ultimately pointless because it undermines the respect for the animals and the closeness of the animal–trainer relationship that the rest of the presentation fosters.

Given the protests over Lacey's elephants it's ironic that, within the circus world, Britain has a reputation for producing the best animal trainers. Every circus speciality tends to be associated with a particular country. Trapeze artists often come from Mexico or Brazil, springboard acts from Hungary, contortionists from Mongolia and jugglers from France. With Britain it's clowns and animal acts.

Lacey's sons, Alex and Martin Jr, both big-cat trainers, are big names in Germany. Yasmin Smart, equestrian director of the Great British Circus, is famous globally for her horses. In 1985 Yasmin was the first Briton to win the coveted Silver Clown at circus's equivalent of the Oscars, the International Circus Festival in Monte Carlo.

At thirty-two, but already a director of the Great British Circus, Helyne Edmonds is one of the rising stars of the scene. In the ring she cuts a relaxed, unshowy figure. Wearing an understated black trouser suit that wouldn't be out of place in a travel agent's, with her hair pulled back in an unfussy manner, her look is more 'horsy' than showbiz. While most performers live for the spotlight, Helyne gives the impression that working with her horses is a bigger motivation than soaking up the applause.

It's what is known as a liberty act, which means the horses move freely, off the rein, while Helyne stands in the middle of the ring commanding them with just the brush of a long crop. Today, though, one of the stallions is a bit frisky, perhaps because it's the first week of the season. For safety, because the horse could literally step over the ring fence and into the laps of the front-row spectators, ringmistress Sophie Coles joins Helyne in the ring and holds the frisky horse on a long rein as he gallops around with the others. Somehow the rein adds to the raw thrill of seeing these big hard-muscled animals galloping and prancing so close to us. It's more like watching a training session in a roped circle on a farm than a polished theatrical performance.

Helyne's love affair with the circus began when she was six years old. Her stepfather was a circus fan, and visits to the big top were a staple of every school holiday.

'I fell in love with the animals,' she recalls warmly. 'The horses, the tigers – because in those days every circus had animals. One of my strongest early memories is feeding Farley's rusks to two Canadian black bears. As a kid it was a wonderful experience, and all I wanted to do when I grew up was work with animals.'

Her mother insisted she stay on at school to take her A-levels, but as soon as that formality was completed Helyne wasted no time in joining Martin Lacey's Harlequin Circus, as it was then, working in the booking office.

'You can't just walk into a circus and ask them to teach you to train animals,' says Helyne. 'They'd just laugh at you and tell you to go away. You have to work hard and show them you're a genuine person and that you're serious. So I worked in the box office for a couple of years, and then, one day, the guy who looked after the tigers left and I said, "I'll do that." I was a groom for a long time, but then I don't believe you can train an animal unless you know how to look after it and how it ticks. Before I ever worked in the ring I spent many a time just watching the animals, observing their behaviour and learning why they do certain things.

'The first animals I presented were a group of camels that had already been trained by someone else. That's when I discovered how hard it is, because if you give the wrong command they do the wrong thing. I remember standing there in tears, thinking, "Why are they doing this?" After that I presented what we call a "Big and Little", and that time I was involved in the training. Just watching the trainer really and seeing how they did it.'

Today's 'Big and Little' is presented by Sophie, in her blinding white ringmistress's costume of leotard, tailcoat, thigh-length boots and top hat. Aptly billed as Dignity and Impudence in the programme, it's a charming routine, high on the 'Ahhhh' factor, that exploits the comical contrast between the big white-and-brown horse that was giving children's rides before the show and a tiny Shetland pony with almost identical markings.

At the climax, the big horse stands with his front hooves on a pedestal while the Shetland runs under his belly. At the end, the big horse, with a lot of encouragement from Sophie, does the one-legged bow thing that I wish they wouldn't bother with. So full marks to the spirited little Shetland who refuses to do so – he just rolls on his back like a playful dog. Sophie orders him back to his feet to try again – and, living up to his name, Impudence rolls on his back once more. Sophie gives the audience an indulgent shrug, as if to say 'What can you do?' – and gives him his sugar-lump reward anyway.

There are human acts in the Great British Circus. Sophie's teenage son, Ben Coles, brought up in circus rings all over the world, is a remarkable juggler. Running on in a gangster-style pinstripe suit and black trilby with a white band, he dances around the ring, making an effortless blur of three black and white clubs, then burning sticks, then five balls.

His best routine involves three brick-size boxes: one in each hand and the third constantly spun and caught every which way between them. For a gravity-defying finale he leaves all three boxes hanging in the air while he spins a full circle on his heel before catching them again.

In another example of circus's ability seamlessly to weld the tacky to the amazing, a spaceship that looks as though it was knocked up from a bit of tin foil and a set of Christmas lights on *Blue Peter* is wheeled into the ring on an awful old luggage trolley. In a cloud of dry ice it is winched high into the air above us. From its base Bulgarian husband-and-wife team Stefan Nikolov and Neli Nikolova – who go by the name of the Duo Stefaneli – emerge to perform a set of stunning feats of strength and balance on a single trapeze bar.

At one point Stefan is hanging by just his feet and ankles, which are crooked around the ropes at the ends of the trapeze bar. In one hand he holds Neli by her ankle – a head-first drop to the ground a good 15 feet below her. At another point Stefan lies backwards with the trapeze bar in the small of his back being the couple's only point of contact with their 'ship'. Counterbalanced by the weight of her husband's torso, Neli lies lengthways across his feet, held in place only by the strength in his ankles. There is no safety net; no umbilical-cord harness linking them to the spaceship.

Neither Stefan nor Neli is young. They could be in their late thirties or early forties – their bodies honed to perfection, their taut faces worn by the constant training and physical strains of their act. According to the programme, Neli was a nurse before she met Stefan and married into the circus life. For better or for worse, indeed.

During the interval Neli puts a fleece over her costume and works on the burger stand selling teas.

Watching the Duo Stefaneli I'm tempted to wonder once more whether circus really still needs animals. It's hard to imagine a form of entertainment more thrilling than the one Stefan and Neli deliver – especially when performed so close to us.

But then, to close the first half, the elephants come out and, as with the Friesian stallions earlier, I'm struck by the privilege of being brought so close to these exotic giants. The experience of having them right there in your face, their trunks sniffing around curiously, their vast wrinkly hides moving like baggy clothing as they breathe trumps the more distant voyeurism of zoo, wildlife park or television.

Things you remember from childhood as being big are supposed to look small through adult eyes. But the sheer scale of the elephants is staggering – especially when they're swinging their trunks and tusks close enough to make you lean back in your seat. If a dinosaur were brought back to life and led into the ring it could scarcely make more of an impression.

For creatures so big, the elephants move with a hypnotic grace. Stepping down from a metal tub is a deeply considered act. First one foreleg stretches out to a surprising length, its big flat toes feeling for the sawdust with the seeming sensitivity of a human hand. The other legs follow just as slowly, and, with perfect balance, the 4-ton colossus descends with not a sound.

The lightness and precision of the elephants' step is demonstrated when handler Lars Holscher, a slender, youthful man who appears to be in his twenties, lies down while Sonja, a 35-year-old African elephant with enormous tusks, carefully steps over him. The demonstration of trust contradicts suggestions of cruelty behind the scenes. If she didn't like him, there's her chance to crush him.

Although elephants are a long-domesticated species, used as working animals like horses and camels in their native regions, they are more than capable of killing if provoked. Earl Chapin May's 1932 study of early American circuses, *From Rome to Ringling*, includes several tales of rampaging elephants wrecking winter quarters, railroad yards and, after a particularly memorable escape from the big top, even a New York home for old ladies. One bull elephant took its trainer in its mouth and literally shook him to death after the latter was foolish enough to get drunk and stick a pocket knife into the pachyderm's hide.

In those days the preferred method of disposing of a killer elephant was to change its name and sell it to a rival circus. Empress, the War Elephant, reportedly killed nine people in different circuses, including a member of the public who got too close to a parade, before finding a trainer she could get on with and living peacefully ever after. Another rogue – a 6-ton bull called Black Diamond – was such a prolific killer he had to be put down. Too canny to eat an orange laced with cyanide, Black Diamond faced the firing squad. It took 125 rounds just to knock him over. But May also describes the mutually loving relationship between some elephants and their trainers, and the tears of an entire circus when a much-loved long-serving elephant passed away of natural causes at the grand old age of ninety-five.

Today, Lars's extra-curricular activities with his herd include swimming and football. He describes the animals as his family: 'Like children, they always come first.'

In the ring Lars's wife Christine does the splits between the foreheads of Asian pair Delhi and Vana Mana as they carefully walk backwards away from each other, holding each other's trunks in an elephant handshake.

Elephants are intelligent, social animals, programmed to observe the hierarchy of the herd, and it's not unfeasible that they respond to human leadership in the same way that a dog does. Just as a well-trained dog appears happy and content while an untrained pet appears stressed and insecure, it's plausible that the elephants enjoy the challenge of learning tricks.

When the annual elephant polo world championships were instigated in Nepal, the animals initially hated it and would stamp the football-sized ball flat with their feet. They became much more interested when a new rule was introduced allowing them to kick the ball into the goal. They trumpeted loudly when they scored.

I could do without the party-piece 'elephant pyramid', in which two elephants stand with their back legs on metal stands and their forelegs resting on the back of the third elephant, who stands between them, holding Christine aloft in her curled trunk.

Lacey defends the stunt. 'I heard one animal-rights person say it's wrong for elephants to stand on their back legs. Well, elephants have been shagging for years by standing on their back legs. If a female elephant is in season, other female elephants will mount her.'

My objection is artistic. As with the horses, the elephants don't need to be oversold with gimmicks. Just walking into the ring and marching, stopping and turning to command would be enough. The elephant pyramid is a circus tradition, however, and in the circus traditions are slow to change.

In the interval, the camel and the horse return to the ring for children's rides, and Sonja the elephant is brought out so we can have our photo taken with her.

'Ten pounds, please,' smiles Christine, who is wearing a floor-length padded parka over her costume, and I get the feeling the elephant isn't the one being exploited.

There's no doubt Sonja makes a dramatic backdrop. The top of her head is twice my height, and, on Lars's command, she curls her trunk into the air and shows off an impressive display of gleaming tusks. But ten quid seems a bit steep for the shiny little snapshots that Christine hands out at the end of the show. For that price I would have expected a cardboard frame at the very least.

As the lights go down once more, tall sections of steel fencing are being clanged together inside the perimeter of the ring. A netted canopy made from thick ropes is hoisted into place above the cage. The heavy lifting creates a sense of anticipation that is not disappointed as the first of five tigers enters the ring. There's no fanfare, apart from a collective and hushed 'Ahhhh', from the audience, and the low-key entrance only conspires to make the big cat's appearance all the more impressive.

She's a big animal, maybe 8 feet from nose to tail and 300 pounds in weight. Her back is as tall as a man's waist and her coat is as glossy as it is possible to imagine. Her striped fur shimmers in the lights as she pads with a slinky feline nonchalance around the perimeter of the cage, her breath forming in clouds on the chilled air. Moving, undirected, to a pedestal, she sniffs it, exactly as a domestic cat would, as if to check its familiarity, before hopping up and sitting down.

One by one the rest of the tigers file in and move as unhurriedly to their pedestals. Again in the manner of a domestic cat, the nearest one to me licks her paw and washes behind her ear.

In the centre of the ring, surrounded by the cats, Lacey couldn't look more relaxed if he were lying down. There are no snapping whips or brandished chairs. Such accoutrements belong to the American tradition known as *en férocité,* in which wild animals are presented as being untamed and dangerous – the tamer risking his or her life by venturing into the ring with them. The European style of animal training is known as *en douceur,* in which the big cats are presented as being docile and obedient.

Watching such a slow-motion act is mesmerizing. With a sparkly red jacket buttoned across his ample belly and a gentle smile on his rosy features, Lacey looks as benign as Father Christmas. As one cat stalks by he strokes its back and lets its tail trail through his fingers. As another sits poised on a stand, ready to make a seemingly effortless leap through a hoop positioned over three other cats sitting below, Lacey says in avuncular fashion, 'Are you ready? Go on then.' He directs the animals with a wave or a tap of a long, thin stick (he taps the ground or a stool, not the tiger). When a manoeuvre is completed he reverses the stick and rewards the cat with a titbit of pork impaled on the other end.

The effect is not unlike tapping a table and watching a domestic cat jump on to it in return for a stroke, and it's hard not to believe Lacey's assertion that the tigers are enjoying themselves. Yet even a domestic cat can give you a nasty swipe – and, as docile as Lacey's circus-bred big cats appear, they are still tigers.

The very real dangers of working with big cats is made clear after the show, when the audience are invited, for a nominal charge, to visit the animals in their stables and pens behind the big top. The living quarters look perfectly humane, and doubtless they are. In addition to the clean bill of health given to the circus by the government's working group, circuses are inspected by local council vets, along with health and safety officials, at every site they visit, which means every one or two weeks. The Royal Society for the Prevention of Cruelty to Animals (RSPCA) have no right of inspection, but it's unheard of for circuses to deny requests for access.

In one of the cages, two of the tigers have a fleeting spat. Again, it's akin to the behaviour of domestic cats: a bit of hissing, a rapid roll in the dirt and a brief chase. What is striking is the split-second speed with which these briefly combative animals cross the length of their cage – which is essentially the length of an articulated lorry trailer. If one of them moved that quickly in the ring, then the 66-year-old Lacey, who has his back to half of them most of the time, wouldn't stand a chance. That he claims to have had just one 'accident' in his career suggests he's doing something right.

While Lacey takes centre stage with the tigers, Helyne, his protégée, assists in the background, helping with the props and bringing the tigers into the ring. If Lacey is away Helyne does his act. As well as presenting her stallions she is also training a mixed group of lions and tigers – born on the circus last year – that she will eventually present herself. She is currently the only woman tiger trainer in Britain.

The Great British Circus has had great success breeding tigers. They're currently on their tenth generation.

'I hand-reared two, which were born in an early litter,' says Helyne, 'and when you do that they come to see you as their mum. A later litter we left on the tiger mother to rear herself. When you do that they stay wild, in a sense. I did go in and play with them when they were younger, and she allowed me to do that. But as they get older, if you don't go in every day, you lose that closeness. They still talk to me and are pleased to see me, but there's a distance, whereas with the hand-reared ones there's no distance between us at all. I can sit on one and ride him. Normally Martin would have trained them. But because I'd become so close to the hand-reared ones, he felt confident that it was time for me to train them myself.

'We start training when they're eight or nine months old. The first thing we have to teach them is a sign language. Tigers communicate by moving their ears and their tails. We can't do that, so we use sticks with pieces of meat on the end to show them directions, and they follow the meat. Eventually they understand that language. You take the meat away and they work to the stick.

'It's a bit like training a dog. They have to learn to sit and stay while you walk away. It takes a lot of time and patience, and you have to make it fun and interesting for them. To get a tiger to climb on his seat he's got to go over, find a bit of meat on it and think: Cor, this is interesting. Then he'll put one foot up, and all the while you're encouraging him: "That's right, good boy." It's all about lots of rewards and praise and encouragement and nice voices.'

Between her tigers and horses Helyne has a long day, of which the twice-daily shows are just the tip of the iceberg.

'My day starts at 7.30 in the morning. The first thing I do is go to my tigers. I put them in their exercise enclosure and give them some water. Then I go in with one of the boys and clean out their night quarters. Next I go to my horses and put them out in their paddock.

'We practise the tigers early, at ten o'clock. We always train them in the ring, while people are moving about in the big top, picking up the litter, cleaning the seats or repairing things. That way they're prepared for the distractions of an audience.'

After lunch Helyne prepares meat for the tigers; their daily meal, which they eat after the last show, and the titbits used in training and performance. 'It's actually the cheeks from pigs' heads, which I cut into squares.'

Between then and the first show it's office work and, if she has time, cleaning her caravan. The circus is on the road from the end of February to the end of October. During the winter months work with the animals continues at their winter quarters in Lincolnshire.

'For the first couple of weeks they just rest. We all do – we're all knackered. But after a short time, if we don't work with them, they start getting niggly. They're intelligent, educated animals. They're like university students. They need to be learning new things all the time or they get bored.'

Over Christmas Helyne also makes public appearances with a Father Christmas sleigh and real reindeers – which the circus also breeds.

'It's not a job, it's a lifestyle,' says Helyne. 'It can be a hard life. It can be very cold and wet and muddy, and there are times when I wonder: What am I doing here? But when I go and see my animals, whom I absolutely adore, and they express the same pleasure at seeing me, that's all the reward I need.'

It's a pity the anti-circus protestors don't take the time to talk to Helyne, or visit the animals in their quarters behind the big top. But, according to Lacey, they never do. 'It would be like abolitionists attending an execution,' he smiles.

As I leave the showground a fair few campaigners stand either side of the gates, waving their banners and shouting at the cars leaving and those coming in for the evening show. In the paper one of them is quoted as saying, 'We just want to inform members of the public about the lives these animals endure.' They don't look like they want to inform and educate, however. They look like their only intention is to bully and intimidate people into staying away. I don't feel inclined to wind down my window to take a leaflet from a woman who looks like she intends to give me a gobful of abuse. So I drive past without stopping.

It's a shame, I reflect. They missed a good show.

Chapter 4

CLOWNS AND CIRCUS GIRLS

To run away with the circus is to enter a close-knit world where traditions, skills, language and superstitions have been passed down for generations.

Gareth Ellis is a clown, but he's no fool. In the ring, as Bippo, he has the presence and assurance of a man who grew up in the big top. His complete control of the audience is never more evident than when he conscripts a little kid and a burly young man into the ring to participate in a comedy tumbling skit or when he climbs over the ring fence to perform the old 'throwing the popcorn into a volunteer's mouth' routine on an unsuspecting man in the third row.

Off duty, Bippo, as he continues to be addressed by one and all, has such an air of maturity, bordering on earnestness, that it comes as a shock when he reveals his age as nineteen. It would be far less surprising if he said he was thirty-five. In that respect Bippo is far from unique among circus performers. We tend to associate the concept of 'running away with the circus' with the desertion of responsibility. In fact, such is the discipline, self-reliance, responsibility and sheer hard work demanded by life in a travelling show that children who grow up in the circus tend to grow up quickly.

On a dark and frigid evening near the beginning of his first season on a new show Bippo stands beneath the swaying lights among the animal tents at the back of a large blue plastic big top and explains that a circus clown's duties never end at the ring doors.

'On build-up days, which is when we put the tent up, and on pull-down days, we all help out. When we arrive on a new site my job is to set up the water supply. The girls set up the electric paddock for the horses. If the wind gets up in the night everyone has to get up to put more stakes in to hold the tent down. It's not like the artistes think: Aw, it's windy. The workers will get up and put more stakes in. Everybody's up – the girls, everybody. Not through anybody asking – through choice. We're all in this together, and the tent is the most important thing in the circus. If we didn't have a tent we wouldn't be able to work. So everybody pitches in.'

Between performances Bippo's still wearing his ring garb: a pair of loud tartan trousers that end a good distance up his shins, a tweed cap, worn back to front, Norman Wisdom-style, and an absolutely enormous pair of black-and-white clown boots – his 'batts', in circus slang – that Ronald McDonald would be proud of. In off-duty mode, Bippo is so at home in his attire, and so comically unselfconscious about the way it contrasts with his serious demeanour, that it's hard to believe he ever wears anything else.

'The build-up and pull-down on this show is actually the fastest I've ever seen. We start the pull-down at four, when the Sunday show finishes, and we're pulling off the ground by five. We generally only go thirty to fifty miles. The longest is probably seventy miles. So we're on the new ground between six and eight. The next day we start the build-up at 7 a.m. and we've finished by 10. I've heard of shows where the pull-down takes all night, and then you drive, so this feels like a luxury.'

Although he's a first-generation circus performer, Bippo has spent nearly all his life in the big top and speaks fluently the language of the old circus families who have been in the business for generations.

'"Nanti" is look out or watch out,' Bippo explains. 'If you're talking about something private and see someone walking up to you, you say to the other person, "Nanti", and it's like "Be quiet or watch out." "Vardi" is look. "Vardi the chat" as you point at something means "Look at that." Sometimes, if something goes wrong, the ringmistress will say '"Vardi the whatever" on mike, and the boys will know to check it out, but the audience won't know anything is wrong.'

The son of a British Gas engineer and a nursery-school teacher, Bippo didn't just run away with the circus; his parents did, too.

'I went to see Zippos Circus* when I was three years old, and I fell in love – with the circus, with the clowns, with everything to do with it. I think when you walk into the tent as a little kid it's just so awe-inspiring: all the lights, everybody smiling. It's like going to Disneyland. That's when I decided I wanted to be a clown. My mum and dad said, "Tomorrow he'll want to be a fireman", but I stuck with it. When I got to primary school I was still interested. In the school holidays we'd go to the circus in our little caravan and stay for the whole holiday.'

The arrangement became permanent when Ellis senior was made redundant. 'My mum was bored with her job, and my older brothers had left home, so we all went and joined Zippos Circus. My mum got a job as the boss's personal assistant, and my dad became a general handyman. I started off selling stuff before the show, and I learned clowning and juggling from the different acts they had each season.'

As for schoolwork, 'I did distance learning on the road, which is when teachers come out and teach you. Then I'd go back to school for two months in the winter.' By then Gareth had become firmly established as Bippo, even to his non-circus friends. With a chuckle, he recalls, 'I remember one time the teacher told the girl next to me to pass a book to Gareth. She looked at me, and was, like, "*Gareth???* I thought your name was Bippo!" No, my parents weren't that cruel.'

His parents having now retired from the circus, after giving their son the start in life that he wanted, Bippo's home is a lorry and a caravan. 'I live in the caravan, and the lorry is my dressing-room.' The view from his window changes every week, but his commute to work is never more than a short walk across the muddy grass to the big top.

---

* If you are wondering why there's no apostrophe in Zippos, its owner Martin Burton puts it like this: 'Circus as an institution has never been tied down by rules, but instead is free spirited. In the same way Zippos will not be tied down by the rules of punctuation and grammar, so it's always Zippos and never Zippo's.'

During the day he takes turns to go and put up posters in the next town. But he also finds time to relax on his PlayStation, to play football with the Romanian boys who do the heavy lifting for the circus and to go riding on the circus's stable of horses.

'We move every week, which is nice. Sometimes if you really like a place you think: Oh, can't we stay? But in general I think everyone looks forward to moving on to a new ground. I think that's one of the reasons people are in circus, really. Number one, because it's their life, it's what they've done all their life. And, number two, it's the travelling, meeting new people and seeing new places. There's circus all over the world, so you can see the world.'

For the future, Bippo says, 'I would like to try my hand at different things. Not next year, not the year after, but at some point I'd like to try television. But I think circus will always be my main career, my main love. There are people doing this in their late seventies. I think once the circus grabs you it's in your blood.'

I first saw Bippo in a Christmas season at the Yarmouth Hippodrome when, I now realize, he must have been just sixteen. He was already handling himself like a veteran. Particularly memorable was his wandering spotlight routine: he starts off singing a song like a straight balladeer, only for the spotlight to wander off him a few feet to the right. He quickly steps over into the spotlight and recommences singing . . . only to have the spotlight move away again and again, until he's chasing it all over the ring and out into the audience.

Between seasons with Zippos, Bippo has also toured the UK with the Moscow State Circus and appeared at the Blackpool Tower Circus. Just back from a Christmas season at a theme park in Malta, he's currently working with Circus Mondao, a traditional animal circus started three years ago by the sisters Carol Macmanus and Gracie Timmis, and their husbands Ryszard and Jason.

I come across Circus Mondao by chance, which tends to be the way. Travelling circuses are notoriously secretive about their route, seldom advertising their locations more than two towns in advance for fear that a rival will jump in ahead of them and steal their business. As Martin Lacey puts it: 'Circuses are like pantomimes. Families can only afford to go to one. The first in town gets all the business. The rest starve.'

The advertising of circuses has also become low key. Some shops are reluctant to display posters for animal circuses, and unauthorized flyposting carries heavy financial penalties. The most common form of promotion is for an advance party to visit schools, shops, factories and businesses and distribute leaflets with vouchers for half-price tickets. It draws a crowd, but whereas once a town would be plastered with circus posters these days you could drive through and not know a circus was there.

As it happens, it's a week after my visit to Lacey's Great British Circus that my partner and I are driving home from the coast when we see a mobile advertising hoarding, on a trailer, pulled up on a grass verge beside a roundabout. *Circus Mondao. Traditional Family Animal Show. In Town Now.* There's a painting of a zebra and an arrow. Still fired up by Lacey's tigers and elephants, we exchange a single look and I take a sharp right.

It turns out that in my search for the real circus experience we're in luck. Circus Mondao may not have any elephants or tigers, but although it's a new name on the circus block its proprietors come from a line of circus people that stretches back 200 years, through such famous family names as the Paulos, who ran one of the most prominent circuses of the 1930s, and the Pinders, who performed three times before Queen Victoria, to a great-great-great-grandfather, the Scottish showman Thomas Ord, a minister's son who ran away with the circus when Philip Astley was still alive.

As Carol and Gracie's doughty Aunty Emily puts it proudly, between serving teas in the refreshment wagon, 'I think you're talking to the oldest circus people in Britain.'

The mixture of centuries-old circus know-how and the enthusiasm of a new venture has made Circus Mondao one of the most vibrant and welcoming shows in the country. The big top is a stylish new Italian design. Tall and squareish in profile, it resembles a giant blue jelly mould, with a white star draped over the top. At night it's bedecked with strings of lights. Parked in front of the tent, the walk-through box-office trailer has a big Circus Mondao sign above it and smart white picket fencing, interspersed with tall flagpoles, to either side.

Inside, the upright shape of the tent allows for a cosy, intimate seating area but also the height to accommodate large-scale apparatus such as a towering Wheel of Death. Glitzy ring doors, with illuminated steps leading up to the central artists' entrance and curtained side entrances for the animals, provide a theatrical backdrop to the ring, where a horse and camel are waiting to give pre-show rides.

As we enter the tent Bippo is 'on doors', greeting the patrons and selling flashing windmills. He's also sizing up potential volunteers to pick out during his act.

'The risk you take in getting audience members out is that it could go very well or it could be awful. If the audience see the volunteer isn't having a good time then it becomes more of a taking-the-Mick thing than laughing with them. When I started I used to just think: He'll be fine, and pick him out, and it would be complete rubbish. So now, when the audience are coming in, I always go up to people and ask them, "How are you? You all right?" If a man just sort of goes "Yep" and moves along quickly I know he won't be a good volunteer. It's about reading your audience, and I think it takes ages to know how to do it.'

Kids are the hardest to read, says Bippo. 'Sometimes they come running up to you before the show, then the moment they get in the ring and see all the people they burst into tears.'

Like Danny Adams, Bippo doesn't wear a wig and sports minimum make-up: a white lower lip and white eyebrows defined by a black outline on the outer edge and some subtly applied blusher on his cheeks. The one element of the traditional clown face that no circus clown seems prepared to give up is the upturned bulb of a false red nose, although even that is getting smaller. I remember Peter Jay telling me about another clown, a Mexican, who worked at the Hippodrome one year. 'I keep telling him, "Lose the nose. You don't need it." He just sort of looks at me, and I can tell he's thinking about it . . . but he won't take it off!'

Unlike Danny Adams, Bippo uses hardly any words in his act, but he has no difficulty in communicating with his audience and getting them roaring with laughter with his broad and boisterous miming. His funniest routine is a double act with showgirl Kristine who is dressed as a ballerina. She begins with serious, elegant ballet moves. Then Bippo bursts into the ring, wearing a tutu, a blond wig with pigtails and an enormous false bosom, making a mockery of everything Kristine does. The routine is an example of the way the earliest traditions of clowning have been continually updated while remaining essentially unchanged.

Since the mid-nineteenth century clowning has centred on two characters, the 'whiteface' and the 'auguste'. Once defined by his full-face white make-up, pointed hat and elaborate silk costume, the whiteface is the boss or authority figure. He may be laughably pompous and actually inept, but he is trying, with a rigidly straight face and ever-increasing frustration, to do the job in hand correctly. The auguste is his underling who invariably messes up the instructions he is given, through incompetence or mischief. It's a dynamic that defines the interaction of Clive Webb (the whiteface) and Danny Adams (the auguste), even though in their case only one of them is actually dressed as a clown, and countless other comic double acts in which no clown clothes or make-up are worn at all, such as Laurel and Hardy or Morecambe and Wise.

In Bippo's ballet, Kristine, although she is dressed as a ballerina and has none of the physical characteristics of a clown, is unmistakably playing the role of the whiteface. Bippo, although his costume is more akin to a pantomime dame, is playing the classic auguste.

The other human acts in a fast-moving show are mainly drawn from Eastern Europe. Vitalie Eremia from Moldova demonstrates his strength with some one-handed handstands on a narrow pedestal and break-dances to hip-hop music, spinning around and around on his head. In the second half, wearing feathered wings on his arms, he flies around high above the ring fence on a pair of aerial straps wrapped around his wrists, his body held parallel to the ground by sheer muscle as he is winched aloft.

On the massive revolving Wheel of Death the Actros Brothers lack the verve and polish of the Latino Valez Brothers, whom I first saw perform this gravity-defying stunt at the Hippodrome. The short nut-brown Valez brothers danced and laughed in the face of danger. The tall pale Actros Brothers face danger with the sort of wary steeliness you might reserve for a formidable foe you're not quite sure you can get the better of. For the finale one of the brothers walks blindfold around the outside of the enormous revolving contraption, his hooded head almost touching the cupola or central rigid roof section of the tent. When he completes his circuit he rips off his black hood and drops to his knees, gripping the handrails with a palpable sense of relief.

Much more polished are the model-thin and youthful Hungarian sisters Anette and Zsuzsi who perform a series of elegant poses and balances on a version of the static trapeze constructed from two hoops, suspended one above the other. At one point one of the slender blonde girls hangs upside down from her sister's legs. The only thing holding her in the air is the strength with which the upper girl holds her legs open and the lower girl presses hers closed against them, so that each has her ankles locked against the other's knees. Slowly, as the crowd holds its collective breath in disbelief, both girls close their legs, allowing the lower girl's feet to slide down her sibling's shins until she is suspended by just her feet hooked over her sister's feet.

During their more dangerous hangs on the double hoop the lower girl clips a thin, barely noticeable safety harness from her waist to the hoop. It doesn't hold her in place or help her to balance, but it would save her from a head-first fall to a broken neck if she slipped.

Wearing a shiny gold body stocking, Zsuzsi also does a solo aerial silk act. At one point she hangs in an upside-down splits, held up by just a few careful coils of silk around her thighs and ankles. There are no safety wires in this routine, as my inevitable memories of the late Eva Garcia remind me.

'Miss Carol', the circus matriarch, wears a long black sequined evening dress to present a liberty act with a group of fine Appaloosa stallions. White with grey spots, they're true circus horses. To close the routine she gets one to rear up on its hind legs, Lone Ranger style, to show off its size and strength.

Tanned, black-haired and intense, Carol also presents what circus people call an 'exotic' liberty routine with a mixed group of two zebras, two llamas, two camels, a donkey and a mule. The routine is still being rehearsed. Ring boys stand close to the llamas and camels, leading them through their pirouettes on a tight rein. As Petra Jackson, the ringmistress, says by way of a voiceover, 'We believe the best way to train our animals is in front of you, the public.' It's a homely touch that adds to the show's accessibility.

In the interval, wearing a thick Circus Mondao jumper over her evening dress, Carol admits she's feeling a bit tense. The circus is built up on an out-of-town ground normally used for go-karting and car-boot sales. Piles of tyres define the car park, racetrack style, and the ground is hard, unforgiving concrete. They had to use a special drill to get the tent stakes in and have put down coconut matting instead of sawdust in the ring. Carol's worried that one of the horses might slip and hurt itself on the hard ground outside the tent.

What about poor Zsuzsi, hanging upside down from her aerial silk above the concrete?

It's a mark of the love circus people have for their animals that Carol says, dismissively, 'Oh, she's all right. She's holding on.' *Ah, but as for the poor horses . . .*

'Madam Gracie', Carol's younger sister by two years, presents a gentle trained pigeon routine called Fantail Fantasia. Gracie is a voluptuous woman with long and straight pale blonde hair, who moves slowly and elegantly in her high heels. In the ring she never seems to stop smiling, and out of it she never seems to stop laughing. In the spotlight she's wearing a wildly sparkling full-length evening gown.

Her white pigeons perch on a frame at the back of the ring. One by one she brings them into the centre of the ring to perform their tricks: climbing up a ladder, walking on a revolving glitter ball, riding on opposite ends of a see-saw. It's a strangely anachronistic act, conjuring memories of Saturday-night variety shows on black-and-white television in the 1970s. Yet, performed briefly and succinctly, leaving us no time to get bored, it's also charming. The little kids, standing up in their ringside seats, are entranced.

'It's something different, isn't it?' as Gracie puts it.

At the end of each trick the birds fly obediently back to their perches. At least they're supposed to. Some inadvertent but fitting humour is added to the act by a bird that persistently prefers to land on Gracie's head, even as she's taking her bow.

After the show Gracie explains, 'She was landing on my head to tell me she wanted to go back to the trailer to sit on her eggs. People say "bird brain", but they're really quite intelligent. Once you teach them something they've got it.'

There are no animal-rights protestors outside on the day I attend. The attention comes and goes, says Carol; last year it was pretty quiet. And perhaps, with their domestic animals (little different, really, to something like the Horse of the Year Show), they draw less attention than elephants paraded on the national news. But still, the 'antis', as circus people call them, remain an inevitable subject of conversation.

Bippo, who grew up on Zippos, a circus with horses, is typically serious behind his clown face – the unselfconscious, sad-faced clown – as he says, 'I've heard them shout "Child abuser" at a woman for bringing her little girl into the circus. I've seen little kids come in in tears because of them.'

We're standing among the animal pens at the back of the big top. Beside us, a pale-cream llama is pressed against the edge of his pen, his eyes level with mine as if he's trying to join in the conversation. I stroke his long thick neck, and he leans into my hand, like a dog.

'If they were mistreated,' says Bippo, 'they'd shy away from people, wouldn't they?'

A week later I read a newspaper report that Carol's partner, Ryszard, has been arrested during an altercation with protestors outside the show.

Despite the hassles Gracie insists, 'Me and Carol and Jason would not have done a circus without animals. And since Ryszard has been with Carol, he's of the same attitude. A circus isn't a circus without animals.'

Gracie was born on Hoffmans' Circus, which was owned by her husband's family. 'I used to play with my brother-in-law, because my husband wasn't born then. My mother's got pictures, but I don't really remember that. My earliest memories are growing up on Gerry Cottle's circus with all the other kids there. I must have been seven or eight, and there were loads of kids on that circus. We used to go to a different school every week, and it was always "Oh, you're from the circus? Sit there and draw a picture and tell us what your mum and dad do." Then we'd be got up in front of the class and tell everyone what we'd done and what we hadn't done.' As Cottle points out in his autobiography, *Confessions of a Showman*, it was all very educational for the other pupils but wasn't very helpful for the circus kids who had to repeat the routine every week. 'So, because there were so many of us, Gerry bought a double-decker bus. My dad fitted it out as a classroom, and we had different teachers who came and taught us.'

The sisters' real education was in the ring. 'My dad trained horses, elephants, llamas, camels,' says Gracie. 'He's passed that on to my sister more than me, even though I do like the animals and I present the 'Big and Little' on a Sunday. Every circus I ever worked on, I always ended up leading a horse or holding a camel. Because they knew my dad trained animals, they knew I'd know what I was doing and wouldn't end up chasing it across a field. But I was never as into that side of things as Carol is. I wanted to be on the trapeze.'

What was the attraction? 'I don't know. I just hung from everything I could hang from for as far back as I can remember. I was obsessed with it. I used to climb up the rope and play on the trapeze every day. Mum saw me up there one day and went mad at me. Then, after that, she got someone to teach me. She taught me in a year, and I performed it the next year. Gerry Cottle let me perform a couple of times. Then we went and joined my mum's family, who had Pinder's Circus out, and I worked there. I think I was eleven or twelve.'

Gracie worked solo trapeze all over Europe until she had her children. 'I didn't lose weight after them,' she says with a laugh, 'and I wasn't a teenager any more.' She gives her age as 'Twenty-one – twice!' She adds, however, that there's no retirement age *per se*, even at the more acrobatic end of circus. 'I think it's more about the way you carry your age. There was a lady I knew who did a perch act – that's where someone balances a pole on their head and the other person climbs up the pole and does tricks at the top of it. She was sixty and she was fantastic. She looked thirty-five. But then there are some people who are sixty and they look horrendous. You think, what are they doing in the ring? I think fifty-five to sixty is a good age to retire. My mum's eighty, and she'd still be in there if she could.'

At the other end of the age scale, Gracie's daughters Cinzia, nine, and Madalane, twelve, are already a fully integrated part of the Mondao team. In the ring they present a troupe of pygmy goats, leading the animals through the sort of manoeuvres associated with dog shows: jumping over a series of low fences, slaloming in and out of a row of poles, walking over a see-saw. One of the goats walks across the ring on its hind legs, another walks on top of a rolling hollow canister, known in circus slang as a spool. Wearing voluminous Victorian dresses and bonnets, the girls also ride with their Aunty Carol and ringmistress Petra in a *My Fair Lady* number and, in more modern attire, join in the dance routines of showgirls Kristine and Lizzy.

Outside the show, Cinzia is practising to follow in her mother's footsteps as a trapeze artist, while Madalane is learning to ride 'high school', a type of dressage characterized by the horse's rhythmic high-stepping.

'When they're not at school they do the stables,' says Gracie. 'They practise. They help us build up and pull down. They staple tickets. Anything that needs doing, we give them the jobs to do. They get paid for it, but they both muck in. When my little one was six she could lead the zebras up and down, no problem at all.'

Is Mum confident they will stay in the circus when they're older? Gracie calls out to Madalane to check. 'Are you happy to do circus or do you want to do something else instead?'

'Circus,' comes the reply.

Overall, Mondao delivers everything you could want from a modern, traditional family circus. The aerial acts are slick and daring for the adults. There's hip-hop and break-dancing for teens. The animals go down particularly well with the children. Bippo has all ages in stitches. More than the sum of the individual parts, the whole is delivered with a lot of colour and enthusiasm and a real sense of warmth from everyone involved.

The first house of the evening is respectably full, the second more so. As I leave, the big car park is jammed. In circus, though, the size of the audience is never predictable.

'You can build up on a site, sit there all week and not see a soul,' says Gracie, who runs the box office. 'Then you can build up on a site and be packed to the roof. It's a fifty–fifty chance.'

Partly, business changes with the seasons: 'Before Easter it's good. After Easter it drops off, then picks up again in the summer. June and July is normally downhill . . .' Partly it changes with the weather. 'If it's sunshine and we haven't had nice weather for ages, then the public sit in the garden or go to the beach. We do better when it's raining.'

As with stocks and shares, past performance does not guarantee future results. 'Just because you were at a site last year and did really well, it doesn't mean you can go back to the same site and do really well again. Last year we did so well in Norfolk we were all saying, "We've got to go back." This year we went to Yarmouth, had two weeks of really nice weather, and did terrible business because everyone went to the beach.'

A month and a half and half-a-dozen towns later, Gracie is sitting in the box office. How's business?

'Crap!' Gracie lets out a peal of laughter.

But for all the ups and downs of circus life it's clear Gracie could not be more content than she is in her life on the road. None of her family could.

Aunty Emily, sitting beside her niece, says, 'This is the best life. I was telling a lady here the other day, man is meant to wander. He's wandered since ancient times, and it's in his genes. He's not meant to sweat from nine till five. That's why they all hate their jobs. This is the only way we can still wander.'

In her younger days Emily walked the tightrope. She also showed the horses and the dogs. 'Then I used to do the rolling globe act as well. You do everything. You do one thing, then you run around and do something else.'

When I ask Gracie what is the best thing about living on the circus, she says, 'To be honest, there isn't a best thing. I just don't know anything else, because I've done it all my life. When it's sunshine and you're on a lovely ground, it's absolutely fantastic. When it's chucking it down and you're up to your eyes in mud, it's horrendous. But it just goes with the job. You just plod along and get on with it.

'When the first lot of foot-and-mouth disease occurred, we stopped at home and Jason went out and did things like tent hire, and we didn't enjoy that. That's when we decided to do Circus Mondao with Carol and Ryszard. They were interested in doing it, they asked if we wanted to go halves with them, and we said yes. We'd always worked for other people, and we thought: We slog our guts out for everybody else, why not do it for ourselves?'

Between them, the founding foursome had all the fundamental skills. Jason used to present a comedy dog act but now concentrates on coordinating the movement of the circus, putting up advance posters and maintaining the lorries. Ryszard was a stunt driver but also a lorry driver and tent master on the Chinese State Circus. He's now in charge of building and designing the sets and, with Jason, getting the circus from ground to ground.

All they needed was a big top. 'It's a big investment,' says Gracie. 'You're looking at over £20,000 to get started, with a tent and generators and this and that. We bought our first tent from Tony Hopkins – an old tent, which we did our first year in. Then we found boys and artists and whatnot and got ourselves out on the road.'

Circus people love an exotic name. Among the old circus families Gracie's paternal antecedents, the Paulos, were originally the Thompsons. Her husband's family, the Hoffmans, changed their names from the Macks. Circus Mondao sounds as if it might be a revival of an old European circus name. In fact its origins were more prosaic.

'We made it up!' Gracie laughs. 'We were all going "What are we going to call it?" And at the time we had a car called a Mondeo . . . My daughters said, "Let's call it Mondeo." So we changed the spelling so we wouldn't be sued.'

The first show was at Donnington, near Spalding in Lincolnshire. 'We were all as nervous as anything. Everyone was shaking like a leaf. Were we going to get any people in or not? Then, afterwards we all had a glass of champagne and went "Phew! We can all go to sleep now!" Because we'd all not been sleeping for two or three days. We were all, like, "Have you been able to sleep?" "No, I couldn't sleep!" There were so many things going round in your mind.'

Home for Gracie, her husband and daughters is a 40-foot wagon – 'We call them wagons, not caravans,' Gracie is quick to point out – with a large pull-out section on the side to give it extra width when parked and a decent-sized lorry to tow it. 'It's got a kids' bedroom, my bedroom, living-room, bathroom with shower, flushing toilet and hot and cold running water, kitchen with dishwasher, washing-machine, tumble-dryer, fridge-freezer. It's got everything you could have. Carol's is about the same.' The families continue to live in their wagons even over the winter, when they pull on to a field at a farm owned by Jason's family.

'We've got a great big shed we keep all the horses in. We only keep two boys on over the winter, so me and Carol are hands-on with the animals, cleaning them and mucking out. The boys chop and saw and paint and do whatever they need to do to get everything ready for next year. If we have to get involved in that, we'll do whatever we need to do, too. We'll paint, if we have to.'

Before Gracie got her current wagon, home was an articulated lorry trailer that her husband and father converted from scratch.

When will daughters Madalane and Cinzia get their own wagons? 'Normally when they're fourteen or fifteen they'll get their own caravan and live outside.' With a chuckle, Gracie reveals, 'My eldest doesn't want me to kick her out. I keep saying, "I'll buy you a nice caravan." "No, no, I'm fine where I am."'

Because a split-second's 'bad luck' in the circus ring could mean a broken bone or worse, circus people have traditionally been superstitious. It's considered bad luck to wear real flowers in the ring or to go back to your wagon for a prop you've forgotten – you should always get someone else to fetch it for you.

Now that circus is no longer the exclusive preserve of the old circus families, and newcomers can enter the profession through circus schools rather than apprenticeships in travelling shows, some of the older superstitions are less frequently upheld. But in circus nothing dies out quickly.

'We tell people they mustn't sit with their backs to the ring,' says Gracie. 'Some people won't wear green costumes in the ring, and others don't mind.' With a chuckle, Gracie adds, 'Some say, "Oh, I don't mind wearing green", and then something happens and they say, "I'm not wearing green any more!"'

This is said with a pointed look at Kristine, the dancer sitting nearby, who immediately begins laughing. Gracie explains. 'Kristine used to say, "I'm not bothered about wearing green." Then she wore a green costume and fell over and broke her arm. So *she* won't be wearing green any more!'

Warming to her theme, Gracie continues, 'My Aunty Jane, my dad's cousin, wasn't bothered. Then the horse she was riding "high school" fell over and broke her leg. *She* won't wear green any more!'

Despite her trapeze career Gracie says she has never had any broken bones of her own. 'I fell twice, but I was quite low and didn't break anything. Touch wood!'

At least the pigeons can't hurt you, I venture.

'They just poo on you!' Gracie laughs.

Although kept alive by staunch adopted sons of the circus, such as Bippo, the traditional circus lingo Parlari is also fading. Parlari is not to be confused with Polari, the theatrical and homosexual slang that gained popularity in 1950s' and 1960s' London, although some of the words are the same, drawn from a wide range of cultural and geographical sources,

from Romany to Yiddish to Russian and Italian, that reflect circus's itinerant, international nature.

Clowns are called 'Joeys' after Joseph Grimaldi, the early-nineteenth-century father of modern clowning, who pioneered the use of white-face make-up. Born in London in 1778, Joseph was the son of an Italian, Giuseppe Grimaldi, who was a ballet master at Drury Lane as well as a clown himself. Joey was the product of an affair between Giuseppe, who was in his sixties, and one of his many mistresses, a 25-year-old chorus girl called Rebecca Brooker.

Nicknamed Old Grim, Giuseppe was a hard taskmaster who frequently beat his son – even on stage. He introduced Joey to the stage at the age of two and nearly killed him during a performance at Sadler's Wells Theatre a year later. The infant was playing a monkey, being swung around on a chain by his father, when the chain snapped and sent him flying into the audience. Two years later Joey had another on-stage disaster when he broke his collar-bone falling through a trapdoor.

Grimaldi never grew out of his accident-prone streak. As an adult he once nearly blew his leg off when a pistol went off by mistake. As his stocking caught fire the audience roared with laughter, and, despite his pain, Grimaldi carried on as if it was part of the act.

Grimaldi senior died when Joey was nine, from which point the boy supported his mother by continuing to work as an apprentice at Sadler's Wells – which wasn't so unusual in an age when children were sent up chimneys as sweeps or toiled for long hours in mines and workhouses. His first major pantomime role was in *Peter Wilkins, Or Harlequin in the Flying World*, at Sadler's Wells, Easter, 1800. He played Guzzle, opposite panto veteran Baptiste Dubois, who played Gobble. Within a year Grimaldi had replaced Dubois as Sadler's Wells's chief clown, and by the time of his most famous performance, in *Mother Goose* in 1806, he was a major celebrity, hailed as the 'Michelangelo of Buffoonery'.

Dispensing with the masks worn by previous pantomime clowns, Grimaldi wore whiteface make-up with elongated red triangles on his cheeks – the better for his famously mobile facial expressions to be seen by those at the back in smoky candle-lit theatres. More importantly, Grimaldi pushed the role of clown to the centre of pantomime, usurping the dominance of Harlequin, a character whose origins dated from Italy's *commedia dell'arte* (literally 'comedy of art') in the mid-sixteenth century.

The reason for Grimaldi's popularity lay in his satirizing of contemporary politics and social mores, as well as his sheer versatility. Although he mainly performed in mime, he also wrote and sang comic songs and was an accomplished acrobat, juggler, swordsman and dancer. In addition, he wrote scripts, painted scenery and designed and made his own props.

At the height of his popularity Grimaldi performed in two or even three pantomimes on the same night. On one occasion he was unable to get a carriage from Sadler's Wells to Covent Garden, so he set off between the theatres at a trot, in full motley and slap (as clowns call their costume and make-up). By the time he arrived a posse of several hundred fans were running alongside him.

Although he never appeared in a circus, Grimaldi's make-up was quickly adopted by the clowns of Philip Astley's circus, who went by the name of Mr Merryman, whoever was playing them.

Underlining the close links between pantomime, music hall and circus in the nineteenth century and even the first half of the twentieth century, Grimaldi often worked with animals, including a trained donkey called Neddy.

By the end of the Victorian era it was in circus that Grimaldi's influence remained most strong, the dominance of the clown in pantomime having eventually been replaced, like the now-forgotten Harlequin before him, by the dame, who continues to rule Panto Land to this day.

Offstage, Grimaldi fitted the stereotype of the melancholy man behind the make-up. As he punned, 'I am grim all day, but I make you laugh at night.' According to a fanciful but enjoyable legend, he once went to his doctor with depression. 'You just need cheering up,' said the doc. 'Why don't you go and see that very funny Mr Grimaldi?'

Charles Dickens posthumously edited Grimaldi's memoirs. But, despite his fame, Grimaldi died broke in 1837, having retired fourteen years before, an invalid at forty-five from the exertions – and mishaps – of his clowning career. He was buried in the courtyard of St James's Church, off Pentonville

Road in Islington, and although the church was demolished in the 1950s an annual memorial service, followed by a clown festival, continues to be held at his graveside each May, in what is now Grimaldi Park.

Other circus words include 'prad' for horse, 'pig' for elephant and 'His Gills' or 'Her Jillpots' for whatsisname.

'A lot of people still use "Joey",' says Gracie. 'Carol and I will say things like "jigger", which means caravan. "Have you locked the jigger?" "Dinaris" is money. But then people who come new to the circus won't understand that, so it's fizzling out.'

How long does it take newcomers to be accepted as circus people?

'In the old days they were never accepted. They were always "flatties" or "jossers". Nowadays, if you've been on the circus a year I'd say you're accepted.'

Ultimately, being a circus person is more about attitude than parentage, Gracie decides. 'Some people who are not from the circus come and they're "Oh, I can't do that, I'll get my hands dirty." That's when you know they're never going to be a circus person. Someone like Bippo, on the other hand, is like part of the furniture.'

Chapter 5

INSIDE THE SPIEGELTENT

Since the 1970s a new breed of performer has taken circus skills on to the streets and into theatres and arts festivals.

The Chapelfield Gardens is an old bosky park in the heart of Norwich, bordered in part by the flinty remnants of the old city wall. In the centre of the gardens is an oasis of rhododendron bushes – a great hill, so it appears, made up of big clumps of orange, yellow and red. The scent wafts thickly on the warm air of a May evening, and with it comes the hot sound of vintage Cuban jazz.

The Gardens have been occupied as the centrepiece of the city-wide Norfolk and Norwich Festival. Just inside the bunting that bedecks the wrought-iron entrance arch stands the Luminarium – a 10,000-square-foot upmarket version of a bouncy castle. From the outside the giant inflatable is a towering row of grey, red and blue triangular peaks – a design inspired by Islamic architecture. Inside it's a series of squishy walk-through tubular tunnels filled with psychedelic light and ambient surround-sound – a massive, other-worldly chill-out zone.

Deeper into the park, beside the rhododendrons, stands the Spiegeltent. Once a familiar sight in rural Europe, a Spiegeltent – literally 'mirror tent' in Dutch – is a fully dismantleable mobile dance hall that first toured villages and town fairs in the Flemish region of Belgium in the late nineteenth century. Popular until just after the Second World War, they've recently found renewed favour on the arts festival circuit around the globe.

Some original Spiegeltents are still in use. The Famous Spiegeltent, where Marlene Dietrich sang 'Falling in Love Again' in the 1930s, continues to travel the continents in its more than 3,000 constituent parts. Others have found permanent bases: the 1910 vintage La Moulin Rouge in Seattle, the 1920 Palais Nostalgique in San Francisco.

This one, the Salon Perdu, is a reproduction, built about eight years ago, but authentic in every way. From the outside it resembles a round two-tier wedding cake. The walls are made from dark stained-wood panels with a continuous band of stained-glass window around their upper edge. The roof sections are made from sloping grey canvas, the uppermost part rising to a low central peak. Attached to the front is a dark-green walk-through box-office wagon elaborately decorated in an art deco style.

Around the front of the Spiegeltent is a cluster of smaller tents: a large pointy-topped red marquee selling beer, with well-attended wooden trestle tables outside; a white tent selling pizza from a coal-fired stove. A stripy-shirted street vendor is selling cappuccino from the back of a Piaggio Ape – a tiny three-wheel van with the engine of a Vespa scooter, of a design you might expect to see zooming through the back streets of Rome in the mid-1950s.

The hugely infectious good-time Cuban music, loud now we're closer, is being broadcast by Radio Barkas – 'The smallest mobile radio station in the Netherlands'. It's based in an even odder vehicle than the Piaggio. Painted chocolate brown, it looks like the cab of a van that has had its back end sawn off and an unlikely number of wheels added. As well as a door each side, it has a wide side-hinged door on the back. All three doors are open to emit not just the music, which is blaring from speakers connected to one of a number of record decks within, but expanding clouds of dry ice, tinted with ever-changing colours by the disco lights inside.

The Spiegeltent is not a circus tent. All week it will be hosting two different shows a night, from 'opera with a difference' to an adults-only burlesque show compèred by Matt Fraser, an actor born with short arms because of thalidomide. The late show tonight is *The Be(a)st of Taylor Mac.*

'He's a transvestite from New York,' enthuses Daisy, the press officer. 'He rants about politics and plays the ukulele. Would you like tickets?'

Um, maybe not. I'm here for Circa, a contemporary circus ensemble from Australia.

The company could hardly have found a more evocative setting in which to perform. From the carnivalesque atmosphere created by the tents, food smells and good-time music to the canvas sheet screening the Portaloos and the collection of lorries and caravans parked around the back, everything about the scene shouts circus. Even so, I have to confess that, despite the fantastic vibe outside, I'm not entirely sure whether the show I'm about to see will be circus as I know it.

The festival programme describes Circa's show, *The Space Between*, as 'three performers explore love, loss and desire on a journey of explosive acrobatic encounters, lyrical duets and supple physical contortions'. It's a description that makes me pine a little for Martin Lacey's elephants and tigers.

My last encounter with the arty end of circus was the Cardiff-based NoFit State Circus, which pitched its shiny futuristically shaped tent on the university campus during last year's Norfolk and Norwich Festival. There were no ringside seats in the NoFit State tent. There was no ring and there were no seats. The audience stood in the moodily lit interior and were herded around the uneven rubber mat floor to watch the routines from different angles as they were performed around, among and above us.

One performer was dressed as a South American spiv in a crumpled and grubby white suit. With a wild look in his eyes and a reeking lit cigar clenched between his teeth, he spent most of his time scurrying up and down the king poles. The clown was a short pudgy girl dressed as a Gothic street urchin. Periodically she pushed between us, poked her tongue out and lay on the floor showing her knickers. She was received with polite titters from an audience that looked as if it attended a great many avant-garde performance arts, but I can't remember her doing anything I could describe as funny.

On the plus side, NoFit State's show provided a thrilling proximity to the action that made even the ringside seats of a traditional circus seem safely distant. Watching a girl on a trapeze swinging directly above your twisted-back head is a completely different experience to watching the same performance side on. Stepping aside a moment later to let a man roll by on a German wheel, close enough to literally smell the sweat on his Popeye-like arms, brings home the sheer muscular physicality of circus feats.

There was also a technically skilled and engagingly presented tightrope routine performed on a wire that was level with my eyes and no more than a couple of arm-lengths away. But, as stirring as individual moments were, there was an overbearing air of self-conscious artiness to the proceedings and a deliberate dowdiness to the lighting and the costuming that seemed to dampen, or play down, rather than enhance the spectacle of the skills on display. In trying to tell a cautionary tale about a dystopian future ravaged by global warming, the show lacked, for me, the warmth and pizzazz of a shamelessly entertaining night out at the Yarmouth Hippodrome.

Although they do much the same things, just dressed and presented differently, there's a snobbiness on both sides between traditional and contemporary circus performers. It's easy to see why progressive companies should want to distance themselves from the negative connotations that traditional circus retains among a large section of the public, not least over the animals issue but also its image as a rather downmarket and old-fashioned form of family entertainment or even a form of children's entertainment. Even Peter Jay, who presents his self-described 'variety shows for a seaside audience' at the Hippodrome, feels that the C-word has such an image problem that it now barely appears on his posters, which are headlined by just the name of the show, such as *Vertigo.*

It's also easy to see why traditional circuses would be resentful of the large audiences and high-fashion status attracted by the enormously successful Cirque du Soleil and other companies that have styled themselves after it, often substituting style for substance. As Malcolm Clay, secretary of the Association of Circus Proprietors, puts it tactfully, 'If there is any rivalry, I think it's when traditional circus people see what they consider to be less than average displays dressed up to be something which is claimed to be special.' And as showman Gerry Cottle puts it more robustly: 'There's a big difference between commercial circus people who go and make a living at it all year and these people who get grants and float around and pretend to be a tree!'

Perhaps the biggest bone of contention for traditional circus people is summed up by Martin Lacey when he says of Cirque du Soleil: 'If I had funding from the Canadian government I could be wonderful, too.'

In many countries, such as France, traditional circus is regarded as a high art form and receives state funding accordingly. The Chinese owe their high standard of circus arts to their state-run circus schools, as did the Russians before the fall of communism. In Britain, where modern circus began, travelling shows not only receive no financial help, they find themselves persecuted for keeping animals and increasingly hidebound by rules, regulations and licensing issues. The flipside of that is a fierce sense of pride among those who survive without hand-outs, which breeds an understandable sense of superiority towards those who rely on them.

Where funding is available, Cottle says, 'The dear old Arts Council give all the money to the wrong ones, in my opinion.' He recalls a show he describes as 'the worst circus show I've ever seen in my life. The first act was about autism . . . they were all about illnesses. We don't want to see a girl on the trapeze talking about her father dying. They're just trying to be different for the sake of it.

'I'm very pro new circus,' Cottle continues. 'Circus has to evolve, and some of the things new circus is doing are fantastic. Soleil has done a lot of good by changing the perception of circus. It's good to add storylines. But you've still got to entertain the public. You've still got to show them some talent.'

Inside the Spiegeltent, then, I can't help wondering if I will find what the festival programme bills as 'a pioneering ensemble' that has 'redefined circus, embracing the innovative use of music, multimedia, interaction and artistic collaborations'. Or whether I'll find someone pretending to be a tree.

With no reserved seating, there's a long well-dressed queue up the red carpet to the Spiegeltent, where shaven-headed bouncers in Crombie overcoats guard the velvet rope enclosure immediately outside and girls in nineteenth-century saloon-girl dresses stand at the door at the top of the steps to take our tickets.

Inside, the place is buzzing. A continuous row of mirrors around the circular wall magnifies the crowd and makes it difficult to tell where the perimeter of the building actually is. Immediately below the mirrors, on a raised outer circle, are booths with chairs on three sides and a loose but heavy wood table in the centre. The raised area, which is decked in hard dark wood, extends to a circle of mirror-faced columns that hold up the roof. Within the columns is a lower circle, again decked with hard wood, where rows of loose wooden folding chairs surround three sides of a large square central stage finished in black. Above our heads a gold velvet ceiling, richly embroidered with red detailing, rises conically to a central apex. From its highest point hangs a dark blue trapeze swing.

Squeezing about through the noisy pre-show mêlée, the usherettes are wearing what might be described as Wild West whorehouse chic: ostrich feathers in their hats, corsets, frilly white bloomers that meet stout black leather lace-up boots at the knee . . . They're all nicely spoken, well-brought-up young gals, though.

It's a very different audience to the young working-class families, puffy from bad food, sallow from fags, in their fleeces and hooded tops, the men's hair cropped to stubble, the women's scraped back from their foreheads, that predominated around the Circus Mondao ring. Here are slim middle-aged women in evening dress or well-cut trouser suits, their hair expensively cut in the style of Helen Mirren. Their husbands are well-fed apple-cheeked ex-public-school types in linen summer suits or chinos and open-necked button-up striped shirts. There's a sprinkling of straw trilbies and red silk cravats. Some men are dressed down in jeans and check lumber shirts, their hair a mass of wild russet curls, hippyish beards on their chins. But their folk festival appearance still signals 'middle class' a mile off.

'This should be interesting,' smiles one of the bird-thin, smartly dressed Helen Mirren lookalikes, as she takes her seat beside me, a glass of white wine in hand.

'Are you a circus fan?' I ask.

'Good Lord, no!'

She and her husband have been to see South Korean harpist Jimin Lee play a programme of Bach and Liszt at the Assembly House just down the road. Strolling through Chapelfield Gardens on the way home, they chanced upon the Spiegeltent and came in on the spur of the moment. Her husband (neat grey hair, three-piece suit and tie, shy smile, the look of a magistrate about him), it turns out, *is* a circus fan. They tend not to shout about it, but ask a few questions and there's usually one not far away.

The show begins with Darcy Grant standing as still and straight as a flagpole on the very front edge of the stage. His dark hair cut short, his arms by his side, his bare feet together, he's wearing plain black trousers and a white vest. For a long moment he just stands there, his eyes gleaming, a faint smile on his lips, drawing our attention with his stillness and building a sense of anticipation.

I begin to wonder if he's pretending to be a tree. Then, ever so slowly at first (and very much in the manner of a tree being felled), he lets himself fall over backwards. Almost all the way to the ground, Darcy remains perfectly rigid. Then, just as he's about to go splat, flat on his back, he curls his spine and rolls backwards over his head and lands upright on his feet, without so much as using his arms for balance. It's an amazing piece of gymnastics and audibly appreciated as such by the packed crowd. So he does it again, and again, at different angles across the stage.

Ultimately, it's this tendency to repetition that spoils Circa's show for me. There is the suggestion of a story or at least a hint of dramatic tension: Darcy Grant and David Carberry competing for the affection of the wild-haired, punky-looking Chelsea McGuffin. But the dramatic element is so vaguely realized as to be irrelevant. Really we're just watching a series of lifts, balances and contortions, as we would in any circus routine. The difference between what they do and what, say, the Duo Stefaneli do in the Great British Circus is that the latter do a ten-minute floor-based routine in the first half and a similar-length trapeze routine in the second. They run once through each progressively more difficult move, and then the show moves on to a completely different act – a clown, a juggler or an elephant.

Circa's show lasts an hour. And it's a *good* hour, as my partner remarks afterwards, 'good' in this sense referring to length rather than quality. It's certainly a long time to watch three people doing variations on essentially the same thing, and, as rapturously received as they are at the end, I find myself becoming inured to the skill of some of their individual feats.

As tacky as the Duo Stefaneli's spaceship was (and the Roman gladiator costumes they wore in their floor-based routine) I also find myself missing the colour of their act – the sense that we're all, performers and audience alike, here to have a bit of fun; to be not just impressed but entertained. Chelsea's unsmiling face, plain, dull red shorts and singlet, unkempt hair, pale flesh and the odd tattoo may be more 'street' than sparkly circus tights, gleaming lycra and a Colgate grin, but the show's understated look also makes the proceedings feel terribly serious. More like an Olympic gymnastics display than a piece of theatre.

One thing that all circus shows have in common, however, is that no matter how many you see you always see at least one thing you've never seen before and would barely believe was possible. To reach the trapeze swing Chelsea stands on Darcy's shoulders. But that's not high enough. So she shifts her bare feet to the palms of his hands. With the veins and muscles in his arms standing out like steel chain links, he straightens his arms above his head so that she can reach the bar.

Perhaps even more impressively, once Chelsea's on the trapeze and hanging upside down by her ankles, she uses just her slim arms to haul this big muscly bloke, who's a head and chest taller than her, up on to the swing with her – without so much as grunt of exertion. When it's Darcy's turn to hang upside down on the bar he suspends Chelsea dangling by her head – one hand at the base of her skull, the fingers of the other cupped inside her mouth behind her teeth, like a fish hook. All around me I see people shaking their heads in awe or exchanging looks of disbelief.

'Chelsea is a force of nature,' says the show's director, Yaron Lifschitz, the next day. 'She's basically irreplaceable.'

So he's really holding her up by her teeth?

'Yep. You just put your fingers in her mouth and lift.'

So what stops her teeth coming out?

'Hopefully she's been to the dentist!' Yaron laughs, before stating, 'Lots of things in circus just . . . *hurt.* Injury, fatigue, tiredness . . . that's the ambient background noise of circus. Our work is particularly demanding, in a way that's unusual for circus, in that what they do is almost constant. I spoke to Chelsea this morning, and it's not like any of them need any treatment, but they're all pretty sore and tired – exacerbated by jet lag.'

Serious injuries are a rare but ever-present danger. Contortionist David Carberry wears a flesh-coloured support strap on his shoulder during the show.

'He's just come back in,' Yaron explains. 'He was out of circulation for about eight weeks after a training accident. He wasn't trying anything particularly difficult; it just went wrong.

'If you think about the hundreds of thousands of individual things we do right, it's a bit like being an air-traffic controller. You do this all day and nobody says anything. But if you make one little error lots of people notice. We've got a lot better as an organization at both preventing and dealing with injuries. But it's an inevitable fact of life.'

It's lunchtime, and a garden party is in full swing in the Chapelfield Gardens. The sun is out, and great clouds of smoke are rolling across the grass from a barbeque with a queue like a January sale. The Spiegeltent is open for the curious to have a nose around, and it's interesting to see what the interior looks like without last night's crush.

Yaron is squeezed in behind one of the booth tables. He's a big friendly bear of a man, stubble-faced, jet-lagged and dishevelled in a faded grey T-shirt and beret. Because of the technical problems of setting up in the Spiegeltent, he explains that last night's performance was not as it is usually presented.

'The show normally has projections. It's designed to be done in a very dark space and lit in a very different way, but the lights wouldn't work because all the fixtures are in the wrong places. So . . .' The big man lets out a pragmatic sigh. 'Last night we kinda got it . . . somewhere. I think it still works as a show.'

In some respects the bare-bones performance was true to the nature of Circa's work generally. Apart from the trapeze bar, for instance, the performers used no props. The focus was entirely on what they could do with their bodies alone. Save for some matting to roll on, they could have done it on a street corner.

'Some of our shows use apparatus and some have lots more complicated audio-visual. We're developing live music projects that will be coming out next year. But the thing that interests me is the sheer force and beauty of the body in space.'

It was Yaron's interest in performance at its most stripped back that first drew him to circus. 'My favourite line in *The Simpsons* is where Homer goes to a really bad theme park. He sees a bear in a cage and says to the bear,

"I've seen *plays* that are more interesting than this!" It's a bit like that with me. I trained as a theatre director at the National Institute of Dramatic Art in Sydney, but I was never very interested in the well-known plays as an art form. I wanted to find a place where my vision and aesthetic – which can tend towards being a bit dry and sparse – could find a complimentary medium to work in.

'That led to a tendency towards the spectacle of circus combined with how I see things. Those two things are not always entirely in sync, and there are definitely creative tensions between the two, but I think that's healthy and one of the things that make Circa's work powerful. We start with the very formal languages and skills of circus, think about them and question them and then take that in many different directions.

'I founded Circa with the bones of another company, Rock'n'Roll Circus, which had been around since 1987. It had been a pioneering adult contemporary circus. They brought me in as artistic director in 1999, and in 2004 we changed the name to Circa.'

While Yaron is in England the company has another unit on tour in Australia. But last night's performance offers a glimpse of the company's beginnings.

'These are the core people who started making this work with me. We haven't actually done this show for a few years – it's three or four years old now. These are the original people who made that work, and this is how we used to tour, just the four of us.

'Chelsea has been with me for eight years now, which is a victory of something over common sense! She has a ballet background and trained in contemporary dance, then got into circus in her early twenties. Dave and Darcy both trained at the Flying Fruit Fly Circus School, which is a kids' circus in Australia, so they share a very broad range of acrobatic skills. I think the four of us came together at a time when we could all further each other in some way, in a shared vision, and that's what this show was.'

The circus scene in Australia is dominated by Circus Oz, says Yaron. I saw them on tour in the UK a few years ago and remember some strong core circus skills – tightrope walking, fire juggling, aerial acts – dressed with a streetwise edge. The strongest emphasis was on broad and brusque Aussie humour.

'They're possibly, I would say, the incumbents who are beyond their time,' says Yaron. 'But they're definitely in the process of reinvention as well. Then there is a panoply of smaller groups and companies coming through. We're kind of in the middle position, which is a nice and exciting place to be.'

As for traditional circus Down Under, Yaron says, 'I think it's as ubiquitous as the Chinese restaurant. Pretty much everywhere in the world has some version of that thing in the tent that goes around. It's kind of charming for five minutes. It's kind of amazing in some ways and atrocious in some other ways. It's kind of the weird spiritual home of some of the languages we use. But increasingly we draw from things like sports acrobatics and contemporary dance.'

Hovering at the end of the table, Daisy the press officer is looking anxious. Jet-lagged as he is, Yaron arrived late for our interview and I'm due to see two more contemporary circus shows on a matinée double bill at the Theatre Royal just down the road. Daisy has arranged for me to interview the Spanish company Circ Panic before the show, so we say hurried goodbyes to Yaron and leg it out of the Chapelfield Gardens at a brisk trot. On the way we hook up with an interpreter – the wife of one of the festival organizers.

It's Circ Panic's first visit to Britain and their first show inside a theatre. They normally perform in the street, all over Europe from Portugal to Norway. Their mobile stage and backdrop (now parked on the Theatre Royal's big stage) is a bizarre metal caravan, shaped like a half-oval and deliberately fashioned to look as if it were constructed from old junk. One side folds down to form a raised stage. On the roof is a drum kit and also a tall pole, like a ship's mast, supported by guy ropes.

The performers are husband-and-wife team Alexa Leconte and Jordi Panareda, plus a pair of musicians who stand atop the caravan throughout the show and provide an accompaniment ranging from flamenco to the surf-rock instrumental 'Wipe Out' on various combinations of violin, guitar and drums. Accompanied by their technical assistant Luis, we find the company around a table in the theatre's posh new café, eating salads and pasta off square plates.

Like most dancers who can appear tall and statuesque on stage, Alexa is a tiny little thing in person. She looks like a bag of bones in her grey cardigan. With her straight brown hair and no make-up, her moon-like face looks a decade or more younger than her years. She could be in her teens. Beside her, Jordi is every inch the European circus macho man. His skin is mahogany, his wiry black curls oiled, his black eyes gleaming and his lean face is set in a permanent grin, like a crocodile. Broad of shoulder and narrow of hip, but no taller than his diminutive wife, his biceps bulge out of his skin-tight T-shirt.

'Who's the boss?' I ask.

Everyone, including the grinning Jordi, points at Alexa, who smiles shyly. Through our interpreter, Alexa explains that she has been keen on gymnastics since the age of eight. As she grew up she became interested in theatre, then met some students who attended a circus school and decided that was where her future lay. From the day she joined the circus school at the age of twenty-one she knew her speciality would be tightrope.

'It's a long process,' she explains: four years in circus school and seven before she was fully confident as a performer. The qualities required? 'A level head and a lot of muscle.'

Circ Panic was formed when Alexa met Jordi in a village 15 miles north of Barcelona. At the time he was the village carpenter, but Alexa taught him the skills they would need to form their own circus company.

Jordi's speciality is Chinese Pole. This involves him shinning up and down the mast on top of their caravan (descending head first in an upside-down position) and striking poses on it, such as the flag position, which means gripping the pole in both hands and holding his body out at right-angles to it. No wonder his arms and shoulders are so big. He also does a comic dwarf routine, walking about on his knees and climbing on to a chair with his ankles strapped to the back of his thighs.

At this point Jordi butts in with a shake of his head and his crocodile grin.

Our interpreter laughs: 'He says she didn't have to teach him; he was born with these skills.'

As for where the couple found their musicians, Jordi doesn't hesitate: 'He says he picked up a stone and there they were!'

Mostly wordless (the occasional Spanish exclamations need no translation), the couple's show is loosely based on scenes from their courtship and relationship. Their stage personas are cartoonish exaggerations of their off-stage personalities. Jordi plays a strutting and preening Victorian-style showman pumped up with machismo. The laughs come from his spectacular and painful come-uppances as he continually overreaches himself. In essence he is the whiteface clown – an angry straight-faced Oliver Hardy or Basil Fawlty character perpetually punished for his own pomposity. Alexa is the auguste – a blushing innocent, whose ineffectual attempts at assistance only worsen the scrapes Jordi finds himself in.

A particularly funny opening sequence finds Jordi trying to fold down the front of the caravan to form their stage. Naturally, he finds himself doing a precarious splits between the roof of the caravan and the folding-out section. Desperately he calls to Alexa to winch the section closed. But of course she innocently turns the winch the wrong way . . .

Alexa's comic tightrope routine – she plays it as if she's nervous and can barely balance – belies her underlying skill. She jumps a skipping rope on the wire, sits on it, lies full length on it and walks *en pointe* in ballet shoes. She also does an attractive abseil ballet routine. Essentially she performs standard ballet moves at right-angles to the flat side of the caravan, suspended on a wire from the top of the mast. It's a neat optical illusion. It looks as if we have a vertiginous aerial view of her dancing on a normal horizontal floor. The leaps, when she swings away from the caravan towards us, especially enhance this disorientating effect.

Equally eye-crossing is the two-headed monster costume that Alexa wears for one of the show's most engrossing scenes.

'What is *that?*' says the kid sitting next to me as a freakish cross between a tarantula and a monkey climbs – more accurately *oozes* – out of one of the caravan's windows. Completely enclosed in a black body-stocking, the creature has two identical and disturbingly featureless heads, one at either end of its trunk. All four limbs are identical, becoming only 'arms' or 'legs' depending which way up it is, for it has no right side up and reverses its position frequently.

The routine works on two levels. First there's the appreciation of Alexa's gymnastic skill and the fun of trying to spot which way up she is. A particularly good bit is when the creature sits on one of its heads and lets its other head sink sadly into its hands – and we realize Alexa is actually standing on her head; the creature's 'arms' and 'hands' are her legs and feet. There's a clever switch at the end of the routine when Alexa goes into the caravan and Jordi emerges from the roof in an identical costume to make a triumphant climb to the top of the mast. But the routine also works artistically. Alexa's movements are so expressive that we forget there's a woman inside the suit and start to believe in the creature before us. We feel for it, in its loneliness and deformity. Played to a violin lament, the slow, sad dance becomes a poetic and moving comment on the tragedy of the circus freak or perhaps the captive circus animal.

In that respect, Circ Panic achieves what Circa tried and failed to – and what most circus never even attempts. It goes beyond impressing us with technique – in fact it sets out to make us forget the technique – and uses its skills as a means rather than an end, to engage our imaginations in a fictional character and narrative, in the manner of a book, play or song.

Overall it's a good show, both artistic and accessible, by turns broad and subtle, packed with incident and colourfully dressed. It gets a good reception from the mums-and-kids audience (it's presented as part of the Children's Festival) but would play equally well to an all-adult crowd in a fringe theatre. As Jasper King, who fronts the other half of the double bill, puts it, 'What is a children's show anyway? Often there is one child and two parents. You've got to do stuff that appeals to everyone.'

Jasper describes his company, the Chipolatas, as musical clowns. Usually they're a trio, but their accordionist is in hospital where his wife is giving birth. He's replaced on stage by a fiddle player, an electric bassist and a DJ making 'scratching' noises on a record deck. The musical line-up is completed by co-founder Sam Thomas on a stripped-down but very loud drum kit. The musical style is lilting folk meets hip-hop. Whereas Circ Panic present a theatrical performance, staying in character and largely ignoring the audience, Jasper plays straight to the crowd, more in the manner of a stand-up comedy gig, only with juggling clubs and a band.

His background is street theatre. He's been making his living at it since his teens, and he knows how to keep a crowd's attention. Typical of his act is a juggling routine in which he takes turns to bounce one of the balls off a different part of his body. 'Fingers, elbow, head . . .' he chants, while Sam and the boys bash out a thunderous accompaniment.

There's also a winning piece of volunteer participation with a girl of about six. While Jasper juggles with balls, her job is to stand on a box and take the balls he hands her one by one, and replace them with clubs, so he seamlessly ends up juggling with the clubs. She plays her part so charmingly she could almost be a plant.

'We always say it's the volunteer who makes our show,' says Jasper. 'People will say, "She was a gift to you, wasn't she?" Yep. She was.'

It's Sam's job to pick the volunteers.

'After seventeen years, you just look for someone who looks up for it,' says Jasper. 'Occasionally you get them up there and they turn around and see hundreds of people, and they go "Waaaaaagh!" So it's a case of very gently getting them back into the audience, saying thank you very much and getting somebody else up. That doesn't happen very often. But it's a case of realizing that of course it can be very scary.'

In the packed foyer after the show, Daisy weaves through the crowd to tell me, 'I've got a Chipolata for you in the café!' The first thing I do is check it's not burnt. During a fire-juggling routine, Sam stood on a chair and, to cringing and wincing laughter from the audience, rested the burning end of a juggling stick on the top of Jasper's head. When he took it away, not only did a thin plume of black smoke continue to rise from Jasper's bonce but for a fleeting moment a 6-inch yellow flame hovered there as well. As he rises from a table to shake my hand the Chipolata dutifully bows his cropped head to reveal not so much as a singe.

How does that work?

'Firstly, I've got very short hair. Secondly, heat goes up not down.'

It must hurt a bit, though?

'Naw. It's like when you're a kid and you can put your finger through the flame of a candle.'

Jasper got his love of performing in public from his father, a church minister. He took his first steps as an entertainer in Christian clowning organization the Holy Fools.

'The appeal for me is just the buzz of performing. Some people jump out of aeroplanes to get it. All I have to do is walk out on stage and I feel great.'

The Chipolatas formed seventeen years ago, when Jasper was seventeen and Sam was fourteen.

'Sam's dad had a street theatre company back in the 1970s and 1980s called the Fabulous Salami Brothers, which is why we got the name Chipolatas. When Sam was nine, he was in the show as Chipolata Salami, the small one.' Since then the Chipolatas have worked in 42 countries: 'We work in theatres, festivals, streets.' Typical of their intensive schedule, they've just come back from three days in Vienna and a weekend in Belfast. Next week they're off to Finland and then on to Romania.

They travel light: 'We can fit all three of us and all our stuff into one car.' And they travel comfortably: 'We used to always demand separate hotel rooms, because you need your space. Now we prefer it if a festival gives us a house, so we have our own rooms and we can cook for ourselves, but we can also come together in the living-room. I've never travelled with a circus. I'd like to. But it's hard work, and they don't pay very much.'

Jasper cites as his mentor an American clown called Avner the Eccentric whom he encountered in Finland just a couple of years ago. 'For the first time in fifteen years I saw someone and thought: I need to learn off that guy. What impressed me was the gentleness of his show. A lot of performers carry an ego, because sometimes it's hard to stand on stage in front of an audience, and an ego helps. Avner has no ego whatsoever. People talk about how you have to own the stage; the stage is yours. Well, Avner's theory is that when he walks on to a stage the audience was there first, so it's *theirs*. He has to ask their permission to come and play on their stage. That's very humble, and such humility is something that I really strive towards in my performance.'

Jasper's other big influence is Rowan Atkinson's silent television creation, Mr Bean. Many of Bean's fans wouldn't recognize him as a clown, any more than they would apply that description to another of Jasper's heroes, the silent film star Charlie Chaplin.

'If Mr Bean did exactly the same things wearing clown make-up they'd say, "That's a clown,"' says Jasper. But then Bean would probably have never achieved his immense popularity. Coulrophobia describes the irrational fear of clowns, and Jasper reckons it's rife in Britain.

'England is the hardest country we work. A lot of other cultures have a beautiful relationship with the clown. We have some friends in Switzerland who do some storytelling and clowning. They travel in a couple of old showman's wagons and put their own tent up. They travel around Europe and they do great. They come into town and it's like, "Hey, the circus is here." They came to England, they were turning up in places and the curtains were twitching. People were calling the police: "The travellers are here."'

It's because of such attitudes that Jasper is a kind of undercover plain-clothes clown. He's recently grown an impressive ginger beard. It gives him a gnome-like appearance perfect for his act. But he wears no clown make-up, not even a red nose.

'When I was sixteen, seventeen and first starting out, I had a white face with very simple make-up. And not heavy white, either. But I soon realized that wasn't the way to go. Straight away it alienates you; you're someone different from them. I'm trying to do things that make people think: I could do that. He's just the same as me. For example, bouncing a football on my head. All of a sudden all the thirteen- and fourteen-year-old boys are going "Oh yeah. I can do that. He's doing it to music." It's about trying to bond with an audience.'

Jasper jerks his thumb towards the foyer. 'A lot of the people in there today will have gone away and not realized they'd seen clowning. They think it's just some guys having a laugh and playing music, you know?'

Chapter 6

FREAK SHOW

In the Victorian era sideshows full of bearded ladies and conjoined twins were part of any circus. Today the human freak show lives on in the Circus of Horrors.

There are three steps to becoming a sword-swallower, says Hannibal Helmurto, the Pain Proof Man. Step One is to overcome your gag reflex.

'I started by sticking two fingers down my throat,' says Hannibal. It took seven months before he could do it without gagging or throwing up.

On stage Hannibal looks like a cross between an undernourished Hell's Angel, a bony psychotic demon and a punk-rock version of the father of clowning, Joey Grimaldi. Stripped to the waist and covered from skull to foot in tattoos, the 38-year-old German has a tangled red Mohican haircut, steel piercings in his lip, nose and nipples, shiny metal teeth and earrings the size of bracelets. His costume is a carpenter's apron filled with chisels and hatchets that look as though they will be used for nothing as innocuous as woodwork and a pair of mesh-covered goggles the size of binoculars, with evil-looking spikes sticking out of them.

Offstage Hannibal is the most gentle, polite and quietly spoken man you could meet and is about to be married to one of his Circus of Horrors co-stars – Anastasia IV, the Blade Walking Beauty, who assists in lowering the longest of his swords down her fiancé's throat.

Step Two is to train your oesophagus to open at will. At this point I had better warn you not to try this at home. Indeed, more squeamish readers might like to skip to the next chapter. That way you'll also miss a man who can pull his neck skin up over his face and a dwarf who does inadvisable things to his private parts with a vacuum cleaner.

On the subject of doing inadvisable things to yourself, Hannibal continues, 'Once you've desensitized your throat so the gag reflex won't go, you start swallowing blunt objects, which is very unpleasant in the beginning. I used a metal coat-hanger which I bent into a sausage shape so it was a long piece of metal and swallowed that.'

The coat-hanger stage took nearly two years before Hannibal was ready to move on to Step Three, which is the swallowing of sharp objects. Today they include a blade 70cm long.

'It's a very weird sensation,' says Hannibal, 'because there's cold metal touching areas where normally nothing ever goes. It feels like you're impaled, because you can't move. There's a straight piece of metal inside you.'

Amazingly, Hannibal didn't learn to sword-swallow under the supervision of an experienced practitioner. Inspired by a visit to his native Munich by his eventual employers, Britain's Circus of Horrors, the then tax office worker went home and taught himself from books.

Hannibal has had one accident in his career: 'I perforated my oesophagus and ended up in hospital for three weeks without any form of food or drink. That wasn't very nice at all.'

So wasn't he scared by the thought of sticking coat-hangers and blades down his throat, on his own, without so much as an accomplice standing by to call an ambulance?

'If you'll excuse my language,' says the ever-polite Pain Proof Man, 'I was shit scared. But that was the only way to do it, because there are not many sword-swallowers around to ask. There are only about eighty in the world.'

What did his friends and family think of his new hobby?

'Most people tell you you're crazy. They say, "Why do you want to do that? It's unpleasant. You're making yourself sick. It's dangerous. Why would you wish to do that?" And at the end of the day you can't really explain why. The only reason is because I want to do it.'

Apart from sword-swallowing and a bit of fire-eating, the Pain Proof Man is also a fakir. He eats broken glass. Then he pushes a knitting needle through his cheeks, fills his mouth with water and squirts it out through the bloody holes. The needle doesn't go through an existing piercing, like an earring.

'I pierce it fresh every night. The needle goes through my flesh every time. When I start touring it takes a week to heal. But the more you do it, the quicker it heals. After ten days it only takes a day to heal. It hurts a bit, and if you do it two or three times a night it hurts much more. The Pain Proof Man is not really pain proof. The art of it is handling the pain. It's about focus and concentration.' Hannibal gives the example of getting an injection at the doctors. 'That's a needle going inside you, but normally you don't jump up and down and scream and shout. But if you stand on a drawing pin, then you scream and shout. The difference is knowing it's coming. You get yourself prepared.'

Freaks of nature, whether by birth – midgets, giants, conjoined twins, two-headed goats – or by choice – tattooed ladies, fat ladies, sword-swallowers and fakirs – have been exhibited for the entertainment of the public since time immemorial. They have been associated with circus since Philip Astley marched solemnly around the first circus ring bearing candles to illuminate a lady from France whose hair was so long it trailed in the sawdust.

Generally, in the UK, freak shows have been more closely linked with funfairs than circus. It was not until the rock'n'roll years of the 1950s, however, that fairs became geared more towards the teenage market and began to separate from circuses, which appealed to a family audience. Before that, circuses and fairs often travelled together, with merry-go-rounds, sideshows, Wild West displays, bear pits and menageries surrounding the big top – or, on a big fairground, four or five big tops. Freak shows were often part of the mix.

George Pinder, whose family has been circus since the dawn of the nineteenth century, remembers from childhood a sheep whose number of legs was commemorated by its name, Fivie, and a horse with an extra hoof growing out of one of its legs. They were genuine birth defects, exhibited as living creatures. But he adds, 'Towards the end a lot of them were stuffed novelties, and some of them were faked. When I was a kid there was a guy who had a two-headed giant. A mermaid. Stuff like that.'

The Victorian era was the golden age of the freak show, when conjoined twins Chang and Eng Bunker toured the world and became wealthy celebrities, as well as giving rise to the term Siamese Twins after their place of birth. Freak shows were most successful in the USA, where they were especially associated with probably the most famous single name in the history of circus, P.T. Barnum.

Barnum never used the phrase most frequently attributed to him: 'There's a sucker born every minute.' It was actually said of Barnum's audience by a jealous competitor – with no small justification, since one of Barnum's greatest draws was the supposed body of a mermaid constructed from the body of a fish and the head of a monkey. He also exhibited a white elephant – courtesy of a bucket of whitewash.

It is often said Barnum was sixty-one before he moved into circuses. But this is only because, as with Astley's Amphitheatre of Equestrian Arts, early circuses weren't often called circuses.

One of Barnum's earliest, unsuccessful, ventures was Barnum's Grand Scientific and Musical Theatre, a travelling tent show with a juggler, singer and horses that was a circus in all but name. So was P.T. Barnum's Asiatic Caravan, Museum and Menagerie, which he promoted for four successful tenting seasons in his early forties. The latter boasted six lionesses, ten elephants, which caused headlines when he marched them through the streets of New York, and one Mr Nellis, the Man Without Arms, who, according to the posters, 'will load and fire a pistol and do other feats with his toes'.

Barnum's most famous late-life circus, Barnum and Bailey's 'Greatest Show on Earth', was actually largely driven by his partner, James A. Bailey, who was the seventy-plus Barnum's junior by thirty-nine years. Fondly remembered by later troupers as a 'little giant' of American circus, Bailey had changed his surname from McGuinness when he joined John Robinson and Bill Lake's Wagon Show (yet another name for circus) as a boy.

Barnum and Bailey became partners after the former tried to buy a baby elephant that Bailey had bred on his then Cooper and Bailey Circus – an upcoming rival to Barnum's dominance of the circus world. Barnum sent Bailey a telegram offering him $100,000 for the pachyderm. Bailey promptly reproduced the telegram on his billboards and newspaper adverts with words to the effect that if this is what the great P.T. Barnum would pay for our baby elephant, how much would you pay to see it? Barnum realized he'd met his match as a showboater and suggested the partnership in the spirit of if you can't beat 'em, join 'em.

The bearded, quietly spoken and slightly built Bailey was happy to let the flamboyant and famous Barnum be the public face of the operation while he provided the real ambition and got on with the real work, such as taking the 'Greatest Show on Earth' across the Atlantic for a successful winter season at London's Olympia in 1889. After Barnum's death, Bailey recrossed the ocean to undertake a five-year tour of Britain and Europe.

Earlier, it was another young and ambitious partner, William C. (Cameron) Coup, who tempted the 61-year-old Barnum out of retirement to start his 'first' great circus, the P.T. Barnum Museum, Menagerie and Circus, International Zoological Garden, Polytechnic Institute and Hippodrome. Barnum, whose only involvement was as a financial investor, is said to have blanched at the size of the operation, which was as big as its name suggests. With three shows daily, plus a morning street parade, it covered a five-acre site, included a 5,000-seat big top, employed 500 men and horses, and travelled on sixty-one specially made railway wagons – the first privately owned circus train in history.

Despite Barnum's initial reservations, of course, once he saw how successful the circus was he was happy, in his several autobiographies, to take sole credit for coming up with the idea, just as he was happy to have only his name on another of Coup's brainchildren that Barnum had initially been resistant to: Barnum's Great Roman Hippodrome – the first Madison Square Garden.

Facing Madison Square, the building was New York's version of ancient Rome's Circus Maximus, with an oval racing track one-fifth of a mile long encircling circus rings, fountains and statues. In 1887 the Garden assembled the largest number of circus elephants ever when a joint Barnum and (Adam) Forepaugh show presented sixty of the 'rubber mules', as US circus men liked to call them.

The reason the Indiana-born Coup wanted Barnum's name on the biggest circus the world had ever seen, rather than simply naming it after himself and a third partner in the venture, Dan Castello, was twofold. First, Barnum was an unparalleled showman and master of publicity who made a fortune as the concert promoter of singing star Jenny Lind. But apart from having the financial wherewithal to fund the circus, Barnum's name was already famous for his museums and, specifically, his freaks.

Born in Bethel, Connecticut, on 5 July 1810, Phineas Taylor Barnum showed early business acumen selling lottery tickets as a twelve-year-old. As an adult he founded a local newspaper and became a ticket-seller, secretary and treasurer on Aaron Turner's Wagon Show, which was one of the USA's earliest successful travelling circuses – for which he took $30 a week and a 20-per-cent cut of the profits.

Barnum's first success with human curiosities was Joice Heth, a blind and almost completely paralysed slave whom he purchased and promoted as being 160 years old and the nurse of the infant George Washington.

After his first disappointing venture in touring shows with his Grand Scientific and Musical Theatre – which he avoided calling a circus because of religious opposition to the term in the Deep South – Barnum moved to New York where he bought a natural history museum on Broadway called Scudder's American Museum, renaming it Barnum's American Museum. Freaks, from the genuine to the fabricated, were his way of attracting publicity and drawing a crowd to the more orthodox exhibits.

The human curiosity with whom Barnum enjoyed his greatest success was General Tom Thumb – real name Charles Sherwood Stratton – who stood just 2 feet 8 inches tall on his eighteenth birthday. Barnum, who was a distant relative, taught Stratton to sing, dance and smoke cigars when he was four years old and still the size of a six-month-old baby. Thumb's fame spread across the Atlantic, where he was introduced to Queen Victoria, and he became one of the wealthiest celebrities of his time, at one point bailing Barnum out of financial difficulties and eventually becoming the showman's business partner.

Another pair of dwarfs made famous – and rich – by Barnum were Waino and Plutano, the Wild Men of Borneo. Their real names were Hiram and Barney Davis, and they were born on a farm in Connecticut. Although mentally disabled, the 40-inch-tall brothers were blessed with enormous strength and performed a strongman act that included lifting and wrestling with members of the public.

At the time of his death, on 7 April 1891, Barnum was probably the most famous American on earth. As he lay on his deathbed he told a friend that his one regret was that he would not live to read his own obituary in the newspapers. The friend called the *Evening News*, which duly did him the favour of printing its obituary early, and, after reading it, the world's greatest showman died happy.

Since the 1970s freak shows have largely disappeared from circuses and carnivals, even in the USA. Some freaks – such as Otis Jordon, the Frog Boy – were banned from exhibiting themselves and found themselves enmeshed in bizarre legal wrangles to defend their livelihood against supposed disability-rights activists who objected to their 'exploitation'. Political correctness, however, will never overpower the public's desire to gawp at the deformity of others or the desire of the freaks themselves to profit from their uniqueness. Today's freak shows camouflage themselves as television documentaries with titles such as *Supersize Teens: Can't Stop Eating*, and *Embarrassing Bodies: Back to the Clinic*, and they have never been more prevalent. Even shows such as *Big Brother* might be regarded as freak shows, parading social misfits for our amusement.

For all the fun of a traditional circus freak show, however, look no further than the Circus of Horrors. The show's chief freak is Gary 'Stretch' Turner, who is in the *Guinness World of Records* for his unique ability to perform the 'human turtleneck' – stretching the skin of his neck up over his nose. With eyes that swivel around like ping-pong balls, Stretch emerges from the wings wearing nothing but a wicked grin and a loincloth. His gait is a kind of cartoon tiptoe – his back hunched and his knees rising to waist height with each step. He's so thin we can count every rib – although a more appropriate word would be 'skinny.'

Licking his lips and rolling his eyes in delight as the audience squirms and watches from between its fingers, he takes a handful of skin from the centre of his chest and stretches it slowly out, 6 inches or more from his breastbone. He then takes a pinch of skin from under his chin and stretches it downwards in the manner of a pelican. During a moment of audience participation he gets a couple of squeamishly giggling girls to pull huge bat wings of skin from the underside of his arms and attach them with bulldog clips to equally large flaps stretched from his sides. The girls – and much of the audience – scream hysterically as they gingerly snap on the bulldog clips, and Gary winces and gurns like a pro.

There's more groaning and gurning elsewhere in the show when Captain Dan, the Demon Dwarf, squats on a potty mid-stage. A busty blonde girl in a crotch-length nurse's uniform screws up her face and fans the air in front of her nose with her hand. Instead of a rabbit from a hat, Dan pulls from the formerly empty pot a very long, grizzled and turd-like sausage – from which he bites the end before tossing it into the audience along with half a pot-full of 'wee'.

Waist high in his bowler hat, another of Dan's stunts is pulling the metal cap from a beer bottle with his eye socket. With his teeth clenched and his eyebrow and cheek screwed together against the cap, it seems to take an age before he finally reels back, with a great snake of white foam gushing from the neck of the bottle.

Dan's party piece involves a tubby 'Henry'-style vacuum cleaner on wheels. Whistling and wearing a kilt, the midget drags the loudly humming cleaner on to the empty stage by its long hose as if he's just doing a spot of tidying up. As he reaches the centre of the stage he flicks up the back of his kilt to reveal that, like a true Scotsman, he's wearing nothing under it. Then, glancing around as if to check that nobody's looking, he lifts the front of the kilt and sticks the vacuum nozzle on his willy. As the audience cross their legs and curl up with shocked and embarrassed laughter, he begins dancing as he drags the Hoover around by the hose hanging out from under his kilt. Ever more gleeful, he begins swinging the hose around like a skipping rope, his hands in the air to prove that the only thing keeping the nozzle in place is suction.

A circus show unlike any other, the Circus of Horrors was the brainchild of its 'undead' ringmaster, the self-styled Dr Haze – a tall man with long peroxide-blond hair and a fetish for top hats, tight-fitting leather trousers, scarlet boas and blood-splattered mad-scientist lab coats. Towards the end of the show, which is set in a lunatic asylum that has been taken over by the inmates, Haze is cut in half by an enormous, although it must be said not terribly convincing, circular saw. He is then wheeled around in a trick cabinet that makes his severed trunk appear to be resting on a shelf, with a long trail of innards hanging like well-sauced spaghetti from its jagged stump. His dismemberment doesn't stop him singing, though, in a baroque'n'roll style that Meatloaf would be proud of.

John Haze was born on a circus. His father was variously an ambulance driver and a bear trainer on funfairs. He persuaded Haze's mother to run away to the circus with him, then ran away from *her*, leaving her literally holding the baby.

'The circus was very good to her and looked after her until the end of the season when they took her back to Preston where my grandma lived, and I grew up there until I was about eleven,' Haze recalls, in a surprisingly soft Northern accent. With sawdust in his blood, his childhood was spent visiting every circus that came to town. 'I remember Billy Smart's marching twenty elephants through Preston. I went to Sanger's Circus in Wales when I was really young. That left a deep impression on my mind.

'When I was eleven my mum decided to find my dad and sue him for maintenance. She found him in prison. He obviously had no money, but the courts advised them to get back together, and, foolishly, she did go back to him, really for my sake, because she thought I wanted a dad.

'Within a few weeks he saw an advert in *World's Fair* for a circus in Ireland that was looking for acts, and off we went to join Circus Della Beck. It was owned by a guy called Jim Beck, a circus fan who owned supermarkets and funded his circus from that. I learned to fire-eat in a day, and away we went. Fire-eater, mind-reader and fakir. I was twelve, and I'd pretty well left school by then.'

The family moved back to England to work with another circus, but before long 'My dad did another runner. My mum, who wasn't really a circus person, went back to live in Preston, but this time I stayed. I stayed in the circus until I was twenty or twenty-one, when I had a burning ambition to play rock'n'roll and start a band. So I left the circus and funded my rock'n'roll career by taking a normal job in a textile company, which I did, reluctantly, for twelve years.'

The first name of Haze's band was Flash Harry. 'We changed the name to Haze. Then we started calling it Haze II and Haze III, like film sequels. All the time the band was becoming more theatrical. I did some fire-eating, we had some illusions and a juggler, and we started calling it, Haze Presents the Circus of Horrors.'

Cult musical *The Rocky Horror Show* would seem an obvious influence. Haze prefers to cite his glam-rock and heavy-metal heroes Marc Bolan and Alice Cooper as inspirations. 'But so was Billy Smart. As was *The Exorcist* – and football, for that matter. All of these things combined helped me to create the Circus of Horrors.'

The rise of the Circus of Horrors as it exists today grew from a tragedy. On Boxing Day 1994 21-year-old Neville Campbell was performing on the Wheel of Death before 1,500 fans at the Blackpool Tower Circus – an ornate arena between the base of the four legs of the Tower, where circus had been presented for exactly 100 years since 1894. As he ran over the top of the wheel Neville slipped and fell. He managed to grab on to the upcoming other end of the wheel but broke both wrists in the process. Desperately, he pulled himself back on to his feet on the still-revolving contraption but fainted from the pain and fell from the top once more. As he hit the ground he broke his neck and died instantly. Neville was Haze's godson.

'I was at home, visiting my mother at Christmas,' Haze remembers. 'I heard on the radio that there had been an accident but didn't make the connection. Then that night, at two o'clock in the morning, I got a call from a friend and was told Neville, my godson, had died in the accident I'd heard about on the radio. I was only 18 miles away, so I called Neville Senior and asked if there was anything I could do, and the next day I went over and just tried to console the family. It was chaos. There was a fight at the police station where everyone had gone to identify the body. Obviously they were in a state of shock. It was a terrible situation. But that's where I met Gerry Cottle, whose son had been a close friend of Neville's. We went to the funeral and became very friendly at that point.'

The timing was fortuitous. Cottle was a stockbroker's son from Cheam who ran away with the circus when he was fifteen. During various shows he learned stilt-walking, clowning and the rola-rola – juggling while balanced on a seesaw made from a plank resting on top of a cylindrical spool.

He married into a famous circus family, the Fossetts. Most of all, he learned the behind-the-scenes tricks of running a circus.

At the age of twenty-five Cottle and his business partner, Brian Austen, had their own circus. Together with Brian's girlfriend, they did virtually all the acts: juggling, magic, tightrope, fire-eating, knife-throwing, a female yogi (Brian's girlfriend) who washed her face in broken glass (and also sold balloons and candyfloss in the interval). Within a year they were featured on television's *Philpott Files* and appeared on the cover of the *Radio Times* with the headline 'The smallest greatest show on earth'.

Cottle always had a talent for creating publicity. He was also a driven man in every area of his life. His autobiography, *Confessions of a Showman*, deals frankly with his addiction to affairs and cocaine. The owner of Britain's *smallest* circus wanted to own Britain's *biggest* circus. And although the eternal risk-taker would have more financial ups and downs than a trampoline act, he quickly achieved his dream.

By the 1980s the name Gerry Cottle was as synonymous with circus as Billy Smart had been in the previous era, not least because of BBC1's Saturday night variety show, *Seaside Special*, which was broadcast from Cottle's big top and regular appearances on programmes such as *The Two Ronnies* and *Morecambe and Wise*. Cottle even appeared on *Desert Island Discs*.

By the mid 1990s, however, Cottle had become frustrated by the animal-rights issue that dogged traditional circus but had been unable to find success with an all-human show. A venture into funfairs had turned sour, and he was looking for something new.

'I told him I was doing this thing called the Circus of Horrors,' says Haze, 'but I really believed we could do it bigger and better in a tent, so I persuaded him to do it. He took a lot of persuading. But eventually he agreed, and we started at the Glastonbury music festival that summer.

'At the time Gerry's daughters had a show called the Cottle Sisters' Circus. So we used their tent and all his family, plus my rock'n'roll band. We had a lot of big acts: a Wheel of Death, a couple of trapeze acts, some Kenyan warriors. We made a couple of big production numbers at the beginning and end and linked it all together with songs and stuff like that. It took a couple of days to get right, but by the third day it had become a very good show. We were packed to the rafters. People were rioting outside to get in.'

From there, the success of the Circus of Horrors built slowly. At Brighton racecourse and Crystal Palace, 'We did terrible business.' The show was also booked on a hugely overambitious three-month tour of South America. 'We were booked into places the size of Wembley Arena for two weeks at a time.'

The big break came when the Circus of Horrors was invited to participate in a television show hosted by Danni Behr. 'It was a series where she did different things each week, becomin g a mercenary and stuff like that, and one of the things was being a circus girl. At that point we still hadn't made up our minds whether to carry on, but we got offered a big arts festival tour. We started doing really good business, got loads of publicity and television opportunities and went from strength to strength.'

Today the Circus of Horrors plays an annual theatre tour from October to March. 'It's a big show, with twenty-eight performers. But because it's in theatres we don't have such big circus acts. You couldn't have a Wheel of Death or flying trapeze. So instead we have more of the bizarre and freaky acts, like Gary Stretch and Captain Dan, doing these amazing things with their bodies.

'All in a funny way,' Haze adds. 'Everything is done with a forked tongue firmly in each cheek.'

The question Haze is most frequently asked is where he finds people like Gary Stretch and Captain Dan.

'The answer is that in a lot of cases they find me. In Gary's case, we were at the Roundhouse in London. We were getting a lot of publicity, so he'd read about us. His wife got in touch and said, "My husband's got really stretchy skin. Would you be interested?" I asked if she could send a video, and he looked amazing. He thought he might do it for a year, but he's been with us for seven or eight years now.'

What was he doing before?

'He was a scaffolder and a sheep farmer. He's got a very strange blood disorder called Ehlers-Danlos Syndrome. Where our blood cells are round, his are all jagged. They don't stick together very well, which means he's got very stretchy skin.

'Dan had been with a couple of the more hardcore freak shows, and although I'd come across him I didn't know him well. I put an advert in *The Stage* looking for all kinds of weird and wonderful things – amputee actors and so on. And one of the people who came forward was Dan. He started off doing the Hoover, and over the years he's added a lot more. This year we're going to be doing an electric act with him: pushing thousands of volts through his body and getting him to light things up with it.'

Is that done for real?

'Absolutely. It's just knowing how to do it, really. People think sword-swallowing isn't real, but I don't know any sword-swallowers who don't do it for real. People think stupid things like the blade retracts into the handle, so with Hannibal we use a sword without a handle so that the audience can see it's not a trick. I don't know why people are so cynical, but I suppose it's the age we live in. Because of the special effects in films they think everything is fake. But everything we do is for real.'

The auditions for Circus of Horrors must be fun, I say.

'We put *Britain's Got Talent* to shame, I can tell you that. You get a lot of people who have absolutely no hope of getting the job. I've had people stick bits of paper on their teeth to make fangs. You can't understand why they even come to audition. But they do, and it's good fun. We try not to take the piss out of them.

'There was a great one in Stockton-on-Tees who said he sets fire to his finger and blows fire. We thought that sounds interesting. We wouldn't let him do it in the tent, so we took him outside. He set fire to his finger and blew fire. But he was using lighter fluid to set his finger on fire, and he was blowing lighter fluid out of his mouth. So his chin caught fire. He tried to put his chin out, and his finger reignited. We managed to put him out, and he went off to a department store for a cup of tea with these other people who told me later how he got up to go to the toilet and left a Coke bottle on the table. This kid came past, picked up the bottle and ran off with it – and it was full of petrol. So he was running around this department store trying to find this kid with a Coke bottle full of petrol. He turned up at the show about three days later with his finger all bandaged up, wearing his McDonald's uniform.'

Asked if he has seen any acts he would consider too dangerous to use in the show, Haze says, 'I wouldn't say too dangerous, but there are things you can't do frequently enough. Again at an audition, these three guys turned up. They were called the Holy Trinity. One of them got his bollocks out. Then he took a 6-inch nail and nailed them to a chair. Then he was nailing his arms to things . . . It was like, *That can't be good for you.* Afterwards we said, "How often can you do it?" He said, "Maybe once every two months." Well, we have two shows a day sometimes, so once every two months was no good to us. So it wasn't that it was too hard core, it was that it was too hard core to be able to do it repetitively enough to warrant giving him a job.'

One of the most wince-inducing moments in the show finds a girl put her tongue out on the edge of a table. A man drives a nail through it, and she runs off with the table hanging from her tongue.

'God help us!' says my partner. 'Did she really do that?'

I suppose that's the reaction every circus performer wants from an audience. But it sounds to me like a lot of pain for a stunt that lasts seconds and is almost a walk-on throwaway gag, likely to be lost among several other things happening on stage in quick succession.

'We do have people putting pins through themselves,' Haze agrees. 'But you do it in a different way' – a different way to the man who nailed his bollocks, I presume he means – 'and your face heals up really quickly.'

Haze says he's pushed plenty of sharp objects through his own skin but adds, 'I don't really like doing it. I've done things like walking on broken glass, jumping on broken glass; having a rope around my neck and being strangled. I used to do that when I was a little kid. Bed of nails. Shoving nails up my nose. All the things they call fakir stuff. You feel the pain, but you try to put it out of your mind. If you do it correctly it will hurt a bit, but it won't hurt that much.

'To be honest, acts like that are really hard to rehearse. If you stand on your own or with one or two people while you try to rehearse, it hurts like mad to the point where you don't want to do it. But when you're stood in front of a crowd of people then the adrenalin takes over and you do it. I wouldn't say comfortably. But you do do it.'

I see the Circus of Horrors at the Yarmouth Hippodrome. On the way out, Peter Jay waits, grinning, in the foyer.

'What did you think of it?' Jay asks.

'Well . . . it was different!'

In all honesty, I prefer Jay's own more family-orientated productions. But that's more a reflection of my personal taste than the quality of the show, which, for what it is, cannot be faulted.

The Circus of Horrors is billed as an adult show. Near the beginning an ominous hooded figure throws off a cloak to reveal a topless girl who runs, screaming, across the ring clad in nothing but a G-string. Obviously you wouldn't want your children to watch Captain Dan sticking a Hoover on his willy or to copy Hannibal sticking pins through his cheeks and knives down his throat. But the fact is that, if they were allowed in, your kids would probably love it more than anybody, for the Horrors is, ultimately, a shamelessly juvenile form of adult entertainment. It's the heavy metal version of circus, with elements of *The Rocky Horror Show*, Screaming Lord Sutch and the Hammer House of Horrors mixed in for good measure. Like heavy metal it has an intrinsic sense of high-camp, gross-out humour that will not appeal to everyone but which certainly appeals to a large and enduring audience that ranges from student-age punks and Goths to businessmen on stag nights.

Since moving out of its big top origins into theatres, where its last tour played more than ninety venues, the Circus of Horrors has become one of the biggest success stories in circus in the past decade and shows no sign of flagging. Certainly its stars have no intention of hanging up their gore-splattered costumes any time soon.

Says Hannibal, 'I'll carry on as long as I have fun with it. If you're an acrobat your joints and muscles get weak. But for the sort of things I do there is no sell-by date. There are sword-swallowers who perform in their late sixties.'

Haze feels the same. 'You can't be a trapeze artist at forty-five or fifty, but if you're singing and playing a part it doesn't matter how old you are. Mick Jagger and Alice Cooper still look fantastic – and I'm not nearly as old as them.'

Having originally wanted to be a rock star, he is particularly proud to add, ' I got my first record deal when I was forty, I've released three albums of music from the show now, and the last one was a double album. Almost all of the music in the Circus of Horrors is original, and it's almost all written by me. Next year we'll have a new show, which will be the biggest tour we've done, and I'll be making a fourth album to go with that.'

Gerry Cottle, who remains a partner in Horrors, attributes its success to its sense of humour and the dedication of its cast.

'They all enjoy being in it, and I think the energy and enthusiasm comes across. It's the type of show we should be producing in this country. We canot compete with the technical marvels of Cirque du Soleil, because we cannot afford to. There isn't the market in this country for a full-time touring show on that scale. But the great British public do like a laugh, and the Circus of Horrors is a fun show. It's fun to talk about: "You won't believe what this guy did . . . I saw this fella with stretchy skin . . . and a guy hanging by hooks in his back . . ." It's one of those car crash things – you can't not look.'

Cottle also cites Horrors as an example of the kind of circus show the Arts Council should be funding – a project that needs investment to get off the ground but which aspires to becoming a self-supporting commercial venture at the earliest opportunity.

'We had a grant the first year we went into theatres,' says Cottle. 'It helped us, and we made money. We offered to give them some money back, as per the agreement, and they didn't know how to accept it because no one had ever given them any money back before.'

Haze agrees. 'The whole thing about our business comes down to two words: "show" and "business" – and the word "business" means you have to make money out of it. Ten years ago people didn't go to theatres to see circus. We devised a show that was completely new to theatre; we were groundbreaking, and we suffered at first. It took us a long time to build up an audience. But once we had built an audience they came back time and time again.

'One of the problems I think you have with the Arts Council is they seem to think art and success don't go hand in hand. A lot of contemporary circuses go all out in terms of what they can get in terms of grants and hand-outs, instead of trying to win an audience over to where they can stand on their own two feet.'

Haze is proud of the contribution the Circus of Horrors has made to the circus scene generally.

'We attract people who wouldn't normally dream of going to the circus, and a lot of people who come to see us then go on to see other circuses. It whets their appetite and they think it might be fun to go to the Chinese State Circus or whatever. So in that respect I think we've done the circus profession in the UK a lot of good.'

Chapter 7

THE UNIVERSITY OF CIRCUS

Want to learn how to walk a tightrope or swing on the flying trapeze? The Circus Space offers Britain's only degree course in circus arts.

London's university of circus grew out of pigeon shit and rubble. Juliette Hardy-Donaldson was there. Today Juliette is Head of Aerial Disciplines at the Circus Space, Britain's only circus school to offer a BA (Honours) degree in circus arts. Twenty years ago she was a former dancer, trained at the Royal Academy, who had gone on to work for a music magazine and manage a band called House of Dolls.

'I stopped dancing because of injury and ended up in the music business where, of course, you drink lots of beer, put on weight and don't exercise,' the Scot recalls with a smile. 'So I took up acrobatics as a way of getting fit again.

'I used to do acrobatics at a little community place in the centre of London, and somebody told me about this place that was being built in North Road in Islington, which was the original Circus Space. It was an old warehouse, a former timber merchant's, which is now the Pleasance Theatre. The deal was, if you go up there and help them knock down walls and clean out pigeon shit during the day, then you get free classes on things like trapeze in the evenings.' The former dancer was attracted to trapeze 'because I had bad ankles. I'd sprained my ankles a couple of times, and in the air you don't have to land.'

Doesn't trapeze involve hanging from your ankles?

'That's traction, though. The compression of landing is what did my ankles in, so the traction of hanging is very good for them.'

Among Juliette's strongest memories is the dust of training in what was effectively a building site. 'It was always dusty. Always, always.'

The Circus Space was founded by a group of new circus performers including Jonathan Graham, Tao Greenstreet and Charlie Holland. Greenstreet was a street entertainer who had discovered circus skills as a student. Holland was originally inspired by a Californian group of jugglers called the Flying Karamazov Brothers, whom he saw opening the show at a Grateful Dead concert at London's Rainbow Theatre. He became a juggler and went on to work in places as diverse as Gerry Cottle's Circus and Japanese theme parks.

Russia and China have a long tradition of state-sponsored circus schools, but in Britain in the late 1980s there was no formal route into circus. You were either born into a circus family, ran away with one or, if you wanted to work outside of traditional circus, had to find an existing practitioner to teach you. Founded with an initial grant of £4,000, the Circus Space was intended to remedy that situation by creating a space where people with an interest in, particularly, new circus could create work, teach and learn new skills.

'They were all teaching each other,' Juliette recalls. 'So I was taught by the professionals of the day on a very friendly, informal basis. It was all very relaxed, because of the state of the building and the fact that there weren't many people. It was quite a small set-up.'

At that point, in 1989, the new circus movement was just beginning, and had yet to gain much public awareness.

'Cirque du Soleil hadn't toured at that point. They were a small outfit just starting in Canada. Britain had its own version of new circus – a few small theatrical circus companies. Then Archaos, a French company, came to the fore when they did the Edinburgh Festival – which was one of the first circus shows I saw, actually.'

Juliette was also present when Cirque du Soleil made its first visit to the UK in 1990, appearing in a blue big top in the Jubilee Gardens beside the Thames. Financially, Soleil's London début was a disaster. It was summer, many Londoners were out of the city on holiday, and those who remained didn't want to spend an evening in a tent when they could be enjoying an uncharacteristic heatwave outside. The foreign tourists, meanwhile, had come to London to see its native sights, not a Canadian circus. After doing similarly poor business in Paris, where sixteen other circuses were in town at the same time, it would be a while before Cirque du Soleil regrouped and returned to Europe on the sort of scale with which it now plays an annual residency at the Albert Hall. For those with an interest in circus, however, the fledgling Soleil's first appearance in the UK was a historic moment.

'It was still a small show, but it was absolutely brilliant,' Juliette enthuses. 'We were all completely mesmerized. It was just different. Different training. Different experiences. Different styles to us. It was refreshing to see such a different style.'

Like many in circus, Juliette has mixed feelings about the way Soleil has grown since those early days. 'It's not always my cup of tea as a show. But the thing is, with Cirque du Soleil, there are so many different shows. You're not going to like everything they do, so there are definitely some shows I like more than others. But they've certainly raised the profile of circus throughout the world. It's generated a lot of interest and a lot of work, and for that we're all eternally grateful, because without Cirque du Soleil there would not be an industry such as there is now.'

Juliette began performing in public in the same year she began her lessons at Circus Space. Initially she appeared in nightclubs, part time, before joining her first touring circus as a full-time trapeze artist in 1991. Until her retirement from performance in 2008, she says, 'I worked on hundreds of shows. I did a lot of contemporary circus, but I did most of my work in traditional circuses, because they're the ones that tour ten months to a year at a time, so it's guaranteed work. We averaged two shows a day, sometimes three, sometimes four and on a nice day just one. It's very hard work, but it's the only way to do the big swinging acts I like on a consistent basis. You get very fit and very sure of what you're doing.'

After 'Entrance of the Gladiators' the most famous piece of music associated with circus is probably George Leybourne's 1867 composition, 'The Daring Young Man on the Flying Trapeze'. The song was inspired by the discipline's founder, Jules Léotard, who was the first to turn a somersault in mid-air and the first to jump from one trapeze swing to another.

Born in Toulouse around 1840 (the exact year is unknown), Léotard was due to go into law when he became more interested in rigging a swing above the swimming pool in his father's gymnasium. He made his public début at the Cirque Napoléon in Paris on 12 November 1859, and his twelve-minute act was so revolutionary that his fellow artistes had a commemorative medal struck in his honour.

Léotard performed without a safety net, which was not introduced to circus until 1871, a year after his untimely death at the age of about thirty (not from a fall but from an illness that was probably smallpox). The first safety net was used by Spanish troupe the Rizarellis, at London's Holborn Empire. Before that, trapeze artists relied on piled mattresses to break their fall. When Léotard first performed in London, however, at the Alhambra Theatre, Leicester Square, in May 1861, he performed over the heads of diners. By then he was the most famous circus performer of his day and a major celebrity.

Today, of course, Léotard's name lives on in the name of the self-designed, wrist-to-ankle skin-tight garment in which he performed. Léotard called it a *maillot*, which the French now use to mean swimsuit. In a style Superman would follow, he preserved his modesty by wearing a pair of shorts over his tights.

There are many types of trapeze act besides the most famous flying variety. Most common in new circus is static trapeze in which one or two performers perform hangs and balances on a stationary trapeze bar. More rare, because it requires the space of a big top, is Juliette's speciality, solo swinging trapeze, in which tricks are performed at the uppermost point of the swing.

Juliette became a solo trapeze act because she couldn't find enough people to put together a flying trapeze troupe. She also performed on the *corde lisse* – or French rope – and aerial silk, although the latter is not one of her favourites.

'It's so popular on the corporate market that, basically, there are hundreds and hundreds of people out there doing silks or tissues, and I feel it's been done to death. It's one of the easiest acts to learn, up to a point. And it's something useful to have in an ensemble production where you might be asked to do a bit of this or that. It's still nice to see a really good act. But there's a lot of mediocre tissue around, and I get bored with it. It's not as dynamic as the kind of acts I lean towards – the big swinging stuff with the release and the catch.'

In 1994 Juliette met her professional and romantic partner Bryan and formed the Duo Vertigo. Their partnership grew out of the same Boxing Day tragedy at Blackpool Tower Circus that introduced Gerry Cottle to Circus of Horrors founder John Haze. Bryan was the other half of the Wheel of Death act in which Haze's godson Neville Campbell fell and died.

'Bryan was devastated. He lost his partner, his best friend and his livelihood in one fell swoop. I was at Blackpool doing my swinging trapeze act, and Bryan came on the next season I did, with Philip Gandey's Cirque Surreal. He didn't have an act, so he had to do other stuff. He's a magician as well, so he worked his way into the show. And while we were there we would rehearse together, just for fun really. We did balance and perch stuff, *corde lisse.* He learned to catch on the flying trapeze. So he developed a lot of different skills, and the year after that we decided to put an act together. For the first couple of years we did balance perch and double rope. Then we came back to London and put together a cradle act.'

A cradle act is a kind of mini flying trapeze performed on a single swing called the cradle. 'The catcher hangs upside down on the cradle, and I'm on the cradle with him,' Juliette explains. 'He'll catch me and swing me and put me back on the cradle, and off the back of the swing I'll do somersaults or pirouettes or whatever.'

Clearly, the death of Bryan's former partner hadn't put him off the dangers of circus. 'He said he would never do Wheel of Death again,' says Juliette. 'But at the same time he's a circus performer, and he had been for many years. So he wasn't going to be freaked out by the idea of doing dangerous things – because the danger is an illusion most of the time. It's a calculated risk, and it's practised to the point where if you're working high, without safeties, you either know you can do it or you just don't do it. We put on a show of it being high risk, with a drum roll to get everybody's heart racing. That's part of the illusion. But I used to swing without safeties, and, believe me, there was no way I was taking a risk up there. I used to do what I knew 100 per cent I could do. It might look like it, but we actually don't have a death wish. Sadly, people do fall, and when it happens it makes headlines. But tragedies are actually extremely rare compared with other industries.'

Lesser injuries are, of course, more frequent. 'You'll get aches and strains and bruises and burns occasionally. Depending what discipline you're working in, you'll get injuries very specific to that apparatus.' With a laugh Juliette adds, 'Dancers, ice skaters, athletes . . . we all have our osteopath on speed dial.'

The Circus Space is fond of the legend that when the founders set up their first trapeze there wasn't enough room for it to fully swing back. With typical can-do spirit they knocked a door into the wall, which was to be opened when the trapeze was in use. Within a couple of years, however, it was clear that the Circus Space needed more space, and in 1994 the school moved across London to new premises in the former Shoreditch Electricity Generating Station in Hoxton. At the time Hoxton was not the trendy borough, full of art galleries and bars, that it is today. It was such a run-down part of Hackney as to be a virtual no-go area, and the former power station was completely derelict. Again, there was a lot of pigeon shit and feathers to clear out of the huge Victorian building, which had lain empty for half a century. The power station was originally fuelled by burning household refuse, and bins full of ash added to the debris that had to be cleared away, along with most of the original machinery.

Although it has since been fully refurbished, the building's origins remain clear from the exposed brick walls, its vertiginous roof space and the names of its two main training spaces, the Combustion Chamber and the Generating Chamber. Various thick and heavy chains and pieces of hard-to-identify ironwork decorate the walls as a reminder of the rooms' former use, while steel girders in the roof provide the perfect support for all manner of aerial apparatus.

The CC, as it's known, has a sprung dance floor with under-floor heating. Other rooms include a couple of dance studios, an acrobatic studio with sprung floor and padded walls and the newly built Creation Studio, which professionals can hire to rehearse new work in privacy. There is also a creative warren of thirteen offices rented out to various circus and theatre companies, including the circus agency Missing Link.

As with the first Circus Space, Juliette recalls fondly, 'I swung in here when it was a derelict building – fighting the pigeons for air space. Me and pigeons – we have a long history!'

Juliette has been teaching at Circus Space almost as long as she's been performing. Before becoming head of aerial disciplines on the degree course six years ago she was head trainer of the eighty-seven aerialists the Circus Space provided for the *Millennium Show* at the Millennium Dome.

'When I was dancing I qualified as a dance teacher. At the old Circus Space they wanted someone to teach ballet, and I used to be a ballerina, so I taught ballet there. Then it was, "Can you have a look at my act? Could you help me with this?" And all of a sudden I began teaching beginners static trapeze. So every time I wasn't touring I would come back to the Circus Space and teach, in order to pay for my training at the Circus Space.' With a smile she adds, 'I have a long history of doing deals with Circus Space, too.'

There are no academic qualifications required for entry to the Circus Space's degree course, just suitability and a successful audition. Now based full time at the school, Juliette personally teaches many of the disciplines. 'Tight wire is one of my favourite things to teach. Balance perch I would teach, but there's no one currently doing it. They all have to choose one discipline to specialize in, and once they've chosen I hire and fire to make sure everyone gets the teacher appropriate to them.'

Juliette describes the intake as a mixed bag. 'We have quite a few English students now, whereas we didn't used to. They're here basically because they want the degree. For the foreign students the degree isn't that important. They're here because they want to train to be a circus artiste. Within that, there are all sorts of different aspirations. Some want to be in companies they already know. Others want to start their own companies or freelance. Others end up going into cabaret or street performance. The events industry is the bread and butter over here. Everyone wants a bit of that, because it's good money.'

No Fit State Circus has proved a popular next step for many Circus Space graduates, traditional circus less so. 'Traditional shows in this country have been stuck in a bit of a time warp,' says Juliette. 'So if they want to go into traditional circus they tend to go abroad, because there are bigger and better shows.' She admits, though, that few graduates are good enough to go straight into a big European circus. 'To be honest, they don't have that much time here, so they tend to go and work elsewhere, to get a bit more experience and skill, and eventually some of them do end up touring with bigger shows.'

Because circus skills take so long to hone, and because they are more easily learned at an early age, it is hoped that many of the future degree students will have first attended the youth programme that the Circus Space has recently instigated for schoolchildren. One of the teachers is Kaveh Rahnama, who graduated from Circus Space two years ago and who has also formed his own company, So and So Circus Theatre, with fellow graduate Lauren Hendry whom he met and with whom fell in love on the course.

Kaveh was a late starter at Circus Space. While most students join straight from school, at sixteen or eighteen, Kaveh had already graduated from the University of Warwick with a degree in English and theatre studies. His interest in circus skills dates back to his teens when he learned to juggle.

'My dad used to go through these fads. One day we were walking through Covent Garden market and we saw this stall called More Balls Than Most. They did a little pack of juggling balls with instructions, and we learned together. It was a father-and-son thing.' Kaveh proved to be a natural, recalling, 'There's something hypnotic about juggling. I enjoyed the distraction from school work.'

Kaveh's first performing experience was with Albert and Friends, a children's circus based in Hammersmith. 'We took a couple of shows to the Edinburgh Festival. They were very much street shows.' Albert and Friends also gave Kaveh the space to progress from juggling balls to hoops and clubs. 'We lived in quite a small council house in Acton, so hoops were difficult to practise with, because we didn't have very much room.'

Having always preferred physical theatre to straight acting, Kaveh set up his first company, Boundless, at university. After graduating and finding sporadic theatrical work, it was an appearance in a production of the musical *Barnum*, in Eastbourne, that led him to the Circus Space.

'I did a bit of singing, dancing, juggling, ball walking, the lot, and some of the people suggested I get a professional qualification. I suppose until that point I'd suppressed my interest in circus because I thought it wasn't cool. At school people would take the mickey out of you for it. But I was doing part-time jobs and a bit of acting, and thought: I want more than this. So Circus Space seemed the right place to go.'

Looking back, Kaveh says simply, 'Circus Space changed my life. In your first term you do a bit of everything: juggling, trampolining, aerial work – which I'm terrible at – acrobatics and acrobalance, which Lauren and I decided to specialize in. Acrobalance is mostly pair work – one person lifting the other in one way or another. There are no props, and that's what appeals to me. There's you and one person and nothing else. I'm also a fan of work that engages an audience, and with acrobalance you can be very close to people, rather than up in the air.'

As well as training in specific skills, Kaveh adds, 'You also do lots of conditioning: circuit training, press-ups, sit-ups, as well as theatre and movement.' There were originally twenty-two students in Kaveh's year, which dwindled to sixteen by the final year. 'It's a tough course. Some people come and think it's going to be a bit of fun, but actually it's incredibly hard work.'

Only half of the class were English speakers. 'There was an American, an Australian, four English people, one Scottish girl (Lauren), an Irish guy, a French girl, an Italian, three Germans and quite a few Spanish. It was a really interesting cultural mix, and, collectively, they came from many different backgrounds. One girl had never done any circus but had been a dancer. Another girl had worked a lot with horses – she'd done vaulting and also some dance. Then Lauren came from a gymnastics background.'

Lauren, who now teaches on the adult recreational course at Circus Space, is six years younger than Kaveh. She joined Circus Space straight from school and admits she had little previous experience of circus and certainly not contemporary circus. 'I'm from Inverness, and no circus goes there that's not traditional circus,' she says. 'So I'd seen the Chinese State, Moscow State, and that was about it. I started gymnastics when I was five and started at Circus Space when I was seventeen, so it was more a way of continuing with something physical as a career, rather than knowing what I wanted to do theatrically.'

'I think one of the good things about Circus Space is they very much look at your potential rather than your existing ability,' says Kaveh. 'They've turned away really good gymnasts because they just wanted to do a load of back flips and didn't have anything else. In me, OK, I could juggle. But, more than that, I think they could see I had ideas and imagination and was quite driven to achieve certain things.'

You might imagine that the athletic demands of circus would produce a cleaner-living atmosphere than a typical university. Kaveh says that's not the case. 'Me and Lauren bonded in the pub. I think most performers like a drink. It's a nice way to relax. But while most of them didn't drink very much, especially in the week, when you're working from 9 a.m. to 4 p.m. or later, quite a lot of people smoke. For a lot of the Europeans, circus is associated with Gypsy culture. A lot of the European students are a bit more hippy than the British ones, and I guess smoking is part of that. Lots of roll-ups, rather than your Marlboro Lights!' The Circus Space's hang-out joint, for students and staff alike, is the aptly named café directly opposite: the Juggler.

Kaveh had a clear vision of what he wanted to do after Circus Space. 'From the moment I left university I knew I wanted to start my own company. I knew roughly what work it would make, and I knew it would be very physical. But I didn't have the tools or the contacts. So before Circus Space it was very much about scrabbling around and hoping for the best in a few little fringe venues. So I went in with the ambition to make my own company, and Circus Space gave me the tools to do that.'

Kaveh has particular praise for the emphasis Circus Space puts on preparing students for the world of work and business. 'As performance arts courses go, I'd say one of the biggest strengths of Circus Space, in the third year in particular, is that they tell you very realistically how to make a living from circus. A lot of my friends have been to the drama schools such as RADA or LAMDA, and they've never had that. At Circus Space you do a whole module on a business plan. They force you to sit down and think about what you're going to do, and give you advice on everything from how to promote yourself to how to fill in a tax return. They also give you an incentive. The top four marks get interviewed by people from Circus Space and people from the Deutsche Bank, who sponsor what's called the Pyramid Award. Whoever wins gets a cash award of £8,000 as well as a business mentor for a year.'

Kaveh used the proceeds of the Pyramid Award to form So and So, and the company was also given a bursary of £1,500 by London Youth Dance to hire a director for their first touring show, *Introducing . . . the Hot Dots.* With a cast comprising just Kaveh and Lauren, the show is based on a pair of fictional vaudeville performers from the 1930s called Frank Johnston and Evie Steele.

'They're both solo performers who meet one day when they're shoved into the same dressing-room,' Kaveh explains. 'She's an acrobat and he's a juggler – just like we are in real life! Neither of them is very happy about having to share, but they eventually begin to like each other and develop some respect for each other and decide it would be a good idea to work together. Over the course of a summer season they fall in love. Then, towards the end of the season, it becomes apparent that she's in the relationship for the fame and fortune and he's in it because he loves her, and in the end she leaves. It's quite a sad ending. I guess it's about what it's like being a performer, and the nature of the double act.'

While *Hot Dots* incorporates circus skills into the performance and rehearsal scenes, Kaveh says, 'Our aim is to make performances that are accessible to people and also have an emotional depth and resonance to them which traditional circus may not have. I'm not taking away from traditional circus – I think it's fantastic. But I also like going to see a really good play and getting that thing you remember for years afterwards. For us it's all about the story and using circus within that.'

At the same time Kaveh stresses he doesn't want to lose circus's ability to present the stand-alone trick. 'I like watching an audience watch a big trick. Sometimes, when you do it every day, you forget the impact it has on people. For instance, we had a couple of hours training yesterday and had a bit of a rubbish day. A lot of the tricks were a bit crap. But you show it to someone who hasn't seen it before – like a little kid – and they're amazed. That sense of wonderment and people getting excited about it is why you do it.'

On that note, Kaveh reflects, 'I think the work is still evolving and hasn't achieved my ambition yet, which is to make work that's emotionally engaging and moving but also spectacular.'

Lauren is the editor of the team, says Kaveh. 'It's often me who comes up with the original idea, then I bounce stuff off her and she'll say, "No, maybe we should do it like this."' Occasionally, Lauren literally bounces off her partner . . . bringing a new meaning to the term 'ead 'itter. The Scots girl suppresses a giggle as she recalls their most bruising rehearsal.

'I started standing on Kaveh's hands. He threw me, and I was supposed to do a somersault and land sitting on his hands and shoulders. But he took a step forward, and I landed on his face. His head snapped back, and the back of his head almost touched his shoulders. That was pretty painful, and we had to go to hospital.'

Asked her view of the current circus scene in the UK, Lauren says, 'I think it's exciting, because it's starting to get on a roll, and as a small company you can influence where it's going. In France I don't think we'd be able to do that. In Britain we're not the only company doing this work, but we're one of the few helping it get where it needs to be.'

Kaveh agrees but adds, 'I also think we've got a lot to learn in this country, not so much in terms of the performers but in terms of audience perceptions. It's an uphill struggle at the moment. In France, if you say you're a circus performer they take you seriously and respect what you're doing as something useful and important. In this country, if you say you're a circus performer most people say, "Yeah, yeah, and what do you do for a living?"' With a grin, Kaveh says, 'The *second* question people always ask is, "Do you want to be in Cirque du Soleil?"'

It's interesting, I remark, that Kaveh and Lauren have chosen to call their company So and So Circus while many contemporary ensembles prefer the word 'cirque'. It's a subject that Kaveh is passionate about. 'There are these huge arguments about traditional circus and contemporary circus and narrative circus and which one's best. People often use the word "cirque" because they want to be associated with Cirque du Soleil and it suggests a more contemporary twist on circus. But I find it a bit ridiculous. I think circus is brilliant. Yes, I want to do other stuff and put theatre in the work I'm making. But I still love going to traditional circuses. I love the smell of candyfloss and popcorn. It's one of those art forms that hasn't changed, and there's something comforting in that. I don't think you should shy away from the word "circus" just because the general public associate it with red noses or . . . I don't know . . . I mean, some people still think all circuses have lions. The way I look at it is, that's their problem, not mine. They need to get out and see more stuff.'

Kaveh catches himself and grins. 'Sorry, I went off on a bit of a rant there! But I think the work we're doing is not cirque. It's circus.'

Chapter 8

THE REAL BIG TOP

Martin Burton was an alternative street clown who went on to found the traditional travelling circus Zippos. When the BBC decided to make a sitcom set in a circus, it asked him, 'Can we borrow your big top?'

Among the many courses offered by the Circus Space is a one-day introduction to circus skills each Saturday. Bruce Mackinnon attended one of them to prepare for his role as East European acrobat Boyco in BBC1's 2009 circus sitcom *Big Top*.

Mackinnon joined the cast of *Big Top* after appearances in *The Office* and *The Catherine Tate Show*. He has been able to juggle since his schooldays, but when it comes to the more physical circus arts he admits, 'I'm terrible at even doing a forward roll. Luckily, I had a stand-in who did some tumbles for the credits and made me look very good. I'm playing a guy who's lived his life on the flying trapeze, and I'm wearing a leotard a lot of the time, but I had a muscle-piece underneath it, so I think we just about got away with it aesthetically!'

As research, Mackinnon says, 'I read some books on circus to get a feel for it. Because none of us knew much about what it's like backstage at a circus – all we knew was from going to see it as a little kid. It's a fascinating world, a crazy world. I don't want to say our version is watered down . . . but if you actually recreated some of what goes on backstage in a circus I don't think it would even be allowed on TV!'

The actor's visit to Circus Space left him with a deep respect for circus's real-life performers. 'I went along just to chat to some of the acrobats training there, and when you talk to them you realize what a dedicated art form it is. They spend their lives training, training and training, and they do a ridiculous number of shows each week. They put us actors to shame.'

Mackinnon also got to try his balance on the tight-wire. 'Once, with my arms flailing like mad, I managed to get from one end to the other. It was only 3 feet off the ground, but I enjoyed it. You read stories about old tightrope walkers or trapeze artists, and they talk about it in such amazing ways. It's such a poetic thing to them. So it was nice to get a small taste of what they go through. Mind you, it's one thing doing it 3 feet off the ground and another knowing there's nothing underneath you but death. I think that would be a lot harder . . . or maybe easier, I don't know!'

Starring sitcom royalty such as Tony Robinson from *Blackadder* and Ruth Madoc from *Hi-De-Hi!* – alongside *Britain's Got Talent* host Amanda Holden, who plays ringmistress Lizzie – *Big Top* is directed and co-produced by Marcus Mortimer whose previous successes include *Jonathan Creek*.

Mortimer's production company Big Bear Films had just come off the success of *My Hero*, a sitcom about a suburban superhero, when, Marcus recalls, 'The BBC said they'd really like an ensemble piece for a mainstream audience. We were trying to come up with a setting when our head of development, Susie McIntosh, came to a meeting and said, "How about a circus?" We kind of sat there and went "Do you know what? That's never been done before. Nobody in this country has done a comedy, or even a drama, about a circus." Which is absolutely extraordinary.'

The idea immediately excited the producers. 'Whenever you think of circus, you think there are a lot of colourful characters there – the sad clown, the various performers with all their insecurities. There's a lot of colour. There are stunts, acrobats, people from Eastern Europe. We thought it was an exciting mix. We decided early on that we wanted to present a traditional circus, because we didn't want to confuse people. We

Shaka the lion with Great British Circus director Martin Lacey

Clowning around: Clive Webb and Danny Adams

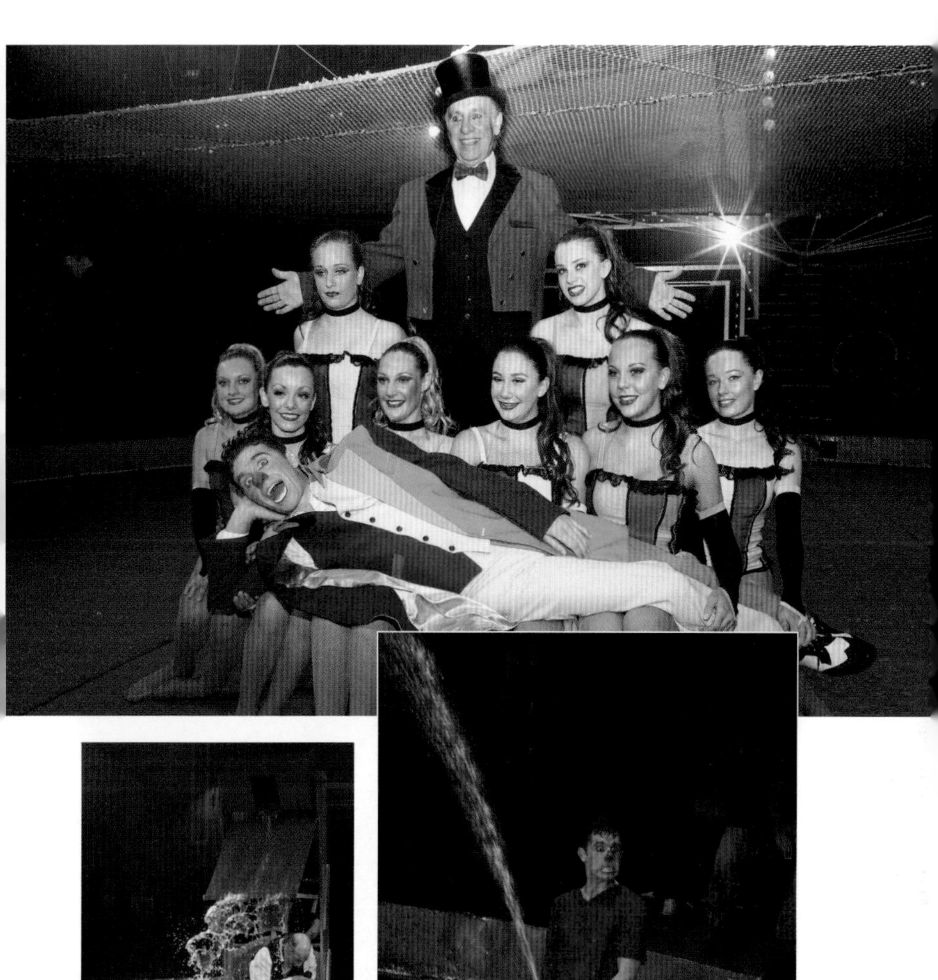

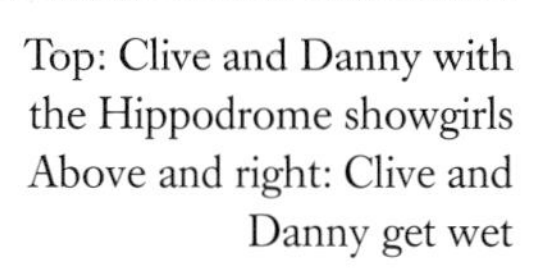

Top: Clive and Danny with the Hippodrome showgirls
Above and right: Clive and Danny get wet

Helyne Edmonds with tiger cubs born at the Great British Circus . . .

. . . and, my, how they've grown!

Helyne with King the Friesian stallion

Above: Jasper King tries not to become a burnt Chipolata
Opposite: Circa's David Carberry (top) and Darcy Grant (below, with Carberry) get bendy

The Great Yarmouth Hippodrome . . .

. . . where the ring becomes a pool . . .

. . . and the Flying Neves take to the air!

Sword swallower Hannibal Helmurto . . .

. . . and the Circus of Horrors

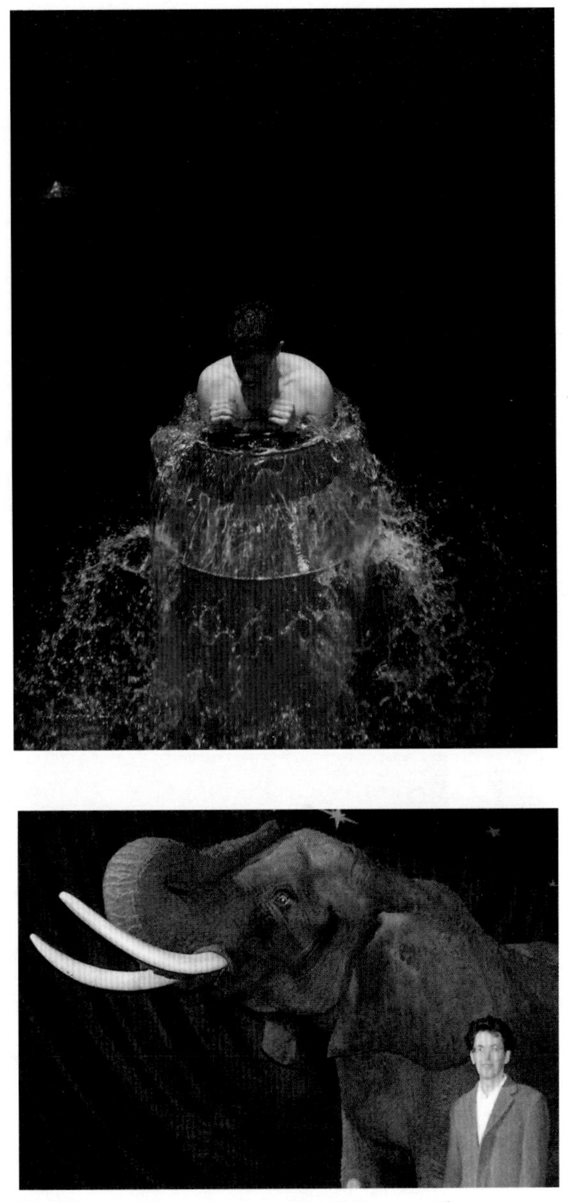

Top: Danny Adams re-creates Houdini's escape from a milk-churn
Above: The author meets Sonja the elephant

The Chinese State Circus: (clockwise from top left)
lion dancing, swordplay, contortionism and bikes

The cast of the BBC's *Big Top*

Miguel Peris takes his sister Alicia for a spin

Gerry Cottle (centre) and his stars of the future . . .

. . . training at Wookey Hole

Above left: Joseph Micheletty, France's 'Diabolist Extraordinaire'
Above: The Bio Brothers from the Ukraine
Left: Danny Adams 'auditions' for the Chinese State Circus

wanted them to recognize the clown and the ringmistress, because when you're making a comedy you need to get to first base very quickly, you need to make it quite clear who you're putting in front of an audience and what their roles are, without too much explanation. That's why a lot of sitcoms are about families. Everybody knows what the relationship is between the husband and the wife.'

To research the circus world the producers visited Zippos Circus. 'We didn't base it on Zippos – we very much came up with our own characters. But we talked to one or two of the people there. We wanted to find out what a typical day was, when they rehearse and all the little details. We had a look at the type of acts they had. Predominantly the acts are from Eastern Europe, and we thought: Ah, that's interesting, because there are a lot of Eastern Europeans coming into the country doing other things, so people will recognize the comedy situations that arise there.'

In the months before *Big Top* is screened, Gerry Cottle – along no doubt with others in the circus industry – has reservations about how circus will be portrayed. 'The trouble is, when you see circus on television, the circus boss is always a crook,' groans Cottle. So I can't help smiling, the very next day, as Mortimer explains, 'The star is the ringmistress, Lizzie, who's played by Amanda Holden, and the reason she's the ringmistress is that her father, the circus owner, is in prison for fraud, so she has to take over. It's about her trying to deal with the everyday traumas and problems that happen in the circus. There are a lot of crazy and quite daft people around her that she has to try and keep in order. So she's kind of our link into that world.

'We're not having a pop at circus, in the way that *Hi-De-Hi!* was not having a pop at holiday camps. Maplin's Holiday Camp was a great, fun place to be. *Big Top* is about a circus that is struggling to exist in the current climate, but they do. They always manage to pull something out of the hat, because they're actually a good circus. What we're doing as a sitcom is creating a world from which no one can escape. A lot of sitcoms have that premise. It could be a bar, like *Cheers*, or a hotel, like *Fawlty Towers*. Ours is a circus. It's a setting for funny characters, some of whom are dysfunctional. But comedy is about dysfunction. People who have problems are funnier than people who don't have problems.'

The scriptwriter of *Big Top* is Daniel Peak, who previously worked with Mortimer on *My Hero*. 'Danny is one of the best of the best of the new young comedy writers. There are very few writers who can write sitcom for a live studio audience, but Danny has that gift. We invited him to a meeting and, amazingly, he said, "I love the idea, because I love circuses. I always go and see the circuses near where I live", which is in Manchester. So we were incredibly lucky to have a really good writer of situation comedy who also loves circuses.

'We took the script to the BBC and they said, "We love it. Who are you thinking of getting for actors?" We told them who we had in mind and they said, "Could you get them together and do a read?" That's the usual way these days, because pilots are so expensive. So we did quite a detailed read, in that I rehearsed the actors. And for that read we had Tony Robinson, Amanda Holden, John Thomson (from *Cold Feet*, who plays the clown) . . . everybody turned up, and they all loved the parts we wanted them to play.

'The Controller, Jay Hunt, was enthusiastic and around six days later said, "I'll have a series, please." I think everyone was genuinely fired up by the sense of fun and colour that you get with circus and that element of family entertainment that perhaps hasn't been around much. A lot of comedies are post nine o'clock. They wanted something at 8.30, and we thought, "Let's give 'em a circus."'

'It was such a great script,' says Mackinnon. 'We had a ball making it. Many of the supporting actors were circus performers or street entertainers. There were lots of juggling clubs around on set. So, between takes, instead of sitting around doing nothing we were entertained a lot.'

Did the actors stay in character between takes?

'Often that happens on set,' Mackinnon confirms. 'A friend of mine was saying how he was in a film about a prison, and at lunch the actors, completely unaware, stayed in their groups as either prisoners or warders. On this show we're all playing versions of ourselves to a certain extent. Ruth Madoc is playing the *grande dame* of the circus and she's the *grande dame* of sitcom. So I, and I think everyone else, treated her as a huge star. Johnny, meanwhile, is the biggest clown I've ever met . . .'

Laughing at the memory, Mackinnon recalls, 'John had these big clown trousers on, and they fell down mid-take and bared his bum! We were backstage and heard the biggest laugh. Bearing in mind the set is soundproofed, we heard this explosion of laughter, and everyone ran out to see what was happening. The whole audience were literally bent double in tears. They laughed for a good five minutes. I don't know whether it will make the show, but I hope it makes the DVD outtakes, because we all said, "You're going to make a fortune out of that clip." He'll probably make more out of that clip than anything he ever does!'

Most of *Big Top* was filmed in a studio dressed as the backstage area of a circus tent. 'The comedy is not about what happens in the big top; it's about the relationships backstage and in the caravans,' Mortimer explains. 'It's a bit like *Hi-De-Hi!* You didn't see much of the knobbly knees competitions or swimming-pool races. Mostly you were in the offices and chalets. But, of course, you do have to have some scenes in the circus ring, so we went back to Zippos and said, "Can we borrow your big top?"'

Martin Burton, the owner of Zippos, was consultant on the circus scenes. Among them was a sequence in which Thomson is pursued across the ring by a dog. It ends up chasing the clown up a ladder to the trapeze rigging, where he manages to set his feet on fire.

'It was totally implausible,' Burton smiles, 'but it's a comedy. That's what works in scripts, so that's what we gave them. We had a lot of fun rigging that scene. And, before you ask, they booked the dog, and, no, it couldn't climb the ladder. If I'd booked the dog they would have got one that could climb the ladder!'

'Amanda Holden was surprisingly good,' Martin concedes. 'At one point we had to tie her on to a knife-thrower's board and spin her around. She needed a bit of hand-holding before she got involved in that, and I can't say I blame her.'

Burton supplied the knife-thrower. So did he throw the knives at Amanda for real?

'No. It's television. But we did strap her on and spin her around for real.'

The circus audience reaction shots were filmed during Zippos' Christmas season. Did Burton share Cottle's reservations about the way circus was going to be portrayed in *Big Top*?

Burton puts it like this: 'We did discuss whether the circus would be called Zippos in the series. I sent a memorable email saying that might be possible unless there were drunken chorus girls and paedophile clowns. An equally memorable email came back saying, "There's all of that and much more . . ." So I said in that case we'd better not call it Zippos, and everything was rebranded as Circus Maestro. But I've had a very long career working with television companies. I started thirty-five years ago, with Tony Hart on *Vision On*, and we've done a series for ITV called *Married, Single, Other* in which one of the characters gets married in a circus tent. I'm very aware that television does what it does in order to get ratings, and I suspected not everything would be as positive towards the circus as I might like and certainly not as positive as the circus fans of Great Britain would like. I'm sure there will be quite a few diehard fans who will be outraged and say it misrepresents circus. But I ignore all that because the truth of the matter is that if you ask the average six-, seven- or eight-year-old today what a circus is, they probably don't know. But I'm sure that after the programme they will know. So, to me, even if it has some elements that don't portray circus in the light I would like, it will still promote circus. I think it's just great that circus is back on telly.'

Burton – more commonly known simply as Zippo – is a new circus performer who became a traditionalist, an alternative street clown who has ended up owning probably Britain's best-known animal circus. Growing up in Oxford, where his parents were shopkeepers, Martin was a keen theatregoer who originally set out to be a drama teacher.

'I knew my plays, but I'd never trod the boards. So when I went to teacher-training college I found they were speaking a different language: stage right, stage left, they called the curtains the tabs. I needed to catch up with the practical side, so I joined a fringe theatre company run by a mime artist called Jonathan Kaye. I wasn't a very good mime artist, but in the summer we used to do clown shows on Brighton beach, and I found I had a strong affinity with clowning.

'When I completed my degree I went for a teaching job, and there were 400 other applicants. I thought, "There's no point in this," and I had to pay the rent somehow, so I went to Covent Garden and became a busker. This was when Covent Garden was still a fruit market and had yet to become the busking haven it is today. I did a ten-minute act, which was a little bit of magic, a little bit of fire-eating – hence the name Zippo – and a little bit of escapology.

At that point my mortgage was £70 a month, and I found I could earn that in a day busking. I promised my mum I would do it for three years and then get a proper job. Well, here I am, thirty-five years later, and I still haven't got a proper job. But I think she's forgiven me now.'

From busking in the street, Burton progressed to theatres and festivals as Zippo and Company. 'Most of our work was in the southern hemisphere: Australia, Singapore, Malaysia. At that point, I swore I would never work in a circus. Circus clowns at that time were very unfunny and boring, and I had a more alternative view of clowning. I'd like to think I was part of a movement that involved a few notable clowns like Mr Sniff, who came from California and appeared in London at the Roundhouse. I thought red noses and baggy trousers were far too mainstream – although I did end up wearing a red nose, if not the baggy trousers, because I realized that kind of exaggeration was necessary to reach an audience that were a long way away.'

After ten years on the international festival circuit, Burton also realized that starting his own big top circus wouldn't be such a bad idea. 'Eventually I got fed up of jumping on and off aeroplanes with hundreds of flight cases of equipment. And while theatres are fun to do, no two theatres are the same. So you never know if it's going to have flies or deep wings or whether you will be able to get all your equipment in. I thought that if I did this in a tent I'd have control over the venue. And while there are many limitations to working in a tent, they're the same limitations wherever you go in the country.'

To find funding for his first big top Burton went to a corporate sponsorship event at the Battersea Arts Centre. 'The principal speaker was the sponsorship supremo from BP. Everyone else were trendy young alternative-theatre administrators from the London area. When it came to lunchtime they all sat in a huddle together. I was from out of town and didn't know anyone, so I was left on my own, and so was this chap from BP. I went up to him and said, "Do you mind if I eat with you?" By the time we finished lunch I'd gained sufficient sponsorship to buy my first circus tent.' With a laugh Burton adds, 'A couple of years later it blew away in Hurricane Charlie. It was a steep learning curve in tents.'

For his first ten years of tenting, Burton ran an all-human circus. Still seeing himself as an alternative circus man, he says, 'It was just out of a determination to be different at a time when every other circus had animals. But, after ten years of comments like "It was very good but we would have liked to see a few animals", I came to the conclusion that while there may be a lot of people who say they don't want to see animals in circus they are, by and large, not the circus-going public. The circus-going public may not want to see bears on motor cycles and lions in cages, but they do actually want to see some animals. Because of that we introduced horses. Strangely enough, it was around that time that all the other circuses started dropping their animals, so that made us unique once again.'

Of course, the reason most circuses gave up their animals was because of council bans. So how was Zippos able to gain a reputation as London's favourite circus, regularly appearing in prime locations?

'I think what was necessary was to take a new approach, and that could probably only be done by someone who wasn't brought up on the circus. The first thing I thought was "I know a lot about clowning, but I don't know anything about animals", so I employed somebody who knew an awful lot, David Hibbling, who is still my consultant on animal welfare. We drew up a very strict code of conduct and a policy, which we will always stick to, of only using domestic, never wild, animals. David then visited all the London boroughs, and, in one memorable winter, we got thirty boroughs to lift their ban on performing animals. We still have a few to go, but we overturned one earlier this year, and I'm pretty confident we're going to overturn another in the next couple of months.'

As for the animal-rights groups . . . 'At the end of the first year we received some criticism from Born Free and some of the other welfare groups. So I said, "Come and meet me and tell me what your problems are." Now, nobody from the circus had ever had a meeting with an animal-welfare group before. We sat down and they said, "We think your stables should be of this design and this minimum size", and I said, "Fine, we'll do it." They also had some comments on diet, and our horses now have a very expensive dietary supplement programme. We stick to it, because what they said made sense and was in the best interests of the animals.'

Not that Burton's efforts have eradicated the problem of protestors at his gates. Burton shrugs. 'The problem with most animal protestors is that they have a much larger agenda than whether an animal is in a circus. They don't believe in the ownership of animals, period. The current big guru in America says the first step to animal rights is worldwide veganism. So these are the people we deal with. It's a shame. But I believe that over the past fifteen years we've overcome a lot of prejudice. We do good business, and I have never in my life seen any protestors turn a single customer away.'

Again, Burton feels it took innovative thinking to challenge public opinion on animal circuses. 'Traditionally, circuses kept the animals at the back of the circus. This was mostly so they could charge the audience an extra 20p to see the animals in what they called the zoo. What I decided to do was put the animals out the front beside the box office. That way people could assure themselves that the animals were in good condition and well looked after before they even bought their ticket. My colleagues in the circus industry thought I was barmy, but now I've noticed a trend worldwide for circuses to have their animals at the front of the circus. We get hundreds of people throughout the day who will come and have a chat and a coffee and just look at the horses, and why not?'

Burton's one regret is that these days he seldom has time to appear in his own ring. 'I try to whenever I can, because I love it immensely. But I spend most of my time administrating.'

Zippos is currently summering in Scotland, and Burton is quick to point out that, despite his reputation as London's circus, Zippos has never been confined to the capital. He also tours a second big top which holds his circus school – the Academy of Circus Arts – and in which his students perform their own shows at the weekend. It was in the Academy's smaller tent that *Big Top* was filmed.

'One of the reasons I started the Academy was I employed two girls who had trained at a circus school in Bristol. I said, "Hang your trapeze there", and they said, "We don't know how to hang the trapeze." They'd trained in a building where they went in each day and the trapeze was already hanging there. So although they'd developed a really great act they hadn't learned one of the key things, which is how to hang a piece of kit that is going to save your life.

'They then proceeded to find it impossible to live on a circus. They couldn't organize themselves sufficiently to cope with the travelling lifestyle.

To give you a very small example, when you're on a travelling circus you'll know by the end of the week where the local supermarket is. So the experienced person will fill their larder with food and water before they move. That way you'll be set up, because when you get to the next town you won't know where the local supermarket is and you won't discover it for a couple of days. If you haven't filled your larder you'll spend the first couple of days running around trying to find the supermarket.

'So we decided to start a school that travelled from town to town. The other part of the ethos is they give performances at the weekend. So the students know that what we teach them on Monday they better bloody well pay attention to, because they're going to be doing it in front of an audience on Friday. It focuses the mind.'

Burton admits there is one drawback to the six-month course, which takes students from the age of eighteen. 'They train fourteen hours a day, seven days a week, and because there's no going home they can't get a job in a bar in the evening to pay their way through; you have to be able to afford the course when you start.' The upside is . . . 'We train ten to fifteen people a year, and in twenty years there has only ever been one person who didn't go on to work in the circus. That was his choice, because he knew from the beginning that he wanted to be a stunt man, and learning circus skills was just another step in getting on the stunt register. Circus directors from around the world queue up to employ my graduates because they know they will be used to sitting in the box office for an hour or two or putting up posters or building up the big top and then taking it down and driving trucks from town to town and all the many, many other things that go with life in the circus besides just doing your act.'

One man who learned those lessons well, of course, was Zippo the clown's former protégé Bippo the clown, even though he was too young to join the Academy when his whole family ran away with Zippos Circus when he was a boy. 'What a great childhood he had,' Burton says warmly, 'when your friends are clowns and acrobats and you live in a caravan and travel. I can't think of anything better. I'm probably an old hippy, but I passionately believe that circus is an exciting and healthy place to live and work. I would rather be at the circus than anywhere else in the world.'

Chapter 9

MAKE 'EM LAUGH

Meet Britain's funniest clowns,
Clive Webb and Daaaaanny Adams!

Clive Webb is wearing his scarlet ringmaster's coat. The spotlight gleams off the top of his slightly sunburned head. His grey hair is swept back at the sides and tumbles on to his black velvet collar at the back.

'And now for a little culture,' he says.

As Clive opens his mouth to continue, his son, Danny Adams, bursts in from the wings in his multicoloured suit. He is slim, pale and wiry, and his short, dark hair stands up in gelled tufts. His clown make-up is limited to a small red nose and a white lower lip.

Brandishing a spear, Danny shakes it violently.

'What's that supposed to be?' Clive splutters.

'Shakespeare!'

A moment later Danny is poking his face through a bright green juggling hoop.

'Grrrrrrrr!' Danny gnashes his teeth through the hoop while making violent karate chops and kung fu kicks with his arms and legs.

'What's *that* supposed to be?' asks Clive.

'A vicious circle!'

Warming to the theme of violence, Danny launches into the story of a man who goes into a supermarket and begins smashing up cornflakes packets, ripping the boxes apart and stamping the contents into the ground. 'He was a cereal killer,' Danny explains.

Infuriated by the interruptions, Clive points at the exit. 'I've had it with you!'

Danny puts his hands on his hips and says, camply, 'Well, I don't remember *that*.'

If today's circus scene has produced any stars capable of crossing over into the wider world of entertainment, it is Danny Adams and Clive Webb. Away from the Yarmouth Hippodrome, they have their own theatre show, Circus Hilarious. This year it's booked into an extensive engagement with Butlin's, on permanent rotation between holiday camps in Minehead, Skegness and Bognor, from February to November. It's a full circus show, modelled closely on the Peter Jay model, with dancers and speciality acts including a magic slot by Danny's brother, Johnny Marx, and a Hungarian juggler and hand-balancer. At Christmas the duo have an annual starring role in pantomime at Newcastle's Theatre Royal. But, whatever show they are appearing in it's not the show people come to see; it's Danny and Clive.

Compared to the personality-driven worlds of music, theatre and even sport, circus has never been good at creating stars. The names we remember are the showmen, not the performers, and even then it's as brands rather than individuals: Billy Smart's, Chipperfield's, Gerry Cottle's and, across the pond, Barnum and Bailey or Ringling. The reputation lies with the brand, be it the Chinese State Circus or Cirque du Soleil, and we buy our ticket without a thought as to who will actually be performing. After the show we may come away enthusing about this act or that stunt, but we will probably have forgotten the names of the artistes the moment they left the ringmaster's lips. One reason is that, while circus artists perform for us, they hardly ever talk to us. What they do is more important than who they are.

The exceptions to the rule are clowns. Clowns engage directly with the audience. Their personality is part of their act. More than any other circus performers, they also have acts that translate easily to media outside the circus ring, such as television. It's no surprise that arguably the two most famous circus performers of the past hundred years have been clowns: Coco, and Charlie Cairoli.

There have been many Cocos, but the original was Nicolai Poliakoff, who was born in Latvia in 1900 and moved to England to work with the Bertram Mills circus in the 1930s. After his involvement in a road accident, Coco used his fame to promote road safety to children and, for his public service, became the only clown to receive an MBE.

Charlie Cairoli was born into a circus family in Milan in 1910. He was in England, appearing at the Blackpool Tower Circus, when the Second World War broke out and ended up staying in the UK. Distinguished by his red nose and bowler hat, Cairoli worked at Blackpool Tower every summer for the next forty years until his retirement in 1979, a year before his death at the age of seventy. Despite his record-breaking association with Blackpool Tower, it was Cairoli's television appearances that made him nationally famous. As well as guest spots on shows from *David Nixon's Comedy Bandbox* to the USA's top-rated *Ed Sullivan Show*, Cairoli starred in his own children's television series, *Right Charlie!* In 1970 he became the only clown to appear on *This Is Your Life*, where he was introduced as the King of Clowns.

'Do you want to see the king of rock'n'roll?' Danny asks. 'Grab a shovel and follow me!'

'We're not children's entertainers,' says Clive, between shows, 'and we're not adult entertainers. I would like to think we're family entertainers, and since the cabaret scene dried up there are not a lot of places you can go as a family, where the entertainment is not blatantly for the kids and Mum and Dad are bored stiff, or the other way around. So we start on the kids, and once they're settled down we move on to Mum and Dad. Nothing's *blue*,' Clive stresses. 'But,' he adds with a smile, 'there's the occasional *double entendre* . . .'

On stage, Danny is wearing an Elvis wig, shades and a sparkly white Vegas jumpsuit. There's no back to his guitar, which allows him to stick his finger out through the sound hole as if it's his willy.

'You're pushing it!' warns Clive.

'I've got to push it to get it through!' says Danny, wiggling his finger.

If Joseph Grimaldi was the original whiteface clown – a clever clown, an alpha figure in a dandyish outfit who could play an instrument, dance, ride a horse or sing a satirical song – then the origins of the whiteface's goofy scruffily dressed, red-nosed assistant, the auguste, in the midnineteenth century are more obscure. Some credit the Victorian whiteface John Albert Griffiths, who used the stage name September and called each of a succession of comic partners August. Many clowns favour the story of Tom Belling, an apprentice on Circus Renz in Berlin. In trouble for some misdemeanour, Belling was confined to his quarters. To amuse himself he donned a wig backwards, an inside-out coat and boots several sizes too big for him. His friends dared him to enter the big top thus dressed. He was just peering through the ring doors when the boss sneaked up behind him and shoved him, tumbling, into the ring. Panic-stricken, Belling promptly fell over his own boots, at which point the audience began cheering and shouting 'Auguste! Auguste!' or possibly 'Dumme August!' either of which translates as a colloquialism somewhere between 'idiot' and 'zany.'

The tale may be as tall as a clown's pointy hat, but, whatever his origins, the auguste quickly became the main clown, with the whiteface swiftly reduced to the supporting role of straight man. By the beginning of the twentieth century, in fact, the whiteface had often lost his whiteface and clown clobber and been replaced by the ringmaster as the auguste's straight-faced foil.

In the USA clowning followed a different course. As big tops grew in size, with three or even five rings, two or three stages and a race track encircling them, US clowns became less verbal and less individualistic than their British cousins, for the simple reason that it was harder for a solo clown to be seen or heard in such a big space. Instead they performed in large troupes, between a dozen and a hundred strong, with the emphasis on tumbling, juggling, horse-riding and other circus skills. Their costumes became uniform, with full make-up and white or spotted full-length satin suits with pom-poms, ruffs and pointy hats.

During the 1920s and 1930s, however, the USA produced a new type of clown, the hobo clown or character clown, who dressed as a tramp (or another non-clown character, such as a policeman or sailor) and didn't wear make-up at all. In a typical routine the hobo would make his appearance as a supposed and perhaps drunken volunteer from the audience, who would proceed through a succession of buffoonery to a daring horse-riding display.

Charlie Chaplin didn't invent the character clown, but he took it out of the big top and into a new dimension on the big screen, where he paved the way for a new breed of silent-movie clown, including Laurel and Hardy, Buster Keaton, Fatty Arbuckle and Harold Lloyd. None of them wore the apparel of traditional clowns, but all of them employed the physical humour and often the whiteface/auguste dynamic of routines developed in the circus ring.

Danny Adams lists his comic heroes as 'Laurel and Hardy, Buster Keaton, Jerry Lewis. More recently, Tommy Cooper. Nowadays, I think Jim Carrey is fantastic.' So it's unsurprising that his make-up is as minimal as a clown's could be. 'I think too much make-up scares the kids. I've never worn a lot, and over the years it's got less and less. When we do pantomime we do it as a double act, rather than ringmaster and clown, so I don't wear any make-up at all. I do exactly the same routines and it seems to work just as well. In fact, even when I'm clowning people often forget I'm wearing make-up because it's so minimal.'

As well as the Grimaldi memorial service held at his graveside each May there is another clown service in his honour at 3 p.m. on the first Sunday of each February at the Holy Trinity Church in London's Dalston, which has been the official Clown Church since the demolition of St James Church (in the yard of which Grimaldi was buried) in 1959. From 1967 clowns were permitted to attend in full motley and slap, and today they gather from all over the world to pay their respects to the man who gave all clowns the nickname Joey.

Until its recent removal to Gerry Cottle's circus museum at Wookey Hole in Somerset, the Holy Trinity was also home to the Egg Gallery, which immortalizes the make-up of every clown who wishes to register his 'face' by having it painted on the side of a porcelain egg. The practice was started by circus fan Stan Bult who founded the International Circus Clown Club at Bertram Mills's annual Christmas show at Olympia in 1946. Stan originally painted clowns' faces on real eggs, some of which still exist, and the practice was continued by Bluey Brattle, then chairman of Clowns International, in the 1960s.

Is Danny in the egg gallery? 'I . . . *am*,' says Danny. Then he pauses, in exactly the way he would pause before unleashing a particularly funny gag in the ring. It's one of those pauses that only the truly great comedians can do: a pause that makes you start chuckling before you even hear what's coming. 'When we were on Zippos in 2001 they came to paint my and Dad's faces on the eggs. They did it there and then and showed us, which was lovely. But between painting the eggs and taking them back to wherever they were taking them . . . mine fell off and smashed. So mine's got a crack in it.' Which is kind of appropriate . . .'

We can make jokes about gags being so old they were first uttered on the gangplank of Noah's Ark, but in clowning it's often the old jokes, or at least time-proven routines, that continue to get the biggest laughs. Thumbing through Earl Chapin May's 1932 book *From Rome to Ringling* I come across a faded photograph of two clowns rehearsing a comedy boxing-match. Their gloves, instead of being round and fist-shaped, like real boxing gloves, are enormous flat leather discs the size of tennis rackets, with which they are busy slapping each other. Even in 1932 the picture is captioned 'An old and sure-fire act'. Nearly eighty years on Danny and Clive are still doing it – their gloves identical to those in the picture.

'There are quite a few routines that go back years and years that people haven't seen and which are now classed as new,' says Danny. 'There are gags from seventy years ago that we do that still get screams of laughter.'

'It's like a film director who gets hold of a book,' says Clive. 'We take the bare bones of the story and put our own stamp on it.'

Another old routine used by many modern clowns is 'You Can't Play Here', in which the auguste keeps starting to play an instrument – or juggle, or skip a rope – and the whiteface keeps trying to stop him.

'Slosh, the decorators routine, has been around for years,' says Danny. 'But very few people do it now because of all the hassle that goes with making it and cleaning it up.'

Danny and Clive, of course, get themselves, and the rest of the Circus Hilarious cast, absolutely covered in white 'wallpaper paste', especially at the Hippodrome, where the water feature also allows them to splash around more water than they could in any other venue. At one point Danny runs around the ring fence while Clive trains a fire hose on him, only Danny's body and some perfect timing stopping the front four of five rows getting completely soaked as well.

'The Hippodrome was a gift!' Clive confirms. 'There's nowhere else you get 100,000 gallons of water to play with, is there? We've had boats, Danny above the water on a big swaying ladder . . .'

They hope the duo will return to the Hippodrome soon, because Clive says he still has in mind a particularly big trick involving the venue's submersible ring.

'I'd like to see members of the audience in there, sitting at tables, and then going down . . .!' The comic cackles with mirth.

Typically Danny embroiders the comedy boxing-match with some audience participation. Every time he takes a resounding slap from his dad he staggers to the front-row seats and gets an embarrassed volunteer – Suzanne – to 'kiss it better'. The first time it's his shoulder. The second time it's his ear. The routine ends with Clive kicking his son in the crotch. After his initial wince of pain, Danny turns to the front row with a lustful and expectant grin. 'Suzaaaaaanne . . . !'

According to Clive, it's their penchant for embarrassing 'volunteers' – perhaps 'victims' would be a better word – that makes the duo so successful.

'It's a British thing. The British love to see somebody suffer. Preferably if it's not *them*.' Front row of a Circus Hilarious show is always a dangerous place to be.

One of Danny's best gags features a leaf-blower with a toilet roll on the end. First of all, he sets it to blow, covering the audience with ribbons and ropes of toilet tissue. Naturally one final person gets the brunt of the assault and ends up covered in so much tissue he looks like an Egyptian mummy. Then, to even louder laughter, Danny switches the machine to 'suck' and hoovers all the tissue back in. Finally, he sets it to 'shred' and covers everyone in a papery blizzard.

'We were writing the radio show routine, where Dad tells the story and I do the sound effects,' says Danny. 'We were thinking: How can we interact with the audience and get them involved? Then one day in the garden Dad had this blower, blowing the leaves, and I thought: That's it. That's where the wind can come from. Then I thought: How can we take it a step further? And that's where the toilet roll came in.'

You don't have to be in the front to get picked on. Danny likes to get right in among the audience, running up and down the stairways and between the rows, spraying everyone with a giant water gun. The highlight of his audience invasion finds Danny sneaking up behind an unsuspecting man with a bald head. There's a great moment when everyone in the theatre except this person knows what's going to happen next. Then, at the precise moment that the man starts to realize he's sitting in a spotlight, Danny lets him have it at point-blank range.

In another skit Danny dresses as a Chinese magician, complete with silk robe and enormous buck teeth. The routine turns – literally – on a swivel chair. Every time Clive sits on the chair and swivels around on it he's fine. Every time the Chinese magician tries it the seat judders down several inches. Wincing, Danny staggers to his feet to reveal an 8-inch steel pole sticking up through the centre of the seat.

'Ah so!' he groans, holding his backside.

Naturally, the buck-toothed magician also finds time to pick on a nearby member of the audience. Making lewd thrusting pelvis movements in the woman's direction, he points out, 'We got the same teeth!'

'The art of it is picking the right person,' says Clive, '. . . and there's no doubt about it, sometimes we get it wrong! I used to do a routine with a guillotine – a great big 10-foot-tall job. I got this guy up and said, "Kneel down here . . ." and he said, "I can't kneel down, I've got a wooden leg!" Another time I tried to get a blind fellow to pick a card . . .'

The joy of Danny and Clive's act is that they make it look so effortlessly off-the-cuff. And some of it is. Having worked together for so long, Danny says, 'It's got to the point where one of us will go off on a tangent and the other will know exactly what we're going to do.'

'We seem to know what the other one is thinking,' Clive confirms. 'It's spooky really.'

Comedy dependent on such split-second timing is a serious business, however. Midway through one of their shows at the Hippodrome I'm backstage as Danny emerges from the ring, his face like thunder. He's just done his 'Shakespeare' gag, and as he stalks back to his dressing-room he hurls the spear into a pile of props in the far corner as if he would quite like to be taking down an antelope with it. Or perhaps his father. Twenty minutes later he's all smiles again.

'There are times when we come off stage arguing,' Danny admits. 'But as soon as we've argued, it's forgotten. I think it's because we're both so passionate about what we do.'

Generally, says Clive, they have a great time.

'How many people get paid to blow up a fire engine every day? Or have pie fights and water fights? *You'd* look forward to coming to work, wouldn't you? It's a beautiful way of life. You get paid for playing with your toys.' As for working with his sons, 'It's like having our very own Crazy Gang.'

The second half of the show features Clown Force, a comedy rock band with Clive on drums, Johnny Marx on vocals and Danny's other brother, Michael Potts, on bass. As with the Chipolatas' musical numbers, the routine features lots of stops, starts and interruptions, with Danny and another clown, Cousin Timoni, doing gags in the gaps. Marx begins singing Johnny Cash's 'Ring of Fire', and Timoni runs across the stage with flames issuing from the seat of his pants.

Is Timoni a real cousin?

'We *think* so . . .' Clive says with a twinkle in his eye. 'That branch of the family tree fell off.'

It was behind a drum kit that Clive began his career. His family had their own firm selling timber and machinery, and he recalls, 'I went through prep school and boarding school, so I think show business was a big shock to my dad. But it was the early 1960s, and I was hooked on rock'n'roll.'

At eighteen Clive was drummer in a rock band. But when a planned tour of army bases in Germany was cancelled he saw an advertisement in a local paper. Roberts Brothers Circus wanted a drummer, so he ran away with the circus.

'The owner's kids were Bobby – who runs Bobby Roberts Super Circus today – John, Beverley, Caroline and Tim. Tim was a very little boy, three or four. But the others were my age, so it was teenagers on the road. I had a great time and said, "Next year I'd like to come back as a clown."'

After a couple of years in the circus Clive returned to the music world in comedy band the North Stars.

'We came third on *Opportunity Knocks.* The winners were The Real Thing, a group that went on to have a lot of hits, and in second place was John Miles, who went on to do songs like 'Music Was My First Love' [*sic*].

It was a massive show at the time, and we got lots of work out of it. It was the era of the variety clubs, and we were top of the bill at all the big places, like Batley Variety Club.'

When the North Stars split up Clive hit the cabaret circuit as a solo comic magician, at which point he was persuaded to appear on *Opportunity Knocks* for a second time.

'I didn't want to do it, but I can remember Hughie Green coming into my dressing-room at a club in Liverpool and saying, "You're gonna do it on Sunday!" This time I came second. And it was the best thing I ever did.'

Among the people watching the show was Michael Hurll, producer of the BBC's top-rated Saturday evening variety show *Seaside Special*, which was filmed in Gerry Cottle's big top and featured a mix of circus acts and 1970s' light entertainment stalwarts such as the Two Ronnies, Ken Dodd, Boney M and Val Doonican.

Hurll had to phone Clive three times. 'I didn't believe it was him!' Clive laughs. 'But I did six or seven *Seaside Specials*, and from that I got a series with Rolf Harris called *Rolf on Saturday*. We did eight of them at prime time, six o'clock. Then the guest spots were starting to come in: *Crackerjack*, *Live at Her Majesty's* and things like that.'

The peak of Clive's television career was a three-year stint alongside Chris Tarrant on Saturday morning series *Tiswas*. 'Nobody thought there was an audience on a Saturday morning,' Clive recalls. 'How wrong they were.' At the time, *Tiswas* was as controversial as it was groundbreaking. Clive defends the show's irreverent approach. 'It wasn't a bad influence. It was lots of custard pies and throwing water about . . . slapstick humour.'

Other television shows followed in the form of *Razzmatazz* and *How Dare You!* By the point in the 1990s 'when the telly dried up a bit', Clive and Danny were ready to form Circus Hilarious.

Like Joey Grimaldi before him Danny has been working with his father since he could walk.

'When I was three or four I used to go with Dad and help him set his gear up. I used to play at comedy magic shows in the front room and pretend I was Dad. The first time I went on stage was when I was five, in pantomime at the Tayside, in Manchester. I was dressed as a little wizard. Dad was doing a comedy magic act and had this cabinet. Every time he opened the door I'd walk out, kick him in the shins, take a bow and walk off. By the fifth time I did it in the show it was getting big cheers and big laughs, and even at that age I can remember getting exactly the same buzz as I do now. I can remember thinking from that moment: This is what I want to do for a living.'

Clive confirms his son's early aptitude for show business. 'I was doing a thing called "Sunday Variety" at Butlin's in Barry Island. At four years old Danny sat in the audience and watched the show all through the first performance, then he wanted to go back and watch it again, all through the second show. Afterwards he came up to me and said, "Dad, that girl singer changed one of the numbers in the second show." That's when I knew he was paying attention.'

Danny joined his father full time when he turned sixteen. 'He left school on the Friday and joined me at Butlin's, Minehead, on the Monday,' says Clive.

It was at that point that Clive adopted the ringmaster role he has today. 'When Danny joined me at Minehead I was a clown, and there were two other guys who were clowns. I realized we had too many clowns and somebody had to be in charge. Or *seem* to be in charge. That's what it's all about, really: the person in authority, getting it.'

So who's really in charge?

'When it comes to the business side, it's Dad. When it comes to the show side, it's fifty–fifty. We're writing next year's show now. We'll come up with a theme and then bounce ideas back and forth throughout the year. For example, we're thinking about a *knife-throwing* routine . . .' Danny does one of his comic pauses, his eyes filled with mischief.

Dare I ask who's throwing the knives?

'I am!' Danny says with relish. 'The trouble is, nobody will stand against the board!'

'Every year we try to top ourselves,' says Clive. Thinking about those knives, I hope he's not talking literally.

The duo's highly physical routines certainly leave them with plenty of bumps and bruises. 'Which at my age, thirty-four, is not good . . .' Clive jokes. In fact, you could add another thirty years to Clive's age, although, as the similarly aged Peter Jay puts it, 'We all still feel like we're nineteen.'

Last year, straight after the duo's Easter special at the Hippodrome, Clive had a quadruple heart bypass. By the summer season at the Hippodrome he was back in the ring in his Union Jack suit and working as energetically as ever. 'I didn't have a heart attack, but they said if I didn't have the operation I would have. Now I'm firing on all cylinders again.'

On stage there are times when Clive looks, and sounds, decidedly breathless. It doesn't seem tactful to mention it to him, but climbing atop a stepladder as it is lowered into a swimming pool, then being bundled into a rowing boat, really doesn't look like the sort of thing a man of his years should be doing twice a day, six days a week, a few months after major heart surgery. Clive, however, has no intention of slowing down, much less retiring. He points to the example of his comic hero Ken Dodd, who is still going strong in his eighties.

'The difficult part is keeping up with Danny,' the old trouper smiles. 'Chasing the little swine around the ring. Because he is very energetic. But Danny does most of the more physical things.'

For Danny the ten weeks that his father was off work was the first time he worked with a different comic partner. As well as any son's anxiety over his father's health, the experience must have brought home the professional vulnerability of being half of a double act in which the age difference is so great – although if it did, he doesn't admit to it.

'Luckily, over the years I've become very friendly with the Jays, and Jack, their youngest son, had seen us working for the past five years at the Hippodrome. He knew how Dad and I worked. He stood in and did a fantastic job. The only person who could have done a better job . . . would have been Dad.'

Danny's dream is to put the duo's mixture of circus and comedy on television. They'd be perfect for the medium – funnier than anything currently on screen. And, although he's been saying the same thing for a few years now, Danny is determined to make his dream a reality. 'With telly it's a case of chipping away and chipping away, and, hopefully, one day you'll get a breakthrough.'

In the meantime Clive and Danny are planning to expand the possibilities of Circus Hilarious with their very own big top: The Mighty Laughter Dome.

'We'll still do the theatres,' says Clive, 'but it would be nice to do the big top in the summer.'

'There are a lot of big props you can't get into theatres,' Danny enthuses, 'like the comedy car. Plus you can build it to your own specification. We can put trap-doors in the stage. There's loads more things you can do in a big top.'

Chapter 10

THE ORIENT EXPRESS

Brian Austen ran away with the circus when he was fifteen. Today he runs the country's two biggest touring shows, the Moscow State Circus and Chinese State Circus.

It's summer, and it's raining. The vast blue pyramid of a big top, with its pointed white peak, appears like a snow-capped mountain against the sodden slate-coloured sky. The sun, if it were visible, wouldn't be going down for a couple of hours yet, but it's already so dark that everyone has their headlights on as well as their windscreen wipers.

Despite the weather, the great snake of cars winding its way around the roundabout and on to the showground is nose to tail. The unflooded half of the half-flooded concrete car park is already full and so is much of the muddy grass beyond. The families in their coats and hoods, hurriedly converging on the tent from the cars parked on all sides, have an excited buzz about them. After more than a decade of perpetually touring the UK the Chinese State Circus remains a big draw.

I first saw the show six months ago during its winter theatre tour. It was playing four performances over a weekend, and the Sunday matinée, which I attended, was packed, with a well-heeled and responsive audience – a typical upmarket theatre audience. The summer tenting season pulls a different crowd, one visibly a couple of notches down the social scale – upper working class, if you like, although, to be fair, you wouldn't expect anyone to be wearing black tie for a tent show on a wet night in a muddy field.

Thanks to half-price ticket deals on vouchers distributed in shops and cafés throughout the city, the big top show is cheaper to attend, and it's easier to park. It's also a much better show. Apart from the authentic circus atmosphere provided by the surroundings, you also get several acts too big for any theatre to accommodate.

At the entrance to the tent we're greeted by a wide open-fronted café/foyer, with an ornate two-tier pagoda-style roof. As we file in through one of the doors to either side of the lengthy food counter, the air is hot with the circusy scents of burgers, fried onions and popcorn – although not, and I think they're missing a trick here, Chinese food. Wouldn't an interval plateful of noodles add to the Chinese State experience?

Inside, the inverted funnel-shaped tent is enormous. It can hold 1,400 people, which is twice the capacity of the average seemingly large provincial theatre. London's Theatre Royal only holds 750. Yet the in-the-round layout brings all the seats into much closer proximity with the action – and the ringside seats into *very* close proximity.

It's not full, but it's only the cheaper side circle grandstand and the restricted view seats to either side of the ring doors that remain empty. A complete half-circle of steeply raked grandstand seating at the front of the ring is rammed solid with people, who burst into lusty applause as the lights go down.

The ringmaster is the Monkey King, a traditional Chinese character. With a face fully made up, old-fashioned clown style or football terrace style, in red, white and blue patterns, he mimes to a cultured English voiceover, partly because hardly anyone in the cast speaks English and partly because it allows him to turn impressive back-flips and baton twirls as he 'speaks'.

The opening sequence is a pageant, with various groups of flag-waving performers marching into the ring in ornate costumes representing the different dynasties, while the Monkey King takes us through a potted history of his country.

It's a nice colourful start to the show and concise, too. Then it's straight into a big, dramatic swinging-pole routine that theatre audiences miss out on. The routine begins with half-a-dozen men, dressed like extras from the Terracotta Army, shinning up half-a-dozen poles hanging from rigging high in the roof of the tent. At the top they strike poses, hanging on with just their legs, then slide down, upside down, arms outstretched to their sides, and stop just short of the ground – again, just using their thighs and ankles for brakes.

The routine hots up when they remove all but one of the poles. Two men leap on to the remaining pole, swinging it right out over the four rows of ringside seating. As it swings back, a third man leaps up to give the pole an extra shove. The pole – which is the length of a telephone pole if not as thick – swings out even further above the heads of the ringsiders. At its highest point it's touching 'four o'clock'. This time when it swings back the innermost man leaps from it. He turns one, two, three somersaults in the air and lands crotch first on a thick rope. Again he grips it with just his legs and sits up there like a monkey. Look, Ma, no hands!

After several increasingly impressive leaps, mid-air pirouettes and upside-down landings, the brutal physicality of the swinging poles is followed by a more genteel display of Chinese plate-spinning. The seven girls in the routine aren't mere window-dressing, however. While perpetually spinning four plates on four sticks in each hand, they perform forward rolls on the floor and turn graceful back-flips. They stand on each other's shoulders. One walks across the heads of a row of her colleagues as if they were so many stepping-stones.

The number of performers filling the ring in every act adds hugely to the spectacle. It's one thing to watch a girl toss a diabolo high into the roof of the tent and turn two or three somersaults before catching it and quite another to see seven girls do it at the same time.

There's no real clowning in the Chinese State Circus, but there's plenty of humour, not least in a very entertaining straw hat juggling routine. Tricks include a seven-strong, three-man-tall human pyramid, each juggling with three hats and two sets of two men standing on each other's shoulders, with all four juggling the hats back and forth across the ring between them. The highlight finds one man juggling with seven hats. As he runs around the perimeter of the ring, the hats fly out ahead of him in a wide circle . . . and curve around back into his hands, like boomerangs.

There's also a certain humour in the martial arts displays of the Shaolin Wu-Shu Warriors. How can you not laugh as you wince at the sight of a monk furiously snapping a metal rasp in half by whacking himself over the head with it? Or as he balances four bricks on his head and a colleague shatters them to rubble with a sharp blow from a sledgehammer? Or as he lies prone, borne aloft on the points of five spears?

The only 'animals' in the Chinese State Circus are the jangly, shaggy, red, green and gold stars of the traditional Chinese lion dance. The three big, playful creatures deport themselves with such character that it's easy to forget there are two men under the skins of each of them. That's two men coordinating their footwork as a lion stands on an enormous ball and rolls it over a see-saw, then one man sitting on another's shoulders as the second lion repeats the stunt while standing on its hind legs and fluttering its eyelashes at the audience. The Chinese music for the lion dance, incidentally, is charmingly melodic and so catchy that it sticks in my head for days. The rest of the show's music retains an oriental character but is often mixed with a rock beat in a pleasing and contemporary amalgam of East and West.

My favourite part of the show is an acrobatic bicycle act that, again, theatregoers miss out on because it could only ever be staged in a circus ring. Clad in shiny and sparkly blue-and-white outfits, with short skirts and Lycra leggings, three stocky little Chinese girls pedal like fury around the perimeter of the ring. Then, with a sudden flip of their bodies, they're all standing upright on their bikes, one foot on the handlebars and the other on the saddle, their arms in the air in a star shape as they continue in a circle.

The Chinese circus tradition evolved from a root independent from that of the Western version. While the father of Western circus, Philip Astley, continued a tradition of equestrianism and animal training that stretched back through the gypsies of Europe to the arenas of ancient Rome, the almost exclusively human-skills-based Chinese acrobatic theatre or variety art, as it is known in its homeland, can trace an until recently self-contained history as popular entertainment back at least as far as the beginning of the Western Han Dynasty (256 BC). Combining gymnastics, contortionism and martial arts, it is so highly regarded and central to Chinese culture as to often be described as 'the pearl of oriental art'.

The cross-pollination of East and West began in the Victorian era as the popularity of circus spread out from London and Paris to North and South America in the west and Russia and India in the east, incorporating local traditions as it encountered them. From Russia came Cossack riders, from the USA came Wild West displays and knife-throwing.

In 1866 the Frenchman Louis Soullier was the first to introduce Chinese acrobats to European circus. In the 1920s Chinese acrobat Su Fuyou returned to China from Russia with a Russian wife and new ideas about how to put on a show. The result became known internationally as the Great China Circus, and toured southern Asia in a big top with a Western-style orchestra and animal acts. In more recent times, the animal-free tradition of Chinese variety art was a major influence on the fledgling Cirque du Soleil.

In the Chinese State Circus the traditions of East and West, old and new, merge perfectly and nowhere more so than in the bicycle routine. As the cyclists fly by, with one foot on the saddle and one on the handlebars, I realize that through the prism of colliding cultures I'm watching the spiritual great-great-great-granddaughters of Philip Astley. In fact, I can almost see him, one foot on his stallion's saddle and the other on its head, his sword brandished in the air.

Other parts of the bicycle routine could equally have come out of Astley's Riding School, where the posters once promised: 'Nearly twenty different attitudes will be performed on one, two and three horses every evening.' One girl stands on the back of a bike while the other pedals – then leapfrogs over her colleague's head so that they change places. One girl stands on a cyclist's shoulders, then leaps into the air and lands on her feet on the shoulders of a second cyclist. I can almost smell the horses, hear the neighing and see the sawdust flying beneath the galloping hooves. For a second, their ghosts, and Astley's, are all around me, and I'm in Lambeth 220 years ago. Except there is no sawdust. The ring has a clean, smooth and shiny wooden floor. And there are no horses, just polished aluminium bicycle frames and wheels. And, somehow, that's better.

I've enjoyed the animal shows I've seen. I've enjoyed the raw proximity to the elephants, tigers, camels and horses. Yet I've never sat there and fully shaken off the feeling that it was an odd thing to be sitting there watching – a spectacle closer to the farmyard than the theatre. There is a place, I now realize, for the liberty horses and the elephant pyramid and the big cat cage, but perhaps it's the place we reserve for museums and Morris dancers and steam railways; a place where we can indulge our nostalgia for the past but a place where only diehard enthusiasts would like to go too regularly. The rest of us, while enjoying our visit and perhaps finding it educational for our children, understand that we can only ever be fleeting visitors because, on the whole, we prefer to live in our present.

The Chinese State Circus has taken the traditions of the circus and moved them fully into the twenty-first century. The big top isn't there out of nostalgia but necessity – to accommodate the stunts too big for theatre or television screen. They have kept the traditional circus format, with feats of strength and skill presented purely as what they are, because there is no need to dress them up in metaphors or storylines. But, by taking out the animals they've stripped away the sense of circus as an anachronism or as something alien, other and off-putting. The girls laying on their bellies across their bicycle crossbars and turning the pedals with one hand present a clean-cut aesthetic close enough to what we are used to seeing on stage and screen to be accepted alongside all the other forms of contemporary entertainment. It just happens to be one of the best forms, which is why it has proved to be so enduringly popular.

The show is so good, in fact, that I decide to see it again a couple of evenings later. I'm not disappointed. There's so much in such a fast-moving programme that you need to watch it more than once just to take everything in. The contortionists, for instance: the monk who can tuck both legs under his armpits and cross his ankles behind his head; the girl who bends over backwards, with her feet and palms on the ground, in the shape of a coffee table. A second girl then does a handstand on the first girl's hipbones. The first girl, while still bent over backwards, takes her hands off the ground.

I'm also taken by a high-altitude aerial silk duet. Set to a romantic pop ballad, it's dressed as the aerial ballet it is – the guy in white trousers and shirt, the girl in a frilly Gothic dress. As they circle the air above the ring fence, sometimes on two silks, sometimes on one, they demonstrate an impressive range of hangs, with each taking turns to be the bearer. At one stage, while they swirl around high above us – and there are no safety wires here – he hangs upside down by his feet from her feet, just the strength in their ankles holding him in the air. Swapping places, he suspends her from a short rope with a loop around the back of her neck, and she becomes a pirouetting blur on the end of his wrist. The audience is entranced and the applause thunderous.

On my second visit I also notice the smaller details otherwise lost in a blur of movement and colour – the intensity in the faces of the performers, for instance. When one of the girls drops her diabolo, the decorous fixed grins of the others disappear in an instant. The girl who retrieves and hands back the fallen top wears an expression of icy fury. The girl who dropped it looks so consumed with shame you half expect her to go back to her caravan and commit suicide in the interval.

The high standard of Chinese circus dates from the foundation of the People's Republic of China in 1949, when state funding of circus schools in every province became a matter of national pride. Today there are around 200 of them, which fiercely compete in regional and national competitions. Pupils attend from the age of six and train between six and eight hours a day, concentrating on strength and flexibility as well as the type of specific skills displayed in the Chinese State Circus.

'I'm not saying they're cruel,' laughs Gerry Cottle, who first took his circus to Hong Kong in the early 1980s, before bringing the Chinese State Circus to Britain in the 1990s, 'but they are very hard on their people.'

In Cottle's opinion the standard of training in China is today challenged worldwide only by the emerging Korean circus schools. 'Now they *may* be cruel . . .' Cottle chortles, but he adds, 'You never see the Chinese running away from the circus. They enjoy being part of the troupe.'

A few days later I try to ask the Chinese themselves about their training. On the phone, as they've already moved to a different town, it doesn't prove easy. The 'translator', Mr Wu (I think that's his name), doesn't seem to speak English any better than Mr Liu, the producer. Pretty much every question goes like this:

Mr Wu: 'Sorry. Please repeat question more simply.'

Me: 'If a performer makes a mistake, do the others get angry with him?'

Mr Wu: 'One moment please.' He shouts in Chinese at Mr Liu for about half a minute. In the background, Mr Liu shouts back for a minute and a half.

Mr Wu: 'Hello? He say yes.'

After five minutes I seriously wonder if I've got Clive and Danny on the line.

At the end of the show I notice something particularly impressive: how few performers come out to take a bow. Distracted by the constantly changing costumes, I'd supposed that each routine was performed by a different group of specialist performers. In fact, apart from the Shaolin monks, there is only one male and one female troupe. The boys on the swinging poles are also the hat-jugglers and the guys in the lion dance. The girls on the bikes are also the diabolists, the plate-spinners and the contortionists. One each of the boys and girls must also be the aerialists, since there's no sign of a separate couple in the all-cast finale.

Once again I'm struck by the talent and versatility of the circus breed. To be able to perform one of the acts I've just seen should be the product of a lifetime's dedication; to be able to do three or four such acts to such a high standard is nothing short of amazing – especially when I learn later that all the performers are around eighteen or nineteen years old.

The only man not amazed by the Chinese State Circus is its promoter, Brian Austen.

'It bores me to sobs!' chuckles the man who has been bringing the Chinese State and Moscow State circuses to Britain for the past decade, together with periodic tours of Circus Berlin. 'But I'm also a realist and know there's a huge audience out there that likes it.'

While Gerry Cottle became the best-known name in British circus over the past thirty years, his sometime business partner Brian Austen has attracted far less publicity on his rise to becoming the biggest player on the scene today. In a sense, Austen's relationship to Cottle was that of a William C. Coup or James A. Bailey to Cottle's flamboyant P.T. Barnum.

Looking back, Austen confesses, 'I suppose I feel hurt sometimes that Gerry always got the recognition for everything we did together, and, actually, behind it all, I don't think he was the key to it. I think he carried the credit for a lot of ideas that were mine and, financially, the money was mine.' Stirring echoes in my mind of Barnum's autobiographies, in which the contribution of his partner, Coup, was played down, Brian continues, 'I would say that some of the things in Gerry's book [*Confessions of a Showman*] weren't true. But I'd never say that to Gerry because he's a great showman, and that's his prerogative.'

As it happens, it's Cottle who puts me in touch with Austen. With a typical sense of fun, Cottle says, 'I could be very naughty and give you his private mobile number . . . but whatever you do don't tell him I gave it to you. Tell him it was Martin Lacey!'

Of course he's joking. Cottle calls Austen to introduce me, and Brian is happy to be interviewed. Although he has seldom spoken to the press in the past thirty years, that turns out to be from shyness rather than the aloofness of a deliberately enigmatic Mr Big.

The interview is delayed for a few minutes, not because of urgent corporate business but because Brian is busy ejecting from his house a mouse that has been menacing his wife.

Although Austen began his career in the ring, where one of his personas was El Briarno, the wire-walker, he admits he never shared Cottle's love of the limelight.

'I came from a poor background, and I probably lacked confidence. I was happy for Gerry to do all the talking, to be the mouthpiece, and the leader if you want, for want of a better word. But in me he had somebody who, whatever he wanted to do, I could back it up. As a team we were unbeatable.'

Like Cottle, Austen ran away with the circus at the age of fifteen, but he came from a very different background. While Cottle was a stockbroker's son educated at a good school, Austen came from a 'very poor' family in Cambridge. One of his brothers went to borstal. Having left school three months previously Brian was working as a panel-beater when he decided life as a horse groom with the Anglo-American Circus had better prospects. It was a ramshackle operation run by the self-styled Count Lazard, a former miner and hair-gel salesman with a penchant for cowboy hats – a fashion he copied from Billy Smart.

With a laugh Brian recalls, 'I always said to Gerry, the one thing I learned from the Anglo-American was to do absolutely nothing they did, because everything they did turned to chaos.' The first time Brian encountered the Anglo-American, it didn't even have a tent. 'They'd had a blow-down, so they circled the lorries and set up the seats in the middle. I don't remember them ever having any artistes. It was Count Lazard and William Lazard – although they weren't really brothers – and Mavis, who was William's wife. Lazard used to do the snakes and fire-eating and that kind of thing.'

The accommodation provided for Austen was a caravan, which he shared with the Count's snakes. 'I never got paid. I never once got a week's money. But I wasn't bothered. They used to feed me and look after me. They wintered in the back yard of a disused pub. There was some storage downstairs where they kept the ponies, and upstairs was a function room where I set up a wire and taught myself wire-walking.' In time he would add stilt-walking, juggling, clowning, knife-throwing, animal training and unicycle to his repertoire – as well as proficiency in the mechanics of building and moving a circus.

Shortly after Austen joined, the Anglo-American Circus embarked on a tour of South Africa – only to find that neither the promoter nor the promised money was waiting for them. Thanks to Austen's increasingly handy technical skills, however, the visit eventually proved successful.

'We moved to a zoo near Port Elizabeth. There was a big Ford car plant nearby, and I built the seats for an outdoor circus from all the discarded wooden pallets. I used to do four acts in the ring, do the whole build-up and drive – as a seventeen-year-old with no licence. It was incredibly hard work – and I still never got paid – but it was a phenomenal adventure. We were the first circus ever to go into Swaziland. I can remember places where they'd never seen a circus and the sight of someone on stilts was frightening to them.'

The African adventure came to an end when Brian ran off with Mavis, who was ten years his senior. To raise the fare back to England, 'I went to work on South African railways, cleaning coaches. I used to collect all the Coke bottles and take them to the shop to get all the sixpences!'

Back in Blighty Austen worked as a labourer for a while before joining James Brothers Circus – where his accommodation proved to be no better than it had been with the Anglo-American: 'They gave me a caravan with no door and absolutely nothing inside it. Absolutely nothing!'

Before long, however, Austen teamed up with his James Brothers colleague Gerry Cottle, who had just married the boss's daughter and decided to start a circus of his own. 'So we set off to a pig farm in Reigate, where I spent all my time building what was to become Embassy Circus.' Embassy quickly became Cottle and Austen's Circus, by which point, Brian remembers, 'I was doing four or five acts. I was the tent-master and the transport manager. I never went to bed two nights a week, because I moved the circus all through the night on my own.'

Among Brian's acts was knife-throwing, with Mavis as the target girl. Asked if he ever nicked her, he confesses: 'Just once, but it was nothing, just her tights. I don't think it actually marked her.' Nor was the knife-throwing the reason for the couple's eventual split – he's now married to a former trapeze artist called Evelyn.

Asked if he was as ambitious as Cottle in the early days, Brian says, 'No. I was never ambitious. I went through life without any great ideas about anything. I just enjoyed what I did. Gerry was always ambitious. He wanted to be a big circus director.' Did Brian take Cottle's ambitions seriously? 'I don't think I ever took much notice, to be honest. I just worked. But I suppose at the end of the day I was aggressive enough to want a little bit more all the time. I wasn't content to sit back with what you've got.'

Within a couple of years Cottle and Austen went from circus outsiders – 'jossers' – to owning Britain's biggest circus, thanks largely to a decision to monopolize London's parks where no other circus had appeared for years.

The 'unbeatable' team parted over Cottle's decision to launch a circus on ice in tandem with their conventional circus. It soon became apparent that the latter was subsidizing the former, but Cottle refused Austen's demands to give up his ice show and the partnership was dissolved with each man taking a circus apiece. Austen was shocked to find that the shared debts they came away with were not the £12,000 Cottle claimed but £48,000.

'We never fell out over it,' says Brian. But he adds with a touch a glee, 'Gerry ran the ice circus for two or three more weeks, then even he gave up and ran an ordinary circus.'

Both ex-partners prospered, but while Cottle's soaring ambitions were frequently accompanied by equally spectacular reversals of fortune, Austen's business climbed a steadier path.

'I've never been bankrupt. I've never had to close the company through financial restraint. I've never been in any sort of financial trouble in my life.

I'm a plodder, a careful person rather than a chancer. I set my sights lower and move on from there, rather than aiming too high.'

Austen also ploughed the profits from his circus into other ventures. His business interests include a 250-acre industrial estate, an engineering business, a timber yard and a company that supplies tents and grandstand seating to some of Britain's most prestigious events, such as tennis championships, rock concerts and the Trooping of the Colour.

Then there's the second-hand helicopter business . . . 'I had a nightmare as a kid of dying in an aeroplane. It was always in the back of my mind, and every time I flew abroad I was terrified. So I thought the only way to overcome this is to learn how to fly.' Initially Austen intended only to buy a helicopter for his own use. His personal transport is a Bell 206 Jet Ranger. 'Then I started buying ex-army helicopters from all over the world. Everybody thought I was mental. I had a shed full of them. But I made a lot of money out of them.'

As Cottle concedes in *Confessions of a Showman*, 'Brian is now a rich man. I am not. Enough said.'

Having formed and successfully run Austen Brothers Circus for a decade and a half, Brian got out of circus in the late 1980s, as the animal issue loomed large.

'Circuses were being forced out of the proper grounds. They were playing farmer's fields, and where you want to be with a circus is in the city centres – as we later proved with the Moscow, when we went back to the proper grounds, without animals, and did phenomenal business. At that point, though, there hadn't been any non-animal circuses. So I closed it because I couldn't see a future for it.'

Looking back, does he feel the anti-animal protests were justified?

'I've seen a lot of cruelty in my time,' Brian admits, 'but it comes from the old families, not the new ones. The Germans were very hard on their animals. But you can have cruel farmers, cruel horse people, cruel dog-handlers. It doesn't mean you have to be cruel to do it, because you don't. You just need a lot of patience. It's no different to training a child really. You can train a child by slapping it. Then it's a question of how hard you slap it, how often you slap it and what you slap it for. But it's actually completely unnecessary.

'I was the first to train lions, from wild, in front of the public. We used to advertise the fact that we would be entering the cage at such and such time and you could come and watch the progress. I did that because I had nothing to hide. The training is about reward and kindness and your voice.' No wonder he had no trouble saving his missus from that mouse.

Of the animal question today Brian says, 'I've never had a problem with the training, but I began to have a bit of a problem with confinement. With some animals I think it's wrong. I don't have a problem with lions and tigers. I don't really have a problem with elephants and horses as long as they're let out. But when you start talking about bears and monkeys and chimpanzees, they're not animals you should confine. But, equally, if I was brave enough I'd start an animal circus now. It would make a fortune, because it's what people want to see.'

Away from circus Austen concentrated on his tent hire and grandstand seating business. He provided the big top for Cirque du Soleil's London début. He also put a canvas roof over the Bolshoi Ballet.

Austen's interest in circus was reignited when the promoters of the ballet brought the Moscow State Circus to the UK. 'It's actually called the Bolshoi Circus,' explains Brian, who would later register the name Moscow State Circus as a trademark, which he now owns. At the time he simply provided the tent and recalls, 'I watched every performance. I loved watching those acts. They were phenomenal.' He also noticed that the then promoter was haemorrhaging money on unnecessary expenses – and that he could promote the circus more profitably himself.

Austen invited Cottle to rejoin him as a partner – 'Gerry's a great administrator' – and the Moscow State Circus became such a success that 'I said, "We've got two tents. Why don't we bring over the Chinese?" Then I said, "Why don't we run three? We can tie up all the grounds on a three-year cycle." It was my idea to start Cottle and Austen's Rock'n'Roll Circus, because I loved rock'n'roll music.'

In 2003 Austen bought Cottle's share in the three circuses, so Cottle could buy the tourist attraction Wookey Hole. At the same time he closed the Cottle and Austen Circus to concentrate his resources on the more successful Chinese and Moscow.

Why does he feel the latter two have remained so popular for so long?

'I think we have a very high standard of performance, and I think we still put a lot into it. I make a lot of money from circuses, but I also put an awful lot back. I spent £200,000 last winter just reorganizing.'

On my second visit to the Chinese State Circus, because I'm not hunched over against the rain I'm able to stand back and properly appreciate the size of the mobile village and the attention given to its presentation. There are a huge number of lorries and bunk wagons for the cast. The latter are articulated lorry trailers, each with a row of windows and doors in the side, like holiday chalets, only much smaller. All the vehicles are painted in bright yellow livery and sign-written with the Chinese State Circus in large green-and-red lettering. They're parked neatly to form three sides of a square around the big top. The front of the square is fenced with neat red railings with arches of coloured lighting above. The ticket-office trailer stands three-quarters of the way along the fence, and uniformed programme sellers flank the walk-through entrance to the grass directly in front of the big top.

This time, on a sunny Saturday evening, I spy a few more yuppies in the crowd, well-heeled women dressed as if for Proms in the Park, grinning at the lark of this big top business. The food counter caters for them by selling green tea and cappuccino alongside the burgers.

As with my last visit, it's a predominantly adult crowd. There are a few kids but far more people in their thirties and forties and a fairly strong contingent in their teens and twenties. Again it's a big turn-out. Most of the side circle is full this time, and there are quite a few cheapskates in the restricted-view seats. At a fiver with a voucher they've got themselves a good deal.

'I've always tried to look after my customers,' says Austen. 'I was the first to have aluminium king poles, the first to put aluminium doors on a tent, or even doors at all, and to have proper heating. The rest didn't seem to care.' Warming to his theme, if you'll excuse the pun, Brian adds, 'I used to go to other people's tents, years ago, and say, "It's not very warm in here." "Oh yeah, but we've got the heaters on." I said, "You know what? For every penny you've spent on heating, you've actually wasted it. Whereas if you'd spent another twenty quid the audience would have been warm and they'd have gone away and said they were warm." I don't think there's any other way than doing things properly. If you're not going to do it properly there's no point in doing it. That's my philosophy on life.'

In Austen's technical prowess there are again echoes of William C. Coup. Coup designed the railway wagons on which Barnum's circus travelled, including innovative ramps for speedy unloading. Coup also designed the original king pole. Barnum's two-ring big top had three central peaks and three main poles instead of the two of earlier tents. Coup put a block and tackle at the top of the central pole – the king pole – so that once it was erect the other poles could more quickly be raised, using horse- or elephant-power. In a twenty-first-century equivalent of Coup's innovation, Austen says, 'About four years ago I made a tent that was all hydraulic, built off a trailer that folded out hydraulically. You put it in the middle of the ground, levelled it on hydraulics, folded down the ring and lifted the king poles hydraulically. You didn't even have to put stakes in the ground.' That's not a bad invention for a man who describes himself as 'very dyslexic and a terrible scholar'. But if you're good with your hands you don't necessarily have to be a mathematician.

'In my view, the problem with circus is the people who run it. They're not prepared to put money back into it, to make it a better circus. Particularly the old families. They're a disgrace. You pull on the ground and see the transport with the paint hanging off . . .' He shakes his head in despair. 'When Gerry and I started we put the lorries around the front, and they were always well painted. We didn't have anything around the back, but it's first impressions, isn't it? These days we're known for our transport. I can go anywhere in Europe and they say, "We know about you. You've got nice transport and nice seating and you do this and you do that."'

Apart from his hands-on attention to technical detail, Austen attributes his success to honesty. 'If I've shook my hand on something, I've shook it. I don't need a lawyer to tell me, and I don't need somebody to write a contract. I think that's the best way to be, because I always believe there's another time. I'm not after a quick buck; I'm after the long haul, and I would like to have the people I deal with around for a long time.'

Perhaps another reason for his success is that while other showmen were born into the circus tradition, or remain in it for romantic or vocational reasons, Austen is first and foremost a businessman. 'I'm not a circus fan. I'm not really interested in going to see other people's shows.'

Nor is he sentimental about his own circuses – especially in the midst of the current economic downturn. 'Merchandise used to be your profit, now you need it to stay alive. In a nutshell, if it doesn't cost me too much money I'll keep the shows going. I have a lot of very loyal people who I feel very loyal towards. But while I'll throw money at the circus to improve it I wouldn't waste money on a loss-maker.

'My audience is a bit more upmarket, and I think those are the people that have been hit the hardest. But, at the same time, a lot of these people will be staying at home this year, so I think we could have a good summer. We've got a good route. We're playing places like the Western Isles, the Orkneys, Fraserborough and Peterhead. Nobody else goes up there because it's too far. So, hopefully, if we've got it right, we'll survive another year.'

At sixty-one Austen certainly has no plans to retire. Claiming to be unmotivated by money, he says, 'The truth is, I'm not very good at doing nothing. I have a big boat in the Med. I've got my helicopter. I've got nearly everything I want. But I still get up at half six every morning and go to work. I'm developing houses, I'm building nursing homes . . . I'm doing all sorts of things.'

Ultimately, the Mr Big of British circus says, 'I think I'm a real entrepreneur in that I see opportunities in all fields, and I have a go at them.'

Chapter 11

THE SUN THAT NEVER SETS

No survey of circus in the twenty-first century would be complete without mention of Cirque du Soleil, a company that grew from a Canadian festival of street entertainment and went on to conquer the world.

Every era has a name synonymous with circus – a name that even non-circus fans will have heard of. In the early nineteenth century it was Philip Astley – even though it was Astley's rival, Charles Hughes, who coined the word 'circus' in a modern context.

It was a pupil of Hughes who was largely responsible for popularizing circus in the USA. The fame of English equestrian John Bill Ricketts's Riding School in Philadelphia (a circus by another name) grew from its endorsement by George Washington, a keen amateur horseman, who became a close friend. But even in the USA it would be the billing 'of Astley's' or 'from Astley's' that lent distinction to circus performers, such as the trick rider and clown Billie Button, for decades to come.

In the late nineteenth century the self-appointed 'Lord' George Sanger dominated British circus, while,across the pond the name Barnum reigned supreme.

In Britain, between the wars, if you went to one circus in your lifetime it was probably Bertram Mills. From the 1950s to the 1970s it would have been Billy Smart's or Chipperfield's. In the 1980s the name that rang a bell with the man in the street was Gerry Cottle.

For the past fifteen years it has been impossible to mention circus without someone saying Cirque du Soleil. If the average generally-non-circus-going Briton has been to one circus, it will have been Cirque du Soleil at the Albert Hall. Even if they haven't been, they will have heard of it. For the past decade Soleil has been the only circus regularly reviewed alongside pop, ballet and opera in the serious press and just about the only circus to receive any positive coverage in the media at all.

Furthermore, unlike the big names of circus before it, Soleil's fame is not confined to one continent. Since the turn of the twenty-first century Soleil has created nine large-scale productions that have never come off the road – they're all still touring on one continent or another. Even in the USA, where the venerable Ringling Brothers and Barnum and Bailey Circus continues to roll around the country at the ripe old age of 130, it is Soleil that has six permanent shows providing year-round entertainment in Las Vegas.

That's not bad for a company founded on the hippy ideals of a bunch of street entertainers with no circus background in a place way off circus's historical map in Quebec, Canada.

Cirque du Soleil – the circus of the sun – was the brainchild of Guy Laliberté, who retains private ownership of the company today. Born in 1959, Laliberté grew up in the hippy culture of the 1960s and 1970s. While still in high school he became interested in entertainment and travel after a visit to Canada by the Cajun singer and accordionist Zachary Richard. Laliberté toured Europe playing folk music in the streets and in Paris met buskers who used circus skills such as acrobatics, fire-eating and stilt-walking.

Back in Quebec Laliberté teamed up with a former high-school friend called Daniel Gauthier and Giles Ste-Croix, who ran a youth hostel. Together they formed a touring company of street entertainers called Les Eschassiers de Baie-Saint-Paul [The Stilt-walkers of Baie-Saint-Paul]. To raise corporate sponsorship for the company Ste-Croix undertook a 22-hour stilt walk from Baie-Saint-Paul to Quebec City.

The company grew to include clowns and puppetry and in 1982 gave birth to a week-long street performance festival in Baie-Saint-Paul called La Fête Foraine (which roughly translates as 'travelling show/fair'). Laliberté was general manager. As well as performances, the festival ran circus skills workshops. The tutors were provided by Guy Caron, a street entertainer who had formed Canada's first circus school in Montreal and who would eventually become one of Laliberté's business partners.

The increasingly successful annual Fête Foraine gave Laliberté the track record and contacts to secure $1.6 million of government funding to create Canada's first home-grown touring circus as part of the national celebrations to mark 1984's 450th anniversary of Jacques Cartier's discovery of Canada. Laliberté came up with the name while watching the sunset on a beach holiday in Hawaii. He called it Le Grand Tour du Cirque du Soleil.

Stylistic influences included the animal-free Circus of China, which visited Montreal in 1982 and impressed the founders of Soleil with its cohesive approach to costuming and music, and the Moscow Circus, which linked its acts with storylines. They also took a cue from Germany's Cirque Roncalli, which had its performers, still in costume, help the stagehands move props and equipment for more fluid scene changes. In time Soleil would take the idea further, removing the traditionally concealed backstage area, so all the performers remained on show and in character throughout the performance. In its second year the company introduced further innovations by recruiting creative staff, such as artistic director Franco Dragone, from the world of theatre rather than circus and acrobats from the world of competitive gymnastics.

The influences took time to gel into the style for which Soleil would become known, however. And in the early days, when Soleil still looked like a fairly conventional circus in an unprofitably small stripy big top, there were more than a few hiccups.

Laliberté knew from the outset that Soleil would stand or fall on the strength of its acts – what he has referred to as the 'acrobatic skeleton' at the core of every show. For the company's first tour he hired professional circus artistes from Europe, who came close to mutiny over the management's inexperience in the basics of running a circus. Things got off to a bad start at the very first show in Gaspé when, having left it to the last minute,

Laliberté failed to secure hotel accommodation for the artistes and had to put them up in youth hostels. They responded by refusing to attend the press launch. At the time Laliberté had worse things to worry about because his inexpertly erected big top had just collapsed in the rain and he had to hire another one, which was only just built up in time for the show.

While developing its artistic vision – and ironing out the technical problems of touring in a tent – the fledgling company took several years to find its financial footing. After a second year's government funding ran out, Soleil survived only through the understanding of bankers who believed in Laliberté's vision and underwrote bad cheques into the hundreds of thousands of dollars. Audience reactions, however, convinced Laliberté that he was heading in the right direction.

The year 1987 was literally the make-or-break year for Soleil. Its future hinged on a one-way ticket to the Los Angeles arts festival. Instead of transportation costs, which the festival couldn't afford to pay him, Laliberté did a deal for 100 per cent of the box office and gambled everything he had on getting the show there. If the show succeeded, the lucrative US and international market beckoned. If it flopped, he wouldn't have the funds to take his circus back to Canada. As it happened, Soleil was the smash of the festival. Its reputation led to profitable runs in Santa Monica and New York, and by the end of the year the formerly struggling company was in profit to the tune of a couple of million dollars.

There would continue to be ups and downs, including a loss-making European début. But a well-received trip to Japan proved Soleil's international viability, and the next decade generally saw Soleil go from commercial strength to strength, not least through the revolutionary artistic input of Dragone and business partnerships with Disney, which hosted a resident Soleil show in Florida, and hotel and casino tycoon Steve Wynn, who hosted the first of many in Las Vegas.

Soleil's first theatre show, *Mystère*, opened at Wynn's new Treasure Island Hotel in Vegas in 1993. In contrast to the Glitter City's tradition of feathers and tuxedos, Dragone's creation was about the origins of life, inspired by concepts such as chaos theory, and featured a cast dressed as exotic insects. When Wynn saw what he had bought, he reportedly commented, 'You guys have made a German opera here.' Dragone took it as a compliment, and the show proved a resounded success. Initially contracted for ten years, *Mystère* is still going strong. Won over by the Soleil formula, Wynn subsequently sank $100 million into a specially built 1,800-seat theatre to hold Soleil's water spectacular, *O*.

Elsewhere along the Vegas strip, Soleil today offers something for everyone. *Love* is based on the music of the Beatles. *Ka* has a martial-arts theme on an immense moving stage that can be lifted into a near-vertical plane by a giant gantry arm. *Zoomanity* explores the sexy side of circus with an adults-only burlesque show.

Away from Vegas, Soleil has resident shows in Florida and Tokyo and is about to develop one in the billionaires' playground of Dubai. The company is also about to take an Elvis-themed show on the road.

As a global operation Soleil dwarfs any circus before it, including the giant circuses of the USA's golden age in the late nineteenth and early twentieth centuries, when the Ringling Brothers toured with a 15,000-seat tent and a menagerie of virtually every animal known to man. But can anything so big ever live up to its own reputation?

On my journey into the circus world, where the name Cirque du Soleil hovers over every interview, I take a long time to get around to seeing my first Soleil show, *Varekai*. When most people who aren't connected to circus hear I'm writing a book about circus, they reply, as if by word association and with a big grin on their face, 'Cirque du Soleil.' Many within the industry greet the words 'Cirque du Soleil' with a more disparaging reaction, perhaps out of an understandable jealousy. I find myself suspicious of both reactions. While the media trendies who first raved about Soleil had probably not seen another circus in years, I want to be sure what the benchmarks are before I go along. Frankly, it has a lot to beat – albeit that it's probably the success of Soleil itself that has been responsible for driving up industry standards in the past ten years. As with my visit to Martin Lacey's elephants, I go as a sceptic. I know it will be good, but can it possibly be *that* good?

The word 'varekai' is Romany for 'wherever' – unfortunately not 'whatever', which would have been a gift to critics. The show is the brainchild of writer–director Dominic Champagne, and its setting is a kind of enchanted forest into which Icarus, the character from Greek mythology, falls from the sky and encounters a bunch of Gypsy-like vagabonds who, essentially, put on a circus show.

The first impression is powerful. You can see the money in the lighting effects and the set (to call it a ring would be far too prosaic, although it's in the round, as a circus ring should be). You can see the cash in the carefully choreographed massed ranks of performers who swarm out from behind the backdrop of what appear to be tall golden bamboo poles.

People, insects, leaves, fairies, aliens? Who knows what the performers are supposed to be as they dance, crawl, roll and strike poses. But their multicoloured costumes, which, like most Soleil productions, take their inspiration from the half-beautiful, half-ugly tradition of the seventeenth-century *commedia dell'arte*, are stunning, as is the mask-like make-up.

Soleil's spending power is also apparent in the standard of the circus performers. They have their pick from the cream of the world. An early highlight is an impressive display of human foot juggling. The jugglers lie on sloped couches, their hips higher than their shoulders and their legs in the air. The flyers sit on their colleagues' feet, then are kicked high into the air, where they perform flips, somersaults and pirouettes over and over again. It's a common circus act, but the grace and precision are exemplary. A high point of the act includes the flyer standing on the juggler's feet doing a somersault, then landing foot to foot once more. Typical of Soleil's lavish scale, the routine is presented in multiple, with four sets of jugglers and flyers performing in perfect synchrony.

The visual strength in numbers continues with a static trapeze display. While most such acts have one or two performers, Soleil fields six women on a specially made rig – all of them identical in shiny blue-and-green costumes, matching face make-up and big blue wigs.

By the time the foot jugglers appear, however, I find myself becoming bored by the extent of the window-dressing – the sheer amount of prancing about by all those fairies, leaves, insects or whatever they are that continues between each of the actual circus acts. As my partner puts it, 'It's all that face pulling I can't stand.' To make her point, she holds her palms up beside her face, fingers spread as if in alarm, pokes her tongue out and goes bug-eyed.

'I think it's supposed to be arty,' I suggest.

Soleil's use of mime in place of verbal communication has been key to its success in crossing language barriers around the world. Early shows were developed through brainstorming and workshops, rather than from the script of a single writer. In Soleil's authorized biography, *20 Years Under the Sun* by Tony Babinsky, Dragone says many of the characters he used were initially inspired by the costume design, while another of the directors, Michel Crête, suggests the dramatic content is often deliberately vague to allow audiences to interpret the action in accordance with their own feelings and experiences. In other words, you see what you want to see. To cynics like me, who like to just sit back and have the story spelled out for them, that sounds suspiciously like the deal offered to the spectators of the king's new clothes.

Early on, and unfortunately reprised several times throughout the show, is an interminable sequence involving a character called the Skywatcher and another called the Guide. The former is a grotesquely grinning character with spiky blond hair, a bare chest, yellow trousers that end in ragged spikes mid-calf and elongated court-jester-style shoes. Around his waist he's wearing a kind of inverted grass skirt, with curved green spikes sticking upwards towards his chest that give him a plant-like appearance. His eerily white-faced pal, the Guide, wears a buttoned-up leather uniform a bit like a spooky art-deco version of a science-fiction policeman, with a light bulb on top of his helmet. I guess they're clowns. But I'm reminded of when I was a child and the television announcer said, 'And now a cartoon . . . from Czechoslovakia.' Whether these occasional offerings from other cultures were designed to broaden our minds, or whether the BBC simply got them cheap, I have no idea, but I remember sitting there watching something numbingly incomprehensible and not remotely funny, thinking: This is not *Tom and Jerry*. If conventional clown make-up is deemed scary, the appearance of these guys would give a kid nightmares.

Varekai is not a children's show, however. The audience titter politely at the antics of the Skywatcher, in the way that arts audiences tend to, either patronizingly, indulgently or, more likely, to broadcast the fact that *they* can see the king's clothes even if nobody else can. But I'm reassured to find I'm not the only thickie who couldn't make head or tale of what the Skywatcher and his mate with the light bulb were up to. In a review in *The Times* in which

Benedict Nightingale reported that *Varekai* generally failed to engage his emotions, he singled out the 'man in a grass skirt', who 'left me feeling pretty murderous'. I have to say I'm with Britain's most eminent theatre critic there.

Fortunately the Skywatcher is not the only 'clown' in *Varekai*. Later in the show a more conventional double act, Claudio Carneiro and Mooky Cornish, provide an engaging silent-comedy magic routine set to the music from 1970s children's television show *Animal Magic*. Although not made up as a clown, Claudio is a textbook whiteface – a straight-faced magician struggling to retain his dignity in the face of perpetual humiliation. Mooky, his assistant, is a textbook auguste – a loveably goofy overweight blonde, a ridiculous sight in a short fur-trimmed négligé and big white knickers, who crashes around the ring messing up every trick. They're not quite in Danny and Clive's league, but they generate plenty of genuine laughter with a routine that would work from Vegas to Yarmouth and bring a relaxed human warmth missing from much of the rest of the show. They also have the best music, the rest mostly being a mixture of foreign-language world music and bad Euro-pop that suits the arty costumes but leaves me pining for the Top 40 soundtrack of Peter Jay's Hippodrome.

Another old-school circus performer who could have stepped out of any big top in the past hundred years is the tanned and grinning juggler Octavio Alegria. At one point he juggles with two footballs in one hand, bounces a third on his forehead and keeps a fourth spinning on one finger. At another point he juggles ping-pong balls with his mouth, spitting them upwards towards the ceiling.

If one performer epitomizes the superlative standard of Soleil's artistes, it's contortionist Olga Pikhienko. Our man at *The Times* wasn't impressed: 'Oh, so here's a contortionist so elastic that each leg moves from 180 to 360 degrees to the other, both of them swivelling on to her forehead,' he yawns from the page, before concluding, 'The problem is that the Cirque has substituted technical expertise for humanity. Bluntly, it lacks soul.' In Olga's case, however, I have to disagree with Nightingale. I've seen many contortionists recently, and Olga outclasses them all. The girls of the Chinese State Circus are impressively flexible and could probably do everything Olga does. The difference is, you can see the concentration on their faces. Watch closely, and you can see the slight kick of exertion as they turn themselves upside down. You can see the slight tremor of their muscles as they hold each pose. In short, you can see them working hard at what they do. Olga, by contrast, makes every move look so effortless she could be computer-animated. With only her face not covered by a skin-tight shiny white costume ribbed with jewels, she looks like an alien, demonstrating her infinitely superior physical mobility to us poor humans. Moreover, the sense of superiority extends to her facial expression.

Unlike the Chinese girls, Olga seems to need no mental engagement with her body's contortions. As she stalks across the ring like a dancer, then does an upside-down splits on a one-handed handstand, her eyes are not on what she's doing; they're on us. Beneath intense eyebrows her eyes are simultaneously fiery and coldly aloof. Her full lips are set in a permanent sullen sneer. More than just a consummate gymnast, Olga is an actress who communicates volumes with a flash of her eyes. Her magnetic presence is such that in the few minutes she is on stage she owns the building.

The finale is a thrilling display of Russian swing by a scarlet-clad Russian troupe that must number a dozen. A Russian swing is similar to a playground swing except that instead of chains the swing is suspended from its frame by four stiff metal bars. Instead of a seat set at right-angles to the direction of the swing, it has a large rectangular platform with the long sides of the rectangle in line with the direction of travel. One or two men stand at the back of the swing to give it momentum. The flyer stands on the front edge of the platform. As the swing reaches its highest point, he is catapulted high into the air, where he performs somersaults or pirouettes. The height the flyers are propelled to is stunning to behold and, in terms of its sheer physicality and daring, Russian swing surpasses even the mid-air daredevilry of the flying trapeze.

I saw a Russian swing act at the Hippodrome where the flyers, used to performing in larger big tops, almost hit the ceiling. With no safety net, they were caught – with a mighty *whompff* – by four colleagues wielding a mattress, like firemen with a blanket catching people jumping from a burning building. Soleil dress the act better. Instead of a mattress, there are two enormous white sheets, suspended almost vertically, like a ship's sails, across the rear corners of the ring. The flyers splat into the sheets like moths, then slide down into cloth hammocks at the bottom.

The act also has two swings. The flyers cross paths in mid-air as they somersault diagonally across the ring. With a rapid succession of flyers coming off each swing, the tumbling, criss-crossing bodies fill the air like artillery fire. Then the swings are spun around so that they face each other. A flyer leaps from one, somersaults in mid-air and, with a miracle of timing, lands on his toes on the platform of the other swing. At this point the audience aren't just applauding; they're hollering in appreciation and amazement.

But still Soleil push the act further. Two flyers leave their respective swings simultaneously. One does a somersault. The other does a mid-air splits as he leapfrogs over his colleague. Both land safely on the opposite swing. It's no fluke. In case anyone missed it, they do the mid-air crossover again. And again. With more dramatic spins and tumbles each time.

This is circus at its breathtaking best, and it brings *Varekai* to an emotionally overwhelming climax – an arena rock-concert climax, a 'Last Night of the Proms' climax. When it's over, the expression on the faces of both the performers and the now standing audience is nothing short of ecstasy.

What's interesting, though, is that apart from an early aerial sequence in which Icarus tumbles from the ceiling and into the world of *Varekai*, there seems to be little connection between the big set-piece circus acts – which are the bits that get the audience going – and the narrative, which I completely lost track of, tending to switch off during the arty bits. The juggler and the Russian swing troupe aren't in character. Nor are they, in any way I can see, metaphors. They're straightforward circus artistes, performing to the crowd, as circus acts have since the days of Astley.

So, would I have enjoyed them as much if they had simply been introduced by a ringmaster? Personally, I would have enjoyed them more. But while it's not for everybody (and what is?) it is Soleil's lavish window-dressing that has elevated the company from the ranks of other top-drawer circuses and made it the phenomenon it is.

If the Circus of Horrors is the heavy-metal version of circus, Cirque du Soleil is the opera version. It's grand, it's enormous, it's extravagant. It's not so much a show as an event to dress up for and make an occasion out of. That you have to travel halfway across the country – or the world – to see it, rather than just down the road to your local theatre or showground, is part of its appeal.

Soleil has spawned many imitators, but when I ask everyone I speak to in the circus world what they think the next Cirque du Soleil will be nobody has an answer. Perhaps, like Barnum, Sanger's and Smart's before it, there simply won't be room in the world for another circus on such a scale until the Soleil finally sets – and that doesn't look like it will be any time soon.

But, for all its commercial success, is Soleil the last word in using circus in a theatrical context? Or could there be a more lucid way of using circus skills to tell a story? I find the answer in a literally cool yet simultaneously hot British production that uses a lot of fire on a stage of ice.

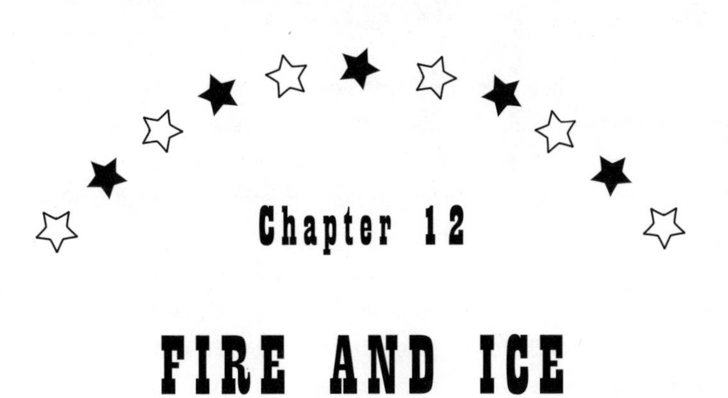

Chapter 12

FIRE AND ICE

The latest incomers to shake up the circus scene are British ice-show producers Wild Rose, who created the circus-on-ice show Cirque de Glace.

The scream fills the dark and nearly empty auditorium. It's a rollercoaster scream – a high-pitched collision of wide-eyed excitement and open-mouthed fear. It's coming from television newsgirl Becky Jago, who is earning her year's salary in the space of a few moments.

The television presenter is hanging from a *corde lisse* rope that has been winched almost to the top of the proscenium arch. One hand is gripping a leather strap that is wrapped around her wrist. The other is gripping the rope itself. She's wearing a white blouse, black trousers and enormous ice-skating boots that are currently being pulled out at right-angles to the rope by centrifugal force.

Below Becky, also wearing skates and a leather and fur cave-girl costume, Katya Belokopytova is spinning the rope as hard and as fast as she can. Katya's not playing. With her sturdy legs braced wide apart and her biceps and shoulders bulging like ostrich eggs, she's really putting her back into it – working the rope as if she's trying to send the television girl hurtling off into the cheap seats at the back of the circle.

High above the frozen ice stage Becky becomes a screaming blur – a black-and-white streak encircling the rope like the rings of Saturn. When the rope finally stops spinning and Becky is lowered to the ice, Katya and her husband Sasha skate in close to her and hold her upright until she is able to stand unaided. It takes a while.

Even twenty minutes later, when she's back in her own shoes and standing on the carpet in front of the stage, Becky looks as 'all shook up' as Elvis. With her eyes standing out like ping-pong balls and her cheeks as red as a woman who has just had ten orgasms and doesn't know where *they* came from, she says, 'I thought they were just going to lift me gently up and gently set me back down again, like a fairy in a pantomime . . .' Poor Becky.

The cast of Cirque de Glace don't do things by half. But you don't have to join in one of their rehearsals to discover that. Watching the circus-on-ice show from the stalls is thrilling enough. Opt for the front row and you get a complimentary spray of ice from the jumps and spins on the edge of the stage.

In two hours the show crams in 4.5 billion years of history, from the formation of the earth, through the origins of life, the birth of man, the discovery of fire and the wheel, the moon landings, the rise of consumerism and the threat of climate change. The story is told, crisply and concisely, in a rumbling, poetic Richard-Burton-in-*War of the Worlds*-style voiceover by Phil Waters. The atmosphere is created by a stirring score by Stu Shaw and floor-to-ceiling cinematic projections across the back of the stage.

The spectacle to match the seismic events in the earth's history is provided by thirty skaters and circus performers who never stop swirling across the ice and through the air in front of the projections. In each scene they wear a dazzlingly different costume. In the formation of the earth's crust scene, as rivers of molten lava flood across the cinema screen and a model volcano belches plumes of real fire centre stage, they're all in shiny red flame costumes. The shredded tinfoil skirts and headdresses of the girls flash in the lights as the men slide around the rink, carrying them, one-handed, above their heads.

In a Wall Street scene everyone is wearing sharp pinstripe suits, with their hair slicked back and a newspaper under their arm, while the back projection shows speeded-up film of car lights zipping through nocturnal canyons of glaringly illuminated skyscrapers. Archive footage of the first moon landing is coupled with a pair of skaters dancing across the stage in authentic bulky helmeted space suits. The result is by far the most accomplished piece of narrative circus I have seen. For pace and clarity it knocks Soleil's *Varekai* into a cocked hat.

'Some of the costume changes are easier than others,' says skater John Hamer, who is one of only two Brits in the predominantly Russian cast. 'After the wheel number, we have the fire number, and we just put cloaks over our existing costumes. But in the second act, between the first and second numbers, it's zips, belts and buttons and a run underneath the stage to where my dressing-room is. In this theatre it's a bit easier, because there's a little more room. In some of the smaller theatres, side stage and backstage can get a little bit not *heated*, exactly . . . but everyone's rushing to get changed and get past each other and there's not room to swing a cat.'

Travelling from theatre to theatre brings problems of choreography, too, says the 25-year-old former junior and senior British champion who swapped competitive skating for show business after the European Championships two years ago.

'Some stages have more width, some have more depth, so the show has to adapt every week. The main problem is we have elements they do in the Olympics and we're doing them on a stage an eighth of the size. When you're performing two-hour shows twice a day mistakes are going to be made. If you're trying to do a triple you might do a double, or maybe your spin will travel a little bit . . .' When that happens the cast cut each other no slack. 'You're going to get it pointed out and you just have to put your hands up and say, "Let's get it right next time."'

As Hamer and I chat in the front row of the stalls, Katya and Sasha are chasing each other around the *corde lisse* hanging above the frozen stage. The low grind and rumble of skates on ice is cut by half as Kayta grabs the rope and is winched spiralling into the air. The scraping sound of the blades disappears completely as Sasha joins his wife in the air – hanging by one hand from her trailing ankle, a fine rain of ice falling like snow from the blades on his feet.

The circus tricks are seamlessly worked into the storyline. A Russian bar sequence is presented as a scene about deforestation. It begins with two men coming on stage in hard hats, visors and high-visibility work clothes wielding noisy chainsaws. One of them cuts down a 'tree', which becomes the Russian bar – a long, narrow springy plank that the two workmen suspend on their shoulders. A pair of acrobats dressed as wood sprites take turns to spring up and down off the bar, turning backwards and forwards somersaults up near the proscenium arch.

The Russian bar guys don't skate. But some of the circus performers do, such as hula-hoopist Yulia Kovina. At one point she has a whole cascade of multicoloured hoops spinning around her body like an undulating tube enclosing her from neck to ankle. At another point she hulas with just one hoop – which is on fire at half-a-dozen points around its circumference.

Hamer denies there's any rivalry between the skaters, who are mostly graduates from international competition, and the circus people. 'I think the most dangerous part of the show is the Russian bar. When you've got a guy upside down 6 or 7 metres above a mat about an inch thick . . . I don't think that's going to do him much good if he misses. But it's difficult to say that what we do or what they do is more difficult, because it's so different.'

Nodding towards the stage where the Russian aerialists are still a rotating blur in mid-air, Hamer says, 'I won't hang off that rope because I know I won't be able to do it as well as Katya, and the circus people won't try to do triples and lifts and pro-jumps because that's not what they do. The only rivalry is between the skaters who jump, myself included. If one man can do this jump, then the next man will try and do that jump or a little bit more. We have our beer bets about who will be able to do this or that, and if you're the third man in the line and the other two get it right and you get it wrong there's some ribbing.'

Despite the competitive spirit, Hamer says the cast all get on well backstage. 'Everybody helps each other out if they have a problem with their credit card or their car.' There is even time for romance. Hamer and fellow skater Rinata Araslanova are about to celebrate the end of the tour by getting married. Generally, Hamer says Cirque de Glace has completely changed his understanding of circus.

'Everyone thinks: red nose, big feet and four clowns in a Mini. But I think circus is more scientific and professional than people imagine. I'm really enjoying being in this show, and I think a lot of people are surprised by it.'

Cirque de Glace is the first venture into circus by Wild Rose, a British company that has been producing traditional ice shows such as *Snow White* and *Carmen* since 1993. According to creative director Julian Deplidge, a whippet-thin bean-pole-tall 32-year-old with a northern accent as broad as the Yorkshire moors, it's by far the most expensive show the company has produced.

'In *Cinderella* we toured twenty-four performers and eleven backstage. In this show we've got twenty-four performers and fifteen backstage. That's an almost 30 per cent increase in wages, 30 per cent increase in air fares, 30 per cent increase in accommodation and transportation. Technically it's a lot, lot bigger show. Our lighting budget is up 80 per cent. There's £300,000 worth of lighting in the roof, not including the control side of it. Then you've got projection, video servers . . . we've got an extra three technical crew.'

In all, Deplidge puts the investment at 'four to five million', which is quite a gamble. But, despite opening slap bang in the middle of a recession, Deplidge says the bet is paying off. 'We've just been to the Lowry in Manchester and outsold any previous ice show or any previous cirque show they've had there. Last year we were in the Palace Theatre in Manchester, so same city different venue, and this year, with Glace, we doubled our box office.'

One of the reasons for the show's artistic success is that Deplidge insisted on using top-quality circus performers alongside the skaters Wild Rose was already renowned for. 'A few years ago there was a production of *Barnum*, and they were trying to get skaters to learn circus skills. But you can't expect someone to learn in eight weeks of rehearsals what a professional has been practising all their life. I think it cheapens the skills and shows a lack of respect for the audience. So I refused to do it unless I could have skaters doing the skating and circus people doing the circus skills. It was a battle. The accountants went mental. But I didn't want a single person leaving the show thinking we'd cheated them. To do that, you have to put on the best.'

Deplidge is the son of Wild Rose founder Vee Deplidge and has been working his way up through the company since the age of sixteen. 'I started front of house, selling programmes for the princely sum of £50 a week. From the beginning I took an interest in the technical side. I pestered people backstage: "How did you do that? Why did you do that?" Eventually they offered me a job as props boy. Over the years various people left, and they'd say, "Do you want to do that job?" So, apart from wardrobe, I've worked in every department: lighting, sound, stage management. I've literally spent half my life on tour with the Russians.'

In all that time he admits he hasn't picked up a word of the language – even though he's married to a Russian, the former star of *Carmen on Ice*. 'We have interpreters on tour, and fortunately a lot of the Russians speak good English. They tend to pick up the rude words first!'

The idea of a cirque-style show first came to Deplidge ten years ago, when Wild Rose was presenting an ice show in a former circus building in Monaco and Cirque du Soleil were first finding global awareness. 'This new genre of circus always fascinated me, because I believe cirque and circus are two totally different genres. Circus, to me, conjures up the image of a big top in a field, with caravans and candyfloss, and "Roll up, roll up . . . without the aid of a safety net". Which is a nice style of presentation in its own right, with the elephants marching down the high street holding each other's tails in their trunks. Whereas cirque is much more of a theatrical presentation, probably in a permanent structure, with more off-the-wall costuming and contemporary movement.'

The two genres have different audiences, says Deplidge, as well as a different audience to his traditional ice shows. 'With our fairy shows we were getting a lot of grandchildren and grannies, and what we were noticeably missing were the twenty- to fifty-year-olds. With Cirque we're still getting our older audience; we don't seem to be getting the children, but we are getting masses of twenty- to fifty-year-olds.'

I first see Cirque de Glace in a ten-day Christmas season at the sizeable King's Lynn Corn Exchange. At a Sunday matinée there's barely a seat to spare. There's an equally strong turn-out when I see the show six months later in a week's engagement at the Theatre Royal, Norwich. But, according to Deplidge, there have been regional differences.

'In the slightly bigger, more cosmopolitan cities where they understand the Cirque du Soleil thing we've done fantastic business. In some of the slightly smaller, more provincial towns we've struggled. The reaction from the people who have come has been the same everywhere, so the problem has maybe been letting people know what to expect. Where we've had a television campaign the business has been phenomenal.' Hence getting people like Becky up on a rope in front of the cameras wherever possible.

After resting the cirque formula for a season, Deplidge is already preparing a new circus-on-ice show that will open in a year's time. In the meantime he promises some circus touches in his forthcoming production of *Snow White*. 'It's going to be a jazzed-up version, crossing what we have traditionally done with some of the highlights that the audience have enjoyed in this show.'

Deplidge hopes, too, that Cirque de Glace may have a future life abroad. 'It's sparked a real interest worldwide. It's phenomenal the enquiries we're getting for Cirque in comparison to what we had for *Cinderella* or *Beauty and the Beast*.'

Most of the music in Cirque de Glace is on pre-recorded tracks, but percussionist Joe Blanks has two big live drum numbers that power some of the most dynamic scenes. His first is a tribal drum routine during a caveman sequence. In the second act he dons a white chemical suit and gas mask and beats on an oil drum that has light and smoke issuing through holes drilled in the side.

After the cast have run through the caveman number for the television crew, Joe joins me in the front row of the otherwise empty stalls. Besides Hamer, the Stafford-born drummer is the only other Englishman in the cast. He's still wearing his caveman gear, his hair in dreadlocks the length of ropes you could moor a boat with, and his arms and chest pale and bare beneath a ragged fur and leather waistcoat.

Away from the show, Joe is in a fledgling band called the Tunics, and he doesn't mind the costume one bit. 'This is the first time I've done theatre, but I love the old bands like Kiss who dress up and wear make-up and put on a show, so this is right down my street. I'm up for it!'

At nineteen Joe is the youngest member of the cast, but he's been drumming his entire life. 'Santa Claus brought me my first kit when I was three. It was a full-size kit, with me reaching over my head to play the drums.'

For Cirque de Glace he had to learn a new non-musical skill. Beside his drum kit are two flaming torches. Periodically, Joe lifts one to his lips and blows a 10-foot stream of fire across the back of the stage. 'Basically, you fill your mouth with paraffin and blow,' Joe explains. 'Like when you fill your mouth with cornflakes and someone makes you laugh and you spurt milk everywhere? It's that kind of tight-lipped pressure. It's no good spitting it out or getting a jet. You've got to atomize it.'

The drummer admits he had reservations. 'I looked it up on the internet and found out how things can go wrong. Some people have burned their airwaves because the particles have caught fire in their mouths. So I was, like, "Aaaaagh, no!" But Chris Wilkey, the effects designer, came over from New Zealand to do the show. He talked me through it, and I felt a bit better about it.' Even so, Joe admits, 'The first time I put the paraffin in my mouth I swallowed it! But you learn as you go along. You start off with a cubic inch of paraffin and a small flame and work up to a whole mouthful. To get where I am now has taken me half the tour, four or five months.'

Joe's fire-blowing isn't the only element of the show that has evolved since the tour hit the road nine months ago. According to Deplidge, new things are being added all the time, most of them originating with the cast. They include a rope that is set on fire, creating a sheet of flame 3 feet high across the entire front of the stage at the end of the first act.

(Fire is a bit of an obsession with Cirque de Glace. During a scene that combines the rise of religion with man's discovery of fire, there are so many flaming torches on stage, and carried through the air by the revolving Katya and Sasha, that the theatre reeks of petrol.)

'We don't use everything they come up with,' says Deplidge. 'But the way I look at it is, the skaters know more about skating than I do and the circus people know more about circus than I do, so if you don't listen to your people you're going to miss out.' It's an attitude that seems to bring out the best in cast and crew. 'Sometimes I'll come in early in the morning to sort out some admin and the lighting guy will already be here, working on something he wasn't quite satisfied with. They all have a pride in what they're doing and want to make the show the best it can be.'

Why is the cast predominantly Russian?

'In truth?' says Deplidge. 'Because we don't support our athletes in this country.'

Circus was introduced to Russia by Philip Astley's great rival, Charles Hughes, who gave a command performance for Catherine the Great. He proved so popular with the Russian nobility that Catherine had two circus rings built for him, and he remained in St Petersburg for a year. During the nineteenth century circus became one of the most popular forms of entertainment in Russia, and after the revolution of 1917 the government invested heavily in state-run circus schools, which made the standard of Russian performers the envy of the circus world.

Only since the collapse of communism, and the subsequent loss of state-funded training, has there been a decline in standards that has allowed China to take the lead. According to Deplidge, the clear link between funding and performance explains why cash-starved British athletes – and circus performers – have traditionally been underachievers on the world stage.

'My passion is skydiving,' says Deplidge. 'I have friends in the British team who qualified to go to the world championships but couldn't get any funding from the governing body or the government. They were expected to pay to go to Brazil to represent their country. In France the team were bought their own aeroplane to train on, and they're paid a salary. They're the world champions.' Closer to home, Deplidge adds, 'John Hamer qualified for the Olympics, and there was no funding to send him. So is he supposed to starve to pay for his ticket? Or does he say, "I was good enough to go and now I've missed my opportunity in life. Why should I bother skating for my country any more? I'm going to go and try to make some money at it, because I need to eat." The fact they didn't send him has been my gain. But for him it must be devastating to have worked hard all your life and reached that standard, then be treated with contempt almost.'

Beyond the question of funding, Deplidge attributes the standard of Russian performers to their work ethic. 'If you talk to some of what I call the golden generation of Russians, who were skating six to eight years ago, and ask them what their proudest moment was, it wasn't collecting their gold medal; it was the first time they put their team tracksuit on; it was representing their country. They were never "Sorry, my alarm didn't go off . . ." or you were off the squad.'

As the television crew pack away their cameras, and most of the cast drift away to get something to eat before the evening's performance, Katya and Sasha are still flying in circles above the ice. Instead of a rope, they're now hanging from a short aluminium step-ladder suspended from the rigging. It's a touch they came up with themselves to enhance a scene about industrialization.

Both born in the Russian town of Saratov, Katya and Sasha grew up in circus school during the golden age that Deplidge refers to. They continued their training at the Moscow Circus College, from which they graduated in 1992, going on to travel the world with the Moscow Circus on Ice. They're older than they look. They have an 18-year-old son who works in computers. But they show no sign of easing off their devotion to their art.

During one scene Katya hangs from the *corde lisse* in an upside-down splits. One ankle is in a loop on the rope, while her husband hangs from her other ankle. It's a position that ought to split her down the middle, like a wishbone.

'We rehearse three or four hours a day,' says Deplidge. 'On a one-show day it's four hours. On a two-show day I give them an hour off. But these guys . . .' he gestures proudly at Katya and Sasha, 'they're the most dedicated people we have. If they've got a couple of hours to spare before a show, they'll use it.'

Another family unit within the cast of Cirque de Glace are Boris and Svetlana Murzak and their daughter Valerie. Boris is one of the men who support the Russian bar. Svetlana appears on a cloud swing in a scene that symbolizes a hopeful future for the planet after Man has reined in his environmentally destructive ways. A cloud swing resembles a double skipping rope strung across the entire width of the stage. Against the cinematic backdrop of a rainbow, Svetlana sits in the centre of the loop and swings out above the first rows of the stalls. Sometimes she uses the two strands like a hammock, laying on her belly or her back – no hands, of course. Sometimes she twists the ropes around her ankles and hangs upside down as she swings. Mostly, she pivots at the waist, revolving over and over like a disc on a string as she swings back and forth.

Valerie, who claims to be nineteen until her mother points out she recently turned twenty ('Oh, yeah, I forgot!') does an above-average aerial silk routine while another pair of performers do elegant but less demanding aerial silk moves in the background. It's a sexy routine. Clad in a flesh-coloured body stocking decorated with swirls of glitter, she could be naked except for a dusting of jewels. It's a dramatic routine, too. With her long blonde hair swirling around her, she does several breathtaking drops from the top of the silk, spinning and tumbling in a blur almost to the stage where the carefully twisted silk catches her at the last moment. Valerie also has a pivotal role as Gaia – Mother Earth. Clad in white, she performs a graceful contortionist routine atop a ball painted to resemble the earth as seen from space.

The latter was actually Deplidge's inspiration for the show's theme. 'I'm not a member of the Green Party,' says Deplidge, 'but I thought we needed a theme to hold the show together. I watched the promo DVD of Val on the ball and thought, what could that ball represent? Well, the earth. The environment is quite an important issue for us, as a planet, so it became a question of how did we get to where we are now? The Big Bang seemed a good place to start, and once we had the first scenes the show sort of put itself together.'

Offstage Svetlana looks very different. On the cloud swing she is ageless. In her tracksuit she's small, middle-aged and mumsy. She has a vivacious personality and is smilingly apologetic (needlessly) about the standard of her English. But if you were to bump into her in the supermarket you would never guess what she does for a living. There's no mistaking Svetlana's pride in her daughter, however.

'One day she's going into Cirque du Soleil,' Svetlana assures me.

Valerie blushes, turns away and rolls her eyes as if to say, 'Oh, *Muuuum*!'

Valerie is also barely recognizable offstage. Born in Moscow, she has lived in Britain since she was ten, when her parents moved here to appear in the long-running circus musical *Eclipse* on Blackpool seafront. In her white tracksuit she could be any slightly awkward British teenager. But there has been nothing ordinary about her life. The statuesque goddess she transforms into on stage has been training since the age of five and on stage since she was six.

Her ability to contort her body in impossible ways isn't something she was born with, she says. 'We stretched her!' says her mother. Svetlana makes gestures with her hands to represent the way she manipulated her infant daughter's limbs. She looks like she's tearing a telephone directory in half.

When she was thirteen Valerie joined her parents in *Eclipse*, where she worked for the next five seasons. 'When I was doing my A-levels I'd do two shows a day. I'd do school work in the morning, finish at one and go and do a show. Do some studying. Do another show, then go home and do some homework. I was never pushed into it. From when I was twelve or thirteen I always wanted to train in my spare time. My A-levels are there if I need to fall back on anything, but so far I'm earning a good living and seeing the world.'

Svetlana leans forward. 'People don't realize that this is our profession. Valerie was doing very well at college, and people were asking me why she wasn't going to university to be a lawyer or a doctor or something. They don't understand that we're circus people and this is what we do.'

Chapter 13

SAWDUST MEMORIES

A ringmaster remembers.

It's getting on for 200 years ago, but George Pinder still talks about it with pride.

'Thomas Ord was the most famous circus man in Scotland of his time. You could equate him with Frank Sinatra or Elvis Presley. There was a very famous circus man called Andrew Ducrow, who was Ord's great rival, and Ducrow wouldn't work anywhere near Ord because he always had a challenge out that he could outride anybody. We haven't got any written proof, but it's said Ord challenged Ducrow and Ducrow wouldn't take him on. Ducrow stayed more in London and England and got more publicity. But in Scotland Ord was the most famous equestrian.' Ord was George's great-great-grandfather, and his family has been circus ever since.

At Circus Mondao Aunty Emily tells me that if I want the full story of her family's circus roots I should speak to her brother Georgie. (Emily, it transpires, is the only person who still calls him Georgie, apart from a nonagenarian aunt who calls him 'Wee Georgie'.) I'm soon glad of Emily's tip. A dozen years retired from the big top, the former ringmaster has lost none of his ability to entertain an audience. Tales from his father's day, his grandfather's day and even his great-great-grandfather's day spill from George

Pinder with the same immediacy as stories from his own youth during the circus boom of the post-war period.

Pinder is one of the most respected names in circus history and, given the tendency of circus folk to marry other circus folk, the names of all the other great circus families, from Sanger to Fossett, pepper George's conversation as well.

Recalling the days when circuses were as frequently staged in purpose-built theatres as tents, he says, 'Henglar's had a circus building in Glasgow with a water spectacle. They had a waterfall running into the ring, and they used to do a Wild West theme, with Indians in canoes paddling around in the ring. The Indians actually paddled the canoes over the waterfall . . . and my dad's cousin used to jump a horse over the waterfall into the ring – sitting on it.'

Listening to George, it's easy to imagine such stories being passed down from generation to generation, together with the wagons and the tents, the circus skills and the pride. Along with the names. 'It gets complicated because of the names,' says George, in his log-cabin-style wagon, now permanently pulled up on the family's old winter quarters. 'Great-grandfather was Edwin, and in honour of him they kept naming people Eddie Pinder. I think there's been fifteen or sixteen Eddie Pinders. There's five at the present time. The other two names you come across all the time are George and William. The original George and William were the two brothers who started Pinder's Circus in 1854.'

George's circus bloodline goes back further than that, though, to Thomas Ord, who is known to have been running a circus by 1812. 'Ord was the son of a church minister, the Reverend Selby Ord, who was the minister at Whitehaven for a while. His father wanted him to go into the church, but he didn't want to. They had a falling out, and he ran away to join the circus. At that time there was a showman in Scotland called McDonald, and Ord joined him as an apprentice. In those days, if you joined as an apprentice you were there for six or seven years, and you didn't leave. If you tried to, you were more or less hunted down and brought back. It was slavery really. But at the end of Ord's apprenticeship he turned out to be McDonald's best pupil. McDonald asked him to stay on, but he left and started his own circus.'

Unlike his descendants, the circus men of Ord's generation didn't sleep in wagons. 'They stayed in digs, as they called them. If you were the showman or the top of the bill you lived in hotels. If you were further down the bill you stayed in lodgings.' Nor did they perform in tents. The big top was an American invention that didn't cross the Atlantic to circus's birthplace until the 1840s. 'Ord performed in the open air. They'd dig out a ring to work in, and what they dug out they'd put in a bank that made a circle. He didn't charge people, because anyone could stand around and watch. So they used to hold a raffle. They'd raffle everything from a gold watch down, and that's where they got the money for the performance.'

That was also, I realize, probably, the origin of the raffle that continues to be held during the interval of every traditional circus to this day.

'In the evening they'd give a performance in the barn or village hall,' George continues. 'If it was big enough, they'd do some of their acts. If it wasn't, they'd do singing and dancing or put on a play. Then, when the circus was doing good, he'd build a wooden circus building and stay until he'd played the town out. Ord had buildings in Edinburgh, Glasgow, Perth . . . In Inverness, I think he was there a year. But they didn't just do a performance. Because of their status as equestrians they'd give riding lessons as well.'

Following the model of Philip Astley's first circus, Victorian circuses were built around riding acts, but tightrope walkers, jugglers and acrobats were also part of the show, as were non-riding horse acts, such as liberty acts, and other trained animals. 'Philip Astley put all those things together in one place,' says George, 'but those sorts of acts had been around for centuries. Trained pigs were very popular. Trained birds. Trained mice . . .

'They always had a fortune-telling pony,' George enthuses. 'They would pick someone from the audience and ask the horse various questions about them, and the horse would answer by nodding or shaking its head.' This was still popular in George's day. As a lad, he presented the act himself. 'The clown would come in with the ringmaster and the pony, and the clown would pick a young lady in the audience. The usual routine would be, "There's a young lady sitting here. Is her coat blue?" The horse would shake his head. "Is her coat red?" The horse would nod. Then you'd say, "How many buttons are on her coat?" And the horse would count with his foot.'

How does the horse know to do that?

'I shouldn't tell you,' says George, 'but it's obvious, really, isn't it? The ringmaster is standing next to the horse, and he can see what colour the lady's coat is, so he gives a cue to the horse to shake its head or nod. Same with the counting. He gives the horse a cue to start counting and another cue to stop.'

Warming to his theme, the old showman continues, 'Another gag was you'd look to see if she was wearing a wedding ring. You'd always pick one without a ring. Then you'd say, "Is this lady married?" The horse would say no. "Would she like to be married?" The horse says yes. "Will it be long before she gets married?" The horse says no. "How many children will she have?" The horse starts counting: one, two, three . . . and, of course, by the time the horse gets to about twenty the girl is getting redder and redder and the audience is in stitches. You couldn't do it today, of course,' George says dryly, 'because instead of getting embarrassed she'd be sitting there rubbing her hands together at the thought of all the benefits and the council house she was going to get.'

Thomas Ord died two days after Christmas in 1859 and is buried in the Scottish town of Biggar, where he lived – the last of his line to actually live in a house, his descendants taking to permanent travel in their wagons and tents. The land George's wagon stands on is, in fact, the first permanent base to be owned by his family for generations.

'We've been here for thirty years. Before that we rented winter quarters all over the place, mostly in Scotland. That all goes back to Ord. When he died, my great-grandmother and her sister fell out over ownership of his house and land. It went on for years, and by the time it was settled there was nothing left; the money had to go to pay the lawyers. So my grandfather saw that and said he would never buy a place, because when he died the same thing would happen and the family would end up fighting over it.

'The difference was, in those days he didn't have to buy, because there were always plenty of places to rent. You could pull up on a showground and enjoy a great social life with all the other circus and fairground people, and if you went into the town and said you were Mr Pinder from the circus they fell over themselves to help you.

'They would take the animals to a farm just outside the town. But, of course, between the wars most of the animals went into theatres during the winter, so at the winter quarters it would just be the horses we used for pulling the wagons. Then they'd be back from the theatre tour, and they'd have about two weeks to do some painting and repairs and be back on the road again. So they didn't need a place. When I was a kid, the family rented a farm just outside of Edinburgh. We had use of the stack yard in the summer to keep things in that we weren't using, and we parked up there in the wintertime.'

Ord's daughter Selina – George's great-grandmother – followed in her father's footsteps to become a bareback trick rider, and in 1861 she married Edwin Pinder, nephew of the founder of Pinder's Circus.

Edwin's uncles became interested in circus through their family business importing wine and ship's chandlery. They supplied and repaired canvas and ropes, and, apart from sailors, the other people who needed those commodities were fairground and circus showmen. 'With all their experience of sailmaking the Pinders made the first tent for George Sanger, when Sanger's started. My great-grandfather helped make it.'

The self-appointed 'Lord' George Sanger was the most famous showman of the Victorian era. He bought Astley's Amphitheatre in London and at one point boasted a circus parade 2 miles long with 200 horses. He also maintained a keen rivalry with the Pinders, says George. 'Old George Sanger was a funny old bugger,' George grins. 'He wrote a book called *70 Years a Showman* and gives a very interesting account of how he started and how life was for the Victorian showman. But, although he's at great pains to drop various names throughout the book, he doesn't mention the name Pinder once – even though two of his brothers married Pinders and all his nephews and nieces were Pinders. He was jealous of the fact that Pinder's had done three command performances at Balmoral. He also didn't like the fact that Pinder's started in 1854 and he didn't start until 1856.'

Edwin Pinder – George's great-grandfather – trained as a sailmaker, but worked in his uncles' circus where he became a horse trainer and bandsman.

The original Pinder brothers expanded their operations to France, where one of their sons, Arthur, established a circus that is still touring today, although the family are no longer connected to it, having sold the

Pinder trade name in the 1920s. 'In France, if you say Pinder, they just think: circus,' George says proudly.

When his uncles headed for the continent Edwin stayed in Britain and formed his own Ord-Pinder's Circus with his wife in a tent he made himself. Their big break came in 1871 when they were working near Balmoral. Queen Victoria spied their big top from a passing carriage and invited them to give a command performance at the Castle. 'Among all the kids there were Edward VII, the Kaiser, the Tsar of Russia . . . From then on they were able to put on their posters that they'd performed by royal command. It became Ord-Pinder's Royal Circus, and it went from strength to strength. In fact, they gave two more performances to Queen Victoria at Balmoral in June 1889 and June 1892. They were the only circus to perform there three times.'

George was born in 1945, just as Pinder's Circus resumed business after a hiatus during the Second World War. His mother was a horse-rider from another prominent circus family, the Connors.

'My mum's sister was Mona Connor, who was reckoned to be the best lady horse-rider in Britain from the twenties to the thirties. She worked with Bertram Mills, Sanger's, went to America and came back again. My mother's mother was Clara Ford, a music-hall artiste. Clara and her sister Anne did an act in the halls.'

George's father, another George, was an all-round circus performer. 'He played drums. He was a horse-rider, an acrobat. He did a Western act: rope spinning, whip-cracking. But clowning was his favourite thing, and that was what he was best known for. My dad for a while did a take-off of Charlie Chaplin, and very good he was, too. It was before I was born, but I've got photographs of him. You show them to people and say, "Who's that?" and they say, "Charlie Chaplin." You say, "No, it's not. It's my dad", and they say, "No, it's not. It's Charlie Chaplin."

'In those days in cinemas they used to have a talent contest during the interval. The prize was something like five or ten bob, at a time when it cost ninepence to get in. Dad used to stick a straw hat and a cane under his coat. Then he'd jump up, do a song and dance, win the ten bob, and that kept him going to the pictures for the rest of the week. Al Jolson was his favourite. If there was a musical on, he'd go in to the matinée and stay there until midnight. Watch it over and over. That's how he learned the songs.

'The clowning was more talking in those days. In fact, all of the great double acts – Morecambe and Wise, Laurel and Hardy, Cannon and Ball – all that sort of thing goes back to the circus: the clown and the ringmaster. The clown was the comedy guy and the ringmaster was the straight man. Morecambe and Wise actually started in Sanger's Circus. In those days theatre, vaudeville, music hall and circus were all mixed together. The acts would be in variety one week and circus the next.'

George followed in his father's clown boots, before moving into the role of ringmaster, which would be his main vocation. 'I first worked as ringmaster when I was seventeen. It was the usual thing: my uncle wasn't well and they said, "You'll have to do it." After that I did it on odd occasions, then went back to it full time around 1974 when I was about thirty. When we were running our own show I used to do half ringmaster, then I'd get changed and do some clown things, because we used to have some big clown numbers. When we gave up running the circus for a while I went and did ringmaster full time for Robert Brothers and Austen Brothers for a few years.'

As well as introducing the acts, a ringmaster is responsible for the day-to-day running of the show. 'The old-time ringmasters had actually done most of the acts and were on the look-out for different things that might go wrong. The ringmaster was also responsible for controlling the horse in the riding acts, so you had to be able to keep the right pace and give the horse the right cues for when to start and stop. The other thing was that years ago, when my Uncle Tommy was ringmaster, they didn't have microphones, so you had to project your voice. You can imagine a tent full of kids screaming. It was no good going in there and whispering. If you couldn't take charge of a tent full of kids you'd be out on your neck, because they'd make an absolute fool of you. With microphones you can take charge of things a lot easier, but with some of the ringmasters today . . .' George laughs, 'if someone trips over the mike lead and the mike goes off, they're standing there lost. "What do I do now?" The old-time ringmaster would just project his voice and carry on.'

George, naturally, married a circus girl. His wife, Christine Fossett, is from another of the most widespread and enduring circus families. As with the majority of circus people, Christine could turn her hand to most circus disciplines, from trapeze and wire-walking to dog-training. 'What happens,' George explains, 'is you go from one act to another. There are a lot of towns in Britain, but after two or three years you're back in the same town, so you have to change the show around. If you can juggle on the ground, then the next step is to juggle on a wire, or the back of a horse.' Circus children grow up with such skills being permanently taught and rehearsed all around them. 'Whatever acts there are on a show, like an acrobatic act, or tumbling . . . if they're teaching their kids, then you get taught as well. If you're getting taught to walk the wire, the other kids will be standing there watching, and it's like "Go on. Have a go." That's the way it is.'

It was as horse-riders that the Fossetts were most famous. 'My wife, her dad and his three brothers were one of the best of what we used to call a jockey act – because they'd go into the ring dressed as jockeys. They'd start with a saddle. Then they'd take the saddle off and ride bareback. Then they'd stand up on the horse and do all these tricks. Her uncle Claude used to do a forward somersault from one horse to another. He'd have two horses running around the ring, one following the other. He would turn around and face backwards. Then he would go up in the air, do a forward somersault and land on the horse behind. Now it's hard enough to do a backward somersault. But, if you think about it, if you do a backward somersault you can see where you're going, because you're looking over your head and you can see where you're going to land. When you do a forward somersault you turn blind. You can't see where you're going to land – and if the horse isn't there you're on the floor.

'The horses have to be trained as well,' George adds. 'The leading horse, on a cue, has to lift its backside up to give you enough height. Then the trailing horse has to look for you and position itself – if you're a bit out, one side or the other – so that it's in the right position as you come back down.'

That's an amazing thing for a horse to be able to do, I say.

'That's training,' says George. 'And of course it's all done with an iron bar and a red-hot poker, as these idiots would have you believe!' Like most circus people George has scant time for the animal-rights brigade.

'Obviously you're going to spend five or six years training a horse and then knock it about, aren't you? Most of the old circus people packed it up because they ran out of money trying to look after their horses. If business was bad, the horses were fed and watered first class and the men went without. In the days of my father and uncle we'd pull on to a site and the men wouldn't be allowed to have a cup of tea until the horses had had a drink.

'My uncle, in the thirties, bred no end of lions and sold them to zoos. He got on great with the old guy who was the director of Edinburgh Zoo. He would come down and ask my uncle all sorts of things about the lions and what they should be fed, because the circus people knew more about animal welfare than a lot of the zoo people.'

Pinder is particularly aggrieved that the media singles out circus as cruel while celebrating horse racing. 'We travel 20 or 30 miles. The horses are perhaps an hour in the box. For the Cheltenham Gold Cup horses are transported from Land's End and John o' Groats and from abroad on aeroplanes. The Grand National is the same. They *kill* horses, going over them jumps. They run them horses at Beecher's Brook. It's 8 or 10 feet high, and when they get over there's a dyke that they can't see before they take off. And at the end of the race the jockey is stood in the saddle whipping the horse as hard as he can to get to the winning post. If you were to take that horse into a circus ring and say, right, we're going to show you how it won the race, and do exactly the same thing to it, everybody would walk out. But your newspapers, which condemn the circus out of hand, what do they do? They give away a ten-page supplement and a free bet. Because they're making millions out of it, whereas the circus doesn't bring them any money.'

It was different in the glory days of the 1950s and 1960s when, George says, 'The three biggest circuses there ever was in this country were on tour.' Somewhere between the giants of Chipperfield's and Smart's and the small family circuses in their one-pole tents, Pinder's was a medium-sized show in a two-pole tent about the size of Mondao's today. 'They probably have more equipment around them today,' George qualifies, 'because they have better and heavier tents and more lights, so you need better transport and a forklift. In the old days we did one-night stands, so we travelled light.' But, George points out, in circus size isn't everything. 'I was talking to Charles Chipperfield the other week, and I told him the circus is like a balloon. You can quickly blow it up, but if you blow it up too big it goes pop. And he said, "You're right, you know."'

'Chipperfield's was, I would say, the biggest circus that ever travelled in this country. In the fifties it seemed that every year it doubled in size, and at one point, around 1955, it was massive. They had a huge twelve-pole tent with a track around it where they used to have chariot races. The tent would seat 6,000 or 7,000 people. They had hundreds of animals and God knows how many lorries. And what happened was, it got out of control, because where do you take a show that size? London, Liverpool, Manchester, Glasgow . . . and then you run out of towns. But with a small circus the size of Mondao, like they all were at one time, you can just keep going, because there's always another village up the road.'

How did the wagons of George's youth compare with the deluxe models his nieces travel in today?

'We always had decent wagons, because that was your home. Of course they weren't as big as they are now. The one I was brought up in was one my dad had made new, when he got married. It was an 18-foot wagon. Inside it was all done out in mahogany. There was a big fireplace with a coal fire. a big mantelpiece, and either side of it were these big chrome fittings with oil lamps in them. I've still got one of the cabinets out of it, which I put in the one I'm in now as a memento. As a teenager I lived in an old converted bus, then when we got married we went up to a 22-foot wagon. The last one we were travelling out on the road in was about 40 foot.'

George built his current home himself, from wood, on top of an existing chassis. 'I was always quite good with my hands, and it's just a shed on wheels, isn't it?' Having always lived in a wagon, he adds, 'I can't sleep in a house. As soon as someone puts the central heating on . . . oh my God . . . I wake up with a headache. I come back and get in my wagon and I fall asleep straight away.' In that, he's not alone. 'The Robert Brothers bought houses but wouldn't live in them. They preferred their wagons.'

Among George's souvenirs of his circus life is an original poster for Thomas Ord's circus in 1832. He also still has the cans in which he would carry water to his parents' wagon as a boy.

'They would hold about three and a half gallons, with a spout and a lid, and you would take them to the tap and fill them up. That was my job. If it was a regular showground there would always be a tap. If it wasn't a regular showground, you would try and get some water put on, bearing in mind that you were only there for a day. If there was a trough in a field and there was a water feed into the trough, you'd go and ask the farmer if you could tap off that. Or you'd go and knock on a house door and ask if you could have some water. You'd give them some tickets for the family, and they'd be only too pleased. You'd either put a hose on their garden tap or stick a pipe out the window and shove it on the tap over the sink. If you were in a field and there was a clean flowing river, you'd take the horse down and let him have a sniff. A horse won't drink dirty water, so if the horse drank it it was all right to let the other animals drink it. You'd use that for the washing as well.'

The Pinders didn't get electricity in their wagons until the 1960s. But they had electric lighting in the big top in the previous century. 'Pinder's was one of the first circuses to have electric light,' George says proudly. 'We had electricity from the 1890s. We had a steam generator that was pulled along the road by horses. It was like a traction engine, and that powered us in the tent. There was an attendant who looked after it and made sure the steam was kept up and the power was kept up during the show. They bought the generator because in the interval they were running a bioscope, showing early moving pictures. The film used to run off the spool and into a sack, and after the picture was over my dad had to sit there with a spool on his finger and wind it back on to the spool for the next show. That was his job when he was ten or twelve years old.

'Before electricity they had flare lamps. They filled them up with lamp oil; it ran down on to a kind of hot plate, and they just flared up. It was quite a high-risk thing, and it filled the tent with smoke. They said that in the olden days there was that much smoke that you didn't notice half the programme because you couldn't see across the tent! I've got a copy of a poster advertising our circus in the 1890s and it says, "This circus is illuminated by the wonder of the age: electricity. No more smoky flare lamps." It was top of the bill, electricity!'

When did motor lorries take over from horses as circus transport? 'Pinder's were the innovators again! We were one of the first to go into motor lorries, just after the First World War. My grandfather was a friend of a man called Gibson who ran a big garage in Edinburgh. He was bringing back army surplus lorries from the war, refurbishing them and selling them on to the haulage industry. They were American lorries, called Peerless, and he persuaded my grandfather to buy some of them.

'Between the two world wars we had motor lorries, but we still had horses as well. I remember saying to my dad, "Them first lorries you had, how fast did they go?" "Oh, about 12 or 15 miles an hour." "So how far behind were the horses when they came in behind the lorries?" "Oh, fifteen or twenty minutes." "So what did you bother with the lorries for?" "Because you didn't have to get up at five o'clock in the morning and catch them!" Some circuses carried on with horses until right up until the start of the Second World War. After the war everyone was on to motor vehicles.'

George and Christine retired from the road a decade ago to look after his mother, who died three years back, aged ninety-nine. But although he no longer travels with the circus, the old showman remains connected to it.

Apart from his nieces at Circus Mondao George has a son who runs Cirk Korona in Poland. 'He went out there, working with the horses, married a Polish girl and stayed. They run their own circus, and it's probably the biggest circus in Poland now. It's certainly the most modern. The only other Polish circus as big belongs to her sister. We're like the British office.' George smiles. 'He'll come back to collect stuff from here, and I'll sort things out for him at this end.'

Another son is a clown with Circus Mascot in Denmark who returns to England and pulls his wagon up alongside his father's during the winter months, as does his sister Emily and another sister working with a different circus.

'My nephew and his wife didn't go out this year, so they're here with me now,' says George. A third sister, Carol and Gracie's mother, lives with her husband Carlos Macmanus – another famous circus name – a fairly short distance away. A former animal trainer, now retired from the road, Carlos continues to make the horse harnesses used on Circus Mondao.

'You never fully retire, do you?' comments George.

Does he miss the travelling?

'People often ask me that, and I say, yes, I do. But I don't miss it as it is today. I miss it as it was thirty years ago. Today is too much hassle over nothing. You've got all these rules and regulations. We last ran a circus about twelve years ago, and I got fed up with people coming down for no reason whatsoever other than trying to shut you down. The problem is that the money you pay a council to rent a ground is insignificant to them. Then, when their inspector comes down he's looking at something he's never seen before and which he knows nothing about, but if he passes it and someone gets hurt he's in trouble. So the councils just don't want you. You're a thing from the past and a pain in the backside, and if they can legislate you out they will.'

Despite his disillusionment George believes the next generation of circus people – people such as Carol and Gracie at Circus Mondao and Gracie's daughters Madalane and Cinzia – will keep alive the tradition that has been in their blood through Pinders and Paulos and Fossetts and Connors since the days of Thomas Ord.

'I think it will keep going because there are that many people determined to keep it going. If I hadn't run a circus in the good times, I'd probably still be doing it, too. I'd push aside all the hassles and just do it. Some of the newer people who've never known anything else thrive on it. It's a challenge to them. And there are very few children who grow up in the circus who don't want to carry on with it when they're older. Quite a lot of them told their kids over the years, "Oh, you don't want to stay in this business. It's finished. You want to go and get yourself a job as a mechanic or a secretary." They'd send them off and spend all this money educating them. Then, when they were sixteen or seventeen, they'd be back in the circus, clowning or wire-walking.'

As for George, he has his sawdust memories and the old stories handed down from father to son. Recalling the days of his Victorian grandfather and great-grandfather with the enthusiasm of one who was there himself – as he doubtless was, many times, in his mind as boy and man alike – he says, 'They used to do re-enactments. Our lot used to do Joan of Arc. Sanger's used to do the Battle of Trafalgar – with elephants as warships. They'd put costumes on these elephants to make them look like the *Victory*, then put cannons on their backs and fire cannons from one elephant to another. Can you imagine that? Sitting in this tent and an elephant coming in dressed as a battleship, firing a cannon off its back. And people firing guns. And all the smoke from them flare lamps, and everybody in the audience smoking a pipe. No wonder they said you couldn't see across the tent. It must have been a fantastic thing to see.'

The old showman shakes his head and says more to himself than me, 'We'll never see it again.'

Chapter 14

THE NEXT GENERATION

Gerry Cottle's
stars of tomorrow.

In a large white former mill building echoing with excited kids' voices, sixty-something circus man Gerry Cottle is refamiliarizing himself with the delights of riding a unicycle. High in the vaulted roof, a pitched ceiling of red-and-orange-striped drapes creates the feel of a big top where Cottle used to do this sort of thing all the time: unicycle, stilts, juggling, a bit of funny business as Scats the Clown.

Today, the twelve- and fifteen-year-old boys all around him are zipping about on the one-wheeled bikes with ease, just as the wiry little eleven-year-old girls are spinning up and down silk threads like spiders or walking on rolling globes taller than they are or balancing on a tight wire rigged on a special stand a foot from the ground. But, propped up on the shoulders of others, the silver-haired Cottle is struggling.

'You do lose it,' he admits with a laugh. 'My old partner Brian Austen did the high wire for a publicity stunt when we were running the Moscow State Circus together, and he said, "I've never been so frightened in my life!" He said, "I can fly helicopters, but I'm never going back on the high wire!"'

For his own part, Cottle says, 'I can show the kids how to juggle.' Most of all, he can share the experience that comes from having lived in the circus since he was fifteen.

'Years ago I was given a tip. If you keep missing a trick, leave it out for a couple of days. Don't upset the whole routine by worrying about that one trick. That's a silly little piece of advice, but it's so true. It's like if you have a fall. Get back on straight away. You might cry, you might bruise your elbow, but get back on straight away or you'll lose your confidence.'

The limestone caves at Wookey Hole, near Wells in Somerset, have been occupied by humans since prehistoric times. They've exerted an eerie fascination for tourists ever since. According to legend, one of the stalagmites in the first chamber is a witch who was turned to stone by a monk, and the ghost of at least one drowned potholer is said to haunt the murky inner labyrinth, accessible only by divers. The makers of *Dr Who, Robin of Sherwood* and the *Harry Potter* films have all employed the mysterious atmosphere of the caves, and *Most Haunted* devoted a programme to searching for ghostly phenomena there.

For many years the caves were run as a tourist attraction by Madame Tussaud's, who incorporated the adjacent paper mill – then the oldest working in Britain, having been powered by the River Axe, which flows from the caves, since 1610. Gerry Cottle sold his share in the Chinese and Moscow State circuses to buy Wookey Hole in 2004 and, with typical entrepreneurial gusto, quickly revived its flagging commercial fortunes, increasing visitor figures from 170,000 to 250,000 a year.

Among his additions were a dinosaur park, a crazy golf course, a 300-seater restaurant and a teddy-bear shop – which he publicized in the inimitable Cottle style. In 2006 the national and even international press carried the story of a guard dog called Barney who ran amok and destroyed a priceless collection of antique bears, including one owned by Elvis. The story had a lot in common with some of the publicity Cottle had generated for his circuses in earlier days, such as the clown picket line that objected to him importing an American clown, and the band members who had heart attacks at the sight of a Russian hula-hoopist's shapely *derrière.* Like P.T. Barnum's stuffed mermaid and white elephant, the stories were products of Cottle's fertile imagination.

Having closed the paper mill, Cottle used the space to open a penny arcade with hundred-year-old vintage machines and, naturally, a circus museum, which also houses Clown International's Egg Gallery.

'I'm not in it yet,' says the former Scats.

Central to the museum is a collection of replica vintage circus wagons. 'We've got a showman's living wagon, which is probably more ornate than they really were; a Bertram Mills saddler's wagon, which we've turned into a wardrobe wagon, full of feathers and sequins. There's Lord Sanger's wagon . . .'

Along the wall, Cottle points out, 'A sign off a lorry for Captain Sydney Howes, who used to be our lion trainer. Sydney was an orphan. G.B. Chapman, who put on shows between the wars, used to recruit from orphanages, so if anything happened to them there were no comebacks.' Next to the sign is a poster of Jeremy Beadle, the television prankster who was Cottle's celebrity ringmaster at one point. 'He was a great friend of the circus and a great mate of ours. Then we've got a wagon full of freaks. Freak shows were never really big in this country, but they seem to be back in fashion. When we opened the museum I wasn't sure about the freaks – I hated them. But the public seems to love them. We haven't had a single complaint.'

It's not circus's past that Cottle is most interested in, however, but its future. Although it is costing him money rather than making it, the most important part of Wookey Hole, for Cottle, is the circus school for nine- to sixteen-year-olds that he has established in one of the former mill buildings. His ambition is to open a full-time school, like a stage school, where circus skills are taught alongside normal schoolwork. For now, for a heavily subsidized nominal charge of £3.50 for three hours, the kids come two evenings a week and perform shows before the public at weekends and throughout the school holidays.

With a range of former circus performers for teachers, including Cottle's daughters and in-laws, the skills taught range from swinging trapeze and Chinese pole to stilts, acrobatics and clowning. That lessons are geared around rehearsals for an actual show is one of the reasons his children learn so fast, just as the children of traditional circus families are introduced to the ring at the earliest possible age. The shows are also a strong motivator for regular attendance, says Cottle: 'Once they're in the show they never miss a lesson.'

The shows draw a good crowd to the rehearsal space, which converts to a 400-seat theatre. 'We're getting a good name. If you said to most people "Do you want to go and see a youth circus?" they'd think it's not going to be very good. But when they come and see all these little smiling faces . . . and then the kids start doing forward somersaults and riding unicycles standing on each other's shoulders, they really do like the show.

'The kids come from all kinds of backgrounds. There's not a lot of money in this area; there's a lot of unemployment, and some of them have got stepfathers galore. But they've all got a great spirit. We've got one kid who is very autistic, but he's in the show, riding a unicycle. The others look after him. We've got another kid who does three diabolos. He just never stops practising.'

These days, Cottle points out, professional circus equipment, from juggling balls to unicycles, is readily available to all. 'When I started I used cut-off broom handles and lemonade bottles. Now you can buy perfectly balanced juggling clubs.'

For children from other parts of the country Cottle is currently building dormitories for summer camps where kids will train for two weeks and then put on a show for their parents. 'It could be for individuals or school or scout groups,' says Cottle, who got the idea from the American circus school Circus Smirkus.

Cottle also runs classes for adults. 'It's mainly young ladies who want to keep fit. All the girls want to do aerial work. They're up and down the silks, building up muscles, all the time. The only trouble is, you do get broad shoulders, rather like swimmers. All of them like acrobatics but find it very difficult. But once they can do it they move forward very quickly. The men and boys seem to like playing with the unicycles or the diabolos. Everybody likes to have a go at juggling. They say, "Oh, I've never juggled", and you say, "Well, you've got the principles, you're doing three, just keep going", and all of a sudden they're doing four and five.'

Cottle himself admits he's far from immune to the circus-skills bug. 'It's like all these things. Now I'm doing it again I'm dead keen on it.'

When I asked Peter Jay why he is so infrequently able to employ British performers at the Yarmouth Hippodrome, he criticized circus schools for producing too many solo performers – particularly on aerial silk or *corde lisse* – 'They don't go to the next stage of putting two or three people together into an original act that I can book.'

Cottle agrees. Actively encouraging his pupils to work together, he says, 'In the current show we've got two young ladies doing a double trapeze. They were neighbours on a housing estate. We've got six girls going up and down the webs, five boys doing an acrobatic number. We've got the whole cast doing a cycle act at the end. The Chinese have got up to sixteen on a bike. We've got eight at the moment.'

Cottle started his first circus school in 1984. He advertised for young hopefuls, gave them a three-month crash course, then took them on the road in a youth circus. As probably Britain's first non-animal circus, it was ahead of its time and only lasted two seasons. But, of the thirty youngsters who took part, Cottle says at least eight are still in the circus business. Among them is Willie Ramsey who is now the shaven-headed chief trainer at Wookey Hole.

'Willie came from a really rough part of Edinburgh, where *Trainspotting* was set. He was taught by Reg Bolton who set up a youth club circus. He learned the basic skills of unicycling, juggling and acrobatics. Then when I started my circus school he came along. He was just sixteen, a tiny little kid, one of the smallest. He was always the one who went up on anyone's shoulders.'

Ramsey became an all-round performer in Cottle's circus, with a particular talent for Cossack horse-riding. For a time he was married to Cottle's eldest daughter, Sarah. 'He's taught all over the world,' Gerry says proudly. 'America, Australia. He was one of the main teachers at the Millennium Dome. He said to me recently, "I've had a great career because of circus, whereas some of my old mates are either dead or still on drink and drugs in Edinburgh."'

Ramsey works with his girlfriend, Lesley, a Circus Space graduate, and Cottle praises the enthusiasm both of them have brought to the school. 'They're always coming up with new ideas for the show. This year they're doing an urban theme, with lots of roller-skating and unicycles. Recently the girls did a show with Moulin Rouge music. We've got about 300 costumes here, and they all enjoy dressing up.'

Another of the pupils from Cottle's first circus school was trapeze artist Andrew Watson. 'He was just a hippy who saw the advert,' Cottle recalls. But he went on to become creative director at Cirque du Soleil. Watson is currently working with Franco Dragone, who broke away from Soleil to create his own Las Vegas productions on an equally grand scale, including the enormous circus and water show *Le Rêve*, which the circus magazine *King Pole* described as 'undoubtedly the most advanced aquatic spectacle the world has ever seen'.

Cottle is confident that his current pupils have every chance of going on to equally glittering careers. 'Circus is big, big business. I thought there were around 1,000 circuses in the world, but in fact it's closer to 3,000. There are 200 in France, 200 in Germany, 300 in Italy. They can join the big boys, Cirque du Soleil, who have got nineteen shows worldwide. They'll be the ideal people for that, as they've been trained in ensemble work and most of them are good all-rounders. Or they can go off with a small circus, like I did when I ran away from home, and be a jack of all trades. It's a good career, a good life.'

Cottle was a director at London's Circus Space for a time but left the board because he thought the school did too little to prepare graduates for the real world of circus. 'I do think they ponce about too much. I'm all for new circus, but they teach them more about being alternative and different than they do about real talent – and you cannot beat real talent. You have to train people to do something that exceeds the norm. They should be teaching them to perform an act, not produce a show. How can you come straight out of a school, apply to the Arts Council, get a nominal grant for £5,000 and produce a show? You need the experience of working for others.'

The logical next step for Cottle is to start a new travelling show, in the style of Martin Burton's Academy of Circus Arts, to give his pupils a stepping stone into the professional world. Cottle admits that when he bought Wookey Hole he thought he'd put his days of running a travelling circus behind him. But while you can take the man out of the big top you can't take the sawdust out of the man. A couple of years ago he produced a circus-cum-variety show called *WOW!* in Blackpool. It wasn't a success, but he's currently rehearsing thirty young Zimbabweans for a new African-themed circus show called *Zambezi Express.* He's by no means certain it will be the next Chinese State Circus. 'But you've got to try, haven't you?'

Asked why he and his former partner Brian Austen are continually driven to new ventures and bigger achievements, while many of the older circus families have been seemingly content to rest on their laurels and fade from prominence, Cottle says, 'That's just the way I'm made. We never stop. You're either like that or you're not.' By contrast, he mentions one old-school circus pal who has been 'going around with the same seating since he started, twenty years ago, and hardly ever fills it. He does three weeks in Sheringham every year and starves. I mean, who goes to Sheringham for three weeks? I said to him, "Your clown's awful", and he said, "Is he? I haven't seen the show since we opened" – and that was three months before. But he said to me, "I've got a nice little farm, nice little bungalow, we go off on a nice holiday every year . . . I'm not doing badly, am I?" He's just doing steady, and I think most people in the business are pretty steady. Me, I'm building a fifty-eight-bedroom hotel! I'm sixty-four years old, and I'm getting into debt to build it, but I'm confident it will do well. This part of Somerset's not really on the map. People go down the motorway and miss us – and if they see a hotel they might stop.'

One selling point is that parents will be able to enjoy a holiday to themselves at the hotel while dropping their small fry off at the circus summer camp. The hotel should also prove popular with wedding guests. Cottle obtained a marriage licence for the caves in 2005. His daughter Polly was the first to be married there. Hannibal, the sword-swallower from the Circus of Horrors, is about to be wed there, too, and doubtless won't be the last from the circus and theatrical worlds to take advantage of the unusual setting and circus connections.

Unlike his former partner Brian Austen, Cottle remains a shameless circus fan. 'I go to every single show that comes within reasonable travelling distance, for the simple reason that there's nothing more satisfying than sitting there for two hours and watching a bloody good show. I get more passionate about circus as I get older, funnily enough, and I don't want to give up.'

Cottle reckons the best show currently on the British scene is the Chinese State Circus. He could be biased. Apart from his previous involvement with the show, one of his daughters runs the box office and a nephew is tour manager (in circus, family connections are part of the wallpaper, even among the new families). Cottle also bigs up the Circus of Horrors in which he remains a partner. But he will talk with knowledge and enthusiasm about any other show you care to mention.

Cirque de Glace, for instance, he enjoyed but missed the element of humour. He also feels 'People are living off this "cirque" word, aren't they? I went to see Le Grand Cirque at the Bristol Hippodrome, and as I was coming out I heard a lady say to her friend, "I'm glad I've seen them. I missed them at the Albert Hall." She thought she'd seen Cirque du Soleil.'

As for Soleil itself . . . 'I'm a big fan of Cirque du Soleil. I've seen most of their shows in Vegas a few times. They keep evolving, and, yes, they make mistakes. They've got a magic-themed show in Vegas at the moment and it's had terrible reviews, but their shows are quite brilliant most of the time. But I think too many people try to copy them, and I don't think any of us can do that.'

Cottle is more enthusiastic about Clive Webb's and Danny Adams's Circus Hilarious. 'I love Clive and Danny. They're a bit naughty at times. They're a bit rough. But they're bloody good: 2,500 people were watching them at Butlin's, and they went absolutely bananas.' Cracking up at the memory, Cottle says, 'Clive did the funniest gag of the year. It's birthday time. He says, "Hello, Johnny, ten years old, congratulations. Lady over there, she's thirty today, marvellous. Lady up there, she's sixty-five . . . Oh, you look older than that." Only Clive could get away with that! 'I think that's the kind of British show that should be touring the small towns and villages. Soleil's absolutely great, but can everybody afford a ticket? Can everybody plan months ahead to go? And if you take the whole family, will they enjoy it? But if you get splashed with a water pistol . . .' Cottle's chuckle says it all.

So is the variety show style of Danny and Clive the future of circus? Will Britain, the birthplace of circus, find the next Cirque du Soleil in a glossy and ambitious production such as Cirque de Glace? Or will we, as a nation, get past the animal issue and see a resurgence of traditional big tops filled with elephants and tigers?

According to David Jamieson, editor of the circus quarterly, *King Pole*, 'Thirty years ago virtually every circus followed a traditional pattern, with clowns and trapeze artists and lots of animals. Now you've got some circuses with animals, wild and domestic, some with just horses, dogs and birds, some without any animals. Some circuses appeal to the traditional family audience, like the Moscow and Chinese State circuses. Some appeal to the teenage audience, like the Circus of Horrors. Then you have the phenomenon of Cirque du Soleil and something like La Clique, which is not necessarily a circus show but which has elements of circus in it. It's more of a cabaret – very adult, with a contortionist and a conjuring striptease. So the market for circus is very diverse, and I don't think you can say it will head in the direction of Cirque du Soleil or animals or whatever. It's going to change and develop and get even more varied.'

David Davies, Chairman of the Circus Friends Association, agrees that the future lies in diversity. 'I think there's a greater awareness of circus creeping through in this country, because of Cirque du Soleil. People think, "That was good. Maybe we'll go and see Zippos when it comes to us." There's a big interest in circus throughout the country at youth level. There's a lot of circus skills being taught at youth clubs and circus clubs and universities. So I think the prospect for the future of circus is good.'

On a lush ground in Halifax, Carol Macmanus of Circus Mondao gazes out of her jigger window at the spotted horses, camels and llamas grazing on the fresh grass of a newly fenced-off paddock. Business has been harder this year than last, she says, but life is good, and the show rolls on. Having presented her first act, a 'Big and Little', in the ring at the age of eleven, Carol has worked with animals all her life. 'I lived in the stables when I was child,' she laughs. 'There are pictures of me with the animals as a toddler.' Today she's passing her enthusiasm and skills on to the children of her sister Gracie. But when she talks about 'everybody', as in 'Everybody's out enjoying the sun today', she's not talking about her human relatives; she's talking about her family of seven horses, five miniature ponies, six pygmy goats, two mules, two llamas, two zebras, two camels and a donkey. That's not counting Gracie's performing pigeons, 'however many of *those* she's got, plus our pet chickens and bunny rabbits and all our pet dogs'.

That's a lot of mouths to feed, I say.

'But look at them.' Carol smiles. 'Everybody munching on the grass . . . and that's *free*!'

Certainly, Carol reckons her four or five animal acts cost a lot less to keep on the road than the equivalent number of human performers. 'Everybody's different,' Carol says of her training. 'Some learn very quickly and some not so quickly. You'll get one pony who can walk very well on its hind legs and another that can't, but maybe that one can do a bow. They'll always learn something, even if they're never going to be the cleverest one in the act. Maybe they'll be the ones that just tag on behind and pirouette and go out.'

As much as she knows about animals, Carol admits the secret of success in the circus is much more elusive. 'If anybody knew that, we'd all be rich,' she laughs. Her plans for the future are just to 'carry on', the way her family has carried on since the days of her great-great-great-grandfather Thomas Ord nearly two full centuries back. 'We haven't got any bigger plans than that,' says Carol. 'Just stay the same size and carry on.'

In London, Jane Rice-Bowen, head of the Circus Space, sits in her office contemplating the past and future of circus. On the wall behind her are two photographs. One shows the derelict Circus Space with its carpet of pigeon poo and feathers, as it was when the school first moved in. The other shows it after the renovations that were finally completed two years ago.

The real future can be seen through the window in front of her which opens into one of the building's main training areas. As the trapeze artists leap and fly and tumble and let out grunts of exertion echoed by the groans and bangs of the straining wires in the rigging, the view reminds Jane of the day she came to be interviewed for her job in 2004. As she stood in the foyer for the first time she gazed through another set of windows that look into the same training area.

Having come with her childhood memories of watching Billy Smart's on television at Christmas with her grandfather – 'He watched it because he loved the animals, and I watched because I just thought it was soooo glamorous, and soooo sparkly and soooo amazing' – the former music-venue manager says, 'I looked through these windows into this amazing world and watched as these artists were training to be the very, very best at what they can do . . . and there was an honest and visceral truth in it that resonated with me and filled me with amazement. Now I get to see that every day, and I feel so privileged. These guys are amazing.'

Have you had a go on the trapeze yourself? I ask.

'I have, and I'm absolute rubbish!' Jane laughs. 'The joke is I've been here for four years and I still can't juggle! But we all have different skills. My skills are in things like lobbying and negotiating with the Arts Council. Ultimately what we want to see is a stronger culture of circus in this country. We want to see circus as an aspirational activity for young people. Instead of them going to ballet classes or youth theatre, we want them to say to their parents, "Actually, I want to go to youth circus." Instead of them wanting to be David Beckham or the latest pop star, we want them to say, "I want to be a trapeze artist."'

Central to that aim is Jane's mission to secure more public funding for training and development.

'We want people to think about circus in the way they think about opera – as a very expensive endeavour. I think we have to talk about circus on that kind of grand scale in order to produce something as successful as Cirque du Soleil.' In the meantime, Jane is encouraged by the prominent use of circus skills in the stage shows of Take That and Britney Spears, both of whom named their latest album *Circus.*

'Circus really is part of the *Zeitgeist.* I think there's a massive appetite for circus and a real demand for it. Audiences are crying out for something new and exciting, and when they see circus they love it.' In fact, Jane feels there is a *need* for circus in our increasingly digitized world. 'We have virtual conversations with people through text and email. Whereas once I'd have walked down the corridor to talk to somebody, now I send them an email. Kids are so into their computers, whereas the *reality* of something as *intense* and as *physical* as circus . . . that's what people have a hunger for right now.'

In Great Yarmouth, the artistes are arriving for Peter Jay's thirtieth anniversary season at the Hippodrome. A Russian swing act from Brazil, a juggler from Mexico, a magic act from South Africa, a contortionist from Mongolia . . . There may be more. At the eleventh hour Jay is still booking people.

'It's Looney Toons here at the moment!' Peter laughs. 'That mad week of putting it all together. But this is the bit I love. It's a magic ten days for me.'

Although hardly anybody in the cast speaks English, Peter says there's seldom a communication problem during rehearsals. 'There's usually somebody who's OK with all the languages. The problem is on the phone before they get here, when we're getting calls from 200 miles north of Rio in the middle of the night. We'll get these emails in broken English and have to read them three times to work out if it's good news or bad!'

During his three decades of running the Hippodrome Peter says the internet has made his job easier. 'It used to be, "Send me a DVD." Now they say, "Look at my act on YouTube." It's instant.'

Peter's 21-year-old son Jack is the ringmaster this year . . . and Peter has finally got rid of the red noses he's been trying to persuade his clowns to ditch for years. This year he's replaced the traditional clown with a stand-up comedian, Johnny Mac, who will be performing a double act with Jack.

'We've been lucky over the years with people like Danny and Clive. But funny clowns are the exception. I've got a room full of DVDs of unfunny clowns. I've also found that lots of people are scared of clowns, especially teenagers who have been brought up on all the horror clowns in films and TV shows like *Psychoville*. But the combination of Johnny and Jack just seems to work. They look good together. They get on well offstage. I'm hoping this is going to be the start of something big for both of them.'

With a chuckle, Peter says, 'Once again, I think I'm going to upset a few circus purists. "That Peter Jay! First he took the band out and put in all this modern music and flashing lights. Then he took the animals out. Now he's even taken the clowns out!" But part of my mission is to turn it into a seaside show that's modern, accessible and easy to watch. It's becoming more of a summer show that has circus acts in it, rather than a circus in a seaside resort. Even though you're going to see the best acts in the world, you don't have to be a circus aficionado to enjoy it.'

As he celebrates thirty years of cutting-edge circus in Britain's oldest circus building, Jay's artistic policy certainly seems to be paying off. 'At long last we've reached the point where it's not just somewhere to go when it rains but something special that people are coming to see. We've had people come from Kent and Doncaster just to see the show and local people who have come four or five times. Last year we were the most successful summer show in Britain.'

The Hippodrome isn't the only circus doing well. According to Zippo, 'In a recession when more people are holidaying in the UK and not buying that new car, they want to take their kids out for a treat, and a trip to the circus is an inexpensive family treat. Week on week, our business this year is up 25–30 per cent.'

To give the last word to Dr Haze of the Circus of Horrors, 'Circus is very much alive and juggling.'

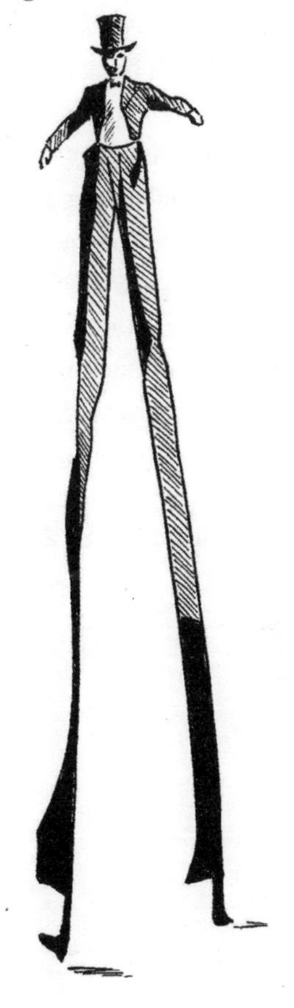

THE END

A final word from your Ringmaster . . .

I hope you've enjoyed reading this book as much as I have enjoyed writing it. If you have, tell your friends. If you haven't, keep it to yourself! It just remains for me to thank all the showmen and artistes mentioned in these pages for sharing their time and memories and entertaining me with their shows. You couldn't meet a warmer-hearted or more talented bunch, and I urge you to visit each and every one of them when they come to your town. Big or small, traditional or modern, with animals or without, in a theatre or a big top, you won't be disappointed.

Until then . . .

May all your days be circus days!

Appendix

CIRCUS CHRONOLOGY

329 BC–AD 549

The Circus Maximus, from which modern circus takes its name, is Rome's biggest amphitheatre. It stages a mixture of chariot races, gladiatorial contests, wild animal displays, acrobats and jugglers.

---

c. 256 BC onwards

Chinese acrobatic theatre or variety art emerges independently of the Western circus tradition.

---

8 January 1742

Philip Astley, the father of modern circus, is born in Newcastle-under-Lyme, Great Britain.

---

9 January 1768

Astley opens his Amphitheatre of Equestrian Arts – the first modern circus – in Lambeth, London. For trick horse-riding displays he establishes the standard size of the circus ring as 42 feet, or 13 metres, in diameter.

1778

Joseph Grimaldi, the father of modern clowning, is born in London.

1782

Charles Hughes opens the Royal Circus in London, becoming the first showman to use the word 'circus' in a modern context.

1793

The USA's first circus building is established in Philadelphia by John Bill Ricketts, a pupil of Hughes.

1800

Grimaldi appears in his first starring role as Guzzle in the pantomime *Peter Wilkins, Or Harlequin in the Flying World*, at Sadler's Wells, London.

1803

Astley replaces his original wooden building with the brick-built Royal Amphitheatre of the Arts, later known simply as Astley's.

1810

The first elephant in a British circus appears at Covent Garden.

---

5 July 1810

Phineas Taylor (P.T.) Barnum, founder of the self-styled 'Greatest Show on Earth', is born in Bethel, Connecticut, USA.

1814

Astley dies at home in France.

1825

In the USA Joshua Purdy Brown stages the first circus in a tent or big top (earlier circuses have been staged in buildings or the open air).

APPENDIX

1837
Grimaldi dies, broke.

1840
Thomas Cooke introduces circus tents to England.

---

c. 1840
Jules Léotard, the father of the flying trapeze, is born in Toulouse, France.

---

12 November 1859
Léotard makes his public début at the Cirque Napoléon, Paris, and becomes an instant sensation.

1866
Louis Soullier introduces Chinese acrobats to European circuses for the first time.

1867
George Leybourne composes 'The Daring Young Man on the Flying Trapeze' in Léotard's honour.

1871
Spanish flying trapeze troupe the Rizarellis are the first to use a safety net, at London's Holborn Empire.

---

7 April 1891
Barnum dies.

---

25 April 1894

Billy Smart, the 'Guv'nor' of British circus, is born in West Ealing, London.

1897–1902

Barnum and Bailey's 'Greatest Show on Earth' tours Europe.

1900

Coco the Clown is born Nicolai Poliakoff, in Latvia.

1904

'Entrance of the Gladiators', the circus 'theme music', is composed by Julius Fucik.

1910

Charlie Cairoli, the 'King of Clowns', is born in Milan.

1919

Russian circuses are nationalized.

1920s

Su Fuyou introduces Western-style circus presentations and animal acts to China and founds the Great China Circus.

1927

The State University of Circus and Variety Arts, better known as Moscow Circus School, opens in Russia.

APPENDIX

1930

Coco emigrates to Britain to join Bertram Mills's Circus.

1939

Cairoli débuts at Blackpool Tower Circus, where he will perform every summer until 1979.

---

5 April 1946

Billy Smart opens his first circus, Billy Smart's New World Circus, after previous success as a fairground operator.

1966

Smart dies.

1970

Gerry Cottle and Brian Austen found their first circus, Embassy Circus.

1970s

Cirque nouveau, an all-human style of circus performance, evolves from street theatre in France, UK, Australia and California.

1980

Charlie Cairoli dies.

1982

ITV broadcasts its last *Billy Smart's Christmas Spectacular*.

1984

Cirque du Soleil is founded in Quebec, Canada.

1990

Cirque du Soleil visits UK for the first time.

1990s

Many British circuses stop using animals following animal-rights protests.

1993

Cirque du Soleil's first theatre show, *Mystère*, opens in Las Vegas.

1990s to present

Promoted by the European Entertainment Corporation, the Moscow State Circus and Chinese State Circus become Britain's most successful permanently touring shows.

2009

Great British Circus reintroduces elephants to the UK circus for the first time in a decade.

THE CAST